LIVES OF THE ANCIENT EGYPTIANS

LIVES OF THE ANCIENT EGYPTIANS

Toby Wilkinson

18 illustrations

 Thames & Hudson

For Emma

Illustration credits

On the cover: Friezes from the tomb of Inerkhau, foreman of a team of artisans who decorated the royal tombs in the Valley of the Kings, 20th Dynasty. Photo © Sandro Vannini

Frontispiece: Vignette from the Great Harris Papyrus: Ramesses III (no. 78) stands before Ra-Horakhty. British Museum, London

Plate illustrations listed by figure number:

Ägyptisches Museum und Papyrussammlung, Staatliche Museen zu Berlin **11, 15, 16**; British Museum, London **3, 7, 8, 10, 13, 14**; Brooklyn Museum of Art **9**; Egyptian Museum, Cairo **1, 6**; Frank Teichmann **17**; Photo Heidi Grassley © Thames & Hudson Ltd, London **12**; © Jürgen Liepe **2, 4**; Werner Forman Archive **5**

Lives of the Ancient Egyptians © 2007 and 2019
Thames & Hudson Ltd, London
Text by Toby Wilkinson

Typeset by Mark Bracey

First published in 2007 in hardcover in the United States of America by Thames & Hudson Inc., 500 Fifth Avenue, New York, New York 10110

www.thamesandhudsonusa.com

This paperback edition 2019

Library of Congress Control Number 2019934320

ISBN 978-0-500-29480-2

Printed and bound in the UK by CPI (UK) Ltd

CONTENTS

INTRODUCTION

What was it really like to live in ancient Egypt? Our impression of pharaonic civilization is dominated by its visible remains, by pyramids, temples and tombs: but what of the people who commissioned and built them, who staffed the offices of central and provincial government, who served in the temples, who fought to defend Egypt's borders, who toiled in its fields? What of the men and women of the Nile Valley who created and sustained its spectacular culture? Individual perspectives on ancient Egypt are rarely encountered in the literature, with the exception of a few well-known pharaohs, such as Hatshepsut or Amenhotep III, Ramesses II or Cleopatra. Yet rulers lived lives heavily circumscribed by ideology and ritual and, for this reason, they are often rather less interesting witnesses than their subjects. It is surprising, therefore, that so little has been written about the ordinary people who actually experienced Egyptian civilization at first hand. For it is only by sharing their viewpoint that we can begin to appreciate the variety and complexity of life under the pharaohs. That is the simple aim of this book: to explore the history and culture of ancient Egypt through the lives of its inhabitants, to give them their own voice.

In selecting our hundred subjects, the aim has been to strike a balance – chronological, geographical and social. The limits of the available evidence have not always made this an easy task. Take the chronological scope of ancient Egyptian civilization: 3,000 years separated the birth of the Egyptian state from its absorption into the Roman empire. Put another way, the era of the Great Pyramid was more remote from Cleopatra's time than she is from our own. If a single generation approximates to thirty years, then ancient Egypt – as an independent and vibrant culture – spanned one hundred generations. Hence, with one hundred lives, this book should be able to cover every phase of pharaonic history in equal detail. Unfortunately, the vagaries of archaeological preservation do not permit so evenhanded an approach. More is known about a single thirty-year span in the fourteenth century BC (the so-called Amarna Period) than about the first half-millennium of Egyptian civilization (the Early Dynastic Period). Hence, in this book, ten personalities have been selected to represent the former whereas the latter has only eight representatives. Nevertheless, care has been taken to ensure that every major phase of ancient Egyptian history is covered, together with all the main turning-points: the collapse of the Old Kingdom, the rule of the Hyksos, the rise of the Ramessides, and so on.

The geographical extent of ancient Egypt was as impressive as its longevity. The state's core territory stretched from the First Cataract in the south to the shores of the Mediterranean in the north, a distance by river of some 1,000 km (625 miles). At particular periods of its history, Egypt extended its borders still further, through conquest and colonization, to take in large parts of Nubia and the Near East. Within this vast empire, administrative and religious life was concentrated in two or three major centres: Memphis at the apex of the Delta; Thebes in Upper Egypt; and, from the thirteenth century BC onwards, various cities in the central and eastern Delta. It is not surprising, therefore, that many of our characters lived and died in these great conurbations. But the provinces were important, too, and even shaped the country's destiny at certain key moments. To get a fully rounded picture of life under the pharaohs, it is crucial to give a voice to the inhabitants of the towns and villages of rural Egypt, from the broad marshlands of the Delta to the narrow valley of southern Upper Egypt. Our witnesses therefore include citizens of places like Busiris, Herakleopolis and Elkab, as well as their metropolitan counterparts.

Although surprisingly extensive, the evidence for ancient Egyptian lives is by no means evenly spread across different sectors of society. Because the majority of monuments and texts were commissioned by men for men, our view of ancient Egyptian culture is filtered almost exclusively through a male lens. A few women gained positions of prominence, especially in the 18th Dynasty royal family, but, in general terms, the lives of half the population remain hidden from view. In this book, eleven out of one hundred subjects are women: less of a gender bias than in many treatments of ancient Egypt, but still far from an ideal balance. Furthermore, most of the scenes and inscriptions on tomb and temple walls, the texts on statues, stelae and other artifacts, and the surviving papyrus documents pertain to the careers and family relationships of Egypt's small, literate ruling class. By contrast, the lives of the illiterate peasantry, comprising up to ninety per cent of the population, are largely unrecorded. Yet, even within the governing elite, many different ethnic backgrounds were represented. Egypt was always a melting pot of peoples and cultures, a crossroads between Africa, Asia and Europe. Indeed, at various times, the kings themselves were Asiatic, Libyan, Nubian or Macedonian. Their stories lift the veil of cultural conservatism promulgated in art and architecture, revealing Egypt as a multi-ethnic and dynamic society.

During the three millennia of Egyptian history, essential continuity and stability were provided, above all, by the bureaucrats: the men who served in the royal household, the central administration and the provincial government. These officials are some of the best-known figures from the ancient past, and they too – from a vizier to a court dwarf – have their stories to tell. Equally influential in pharaonic society were the great priesthoods of the country; no picture of ancient Egypt would be complete without including its religious personnel, from the High Priest of the chief state god to a humble priestess in a provincial temple. Joining them in the following pages are myriad others, including a doctor, a dentist, a draughtsman, a sculptor, an architect, a musician, a soldier, a sailor, a farmer, a housewife, a criminal, an historian, even the first Egyptologist: for these are the real ancient Egyptians, and it is their experiences that give the best idea of what life was like in the Nile Valley twenty, thirty or forty centuries ago.

PART 1

Foundations
Early Dynastic Period

Around 3000 BC, the first nation-state in history was born – in Egypt. In the Nile Valley and Delta (known to the Egyptians themselves as the Two Lands), the various rival kingdoms and territories which had developed over a period of a thousand years were unified into a single country ruled over by a single king who claimed divine authority. This process, known as the unification, seems to have occurred fairly quickly, taking a few generations at most to complete. Although the precise course of events remains a little hazy, the outcome is clear: the kings of This (ancient Tjeni, near modern Girga), one of two or three proto-kingdoms in Upper Egypt (the southern Nile Valley), emerged supreme. They overcame not only their rivals in the south of the country, but also the rulers of towns and cities throughout the marshlands of the Delta. The king known to us as Narmer (no. 1) is the first monarch who can be said with confidence to have ruled over the whole of Egypt, from the First Cataract in the south to the shores of the Mediterranean in the north. He was recognized by his near-contemporaries as a founder figure, and has a special place in Egyptian history as the first king of the 1st Dynasty.

The challenge for Narmer and his immediate successors (nos 2–4) was to develop and prescribe the means for ruling their new, geographically vast realm. Egypt was certainly not lacking in cultural dynamism: two distinctive and vibrant traditions had grown up, in the Nile Valley and Delta, respectively, during the millennium or more preceding the unification. Technologically superior and more in tune with the conspicuous consumption favoured by Egypt's early ruling class, Upper Egyptian culture had supplanted its northern counterpart in the Delta during the late predynastic period, mirroring the process of political unification that was likewise driven from the south. The kings of the 1st Dynasty took this cultural tradition, and refined and codified it as an expression of the court's own power. Art and architecture were carefully deployed to enhance the prestige of the monarchy as an institution, allowing it to overcome challenges such as the regency under Merneith (no. 2) or all-out civil war in the early years of Khasekhemwy's reign (no. 4). The barrage of propaganda worked spectacularly well: kingship swiftly became the ideological glue that bound Egypt together; government without monarchy was unthinkable. One of the great achievements of Egypt's early rulers was thus to develop an iconography and ideology of royal rule that survived, virtually unchanged, for the next 3,000 years.

Relatively little is known about the early kings as individuals, since hieroglyphic writing was still at an early stage of its development and, in any case, monarchy thrived best behind a veil of secrecy and mystery. But the political, economic and religious programmes of these rulers can be deduced from scraps of textual and archaeological evidence. The first three or four centuries following unification – known as the Early Dynastic Period – were a time of great innovation and of rapid developments in Egyptian civilization, when all the major building blocks of pharaonic culture were put in place. Some of the techniques used to extend and maintain the state's power would be familiar to us today. While expounding a creed of strident nationalism to bolster its own legitimacy, the government quietly increased formal contacts with foreign lands, using the revenue from trade to fund increasingly elaborate royal projects (notably the king's tomb). Internally, the state tightened its grip on all areas of administration, in particular ensuring that every aspect of the national economy was subject to state regulation, if not direct control. The inauguration of a regular census of the country's wealth combined with meticulous record-keeping set the pattern for Egypt's enduring love-affair with bureaucracy.

The two interlinked policies – of economic and political centralization, and an obsession with monumental architecture – came together in the reign of Djoser (no. 5) with the construction of the first Egyptian pyramid. The enormous feat of engineering required to erect a mountain of stone high on the Saqqara plateau was matched by the logistical operation needed to quarry and transport the blocks, and recruit, house, feed and direct the massive workforce. The sheer administrative complexity of pyramid-building necessitated a more professional bureaucracy, rather than the small cabal of royal relatives with shifting areas of responsibility which seems to have character-ized government in the first two dynasties. Men like Hesira (no. 6) and Metjen (no. 8) show the changing nature of high office in the 3rd Dynasty. The titles lovingly recorded on their funerary monuments allow us a glimpse of individual careers, for the first time. The most famous official of Djoser's inner circle, Imhotep (no. 7), achieved even greater prominence and was venerated as a god of learning and wisdom by later generations of Egyptians. His great creation, the Step Pyramid complex, dominates the 3rd Dynasty, and marks it out as a transitional era, when the achievements of Egypt's formative period were consolidated and the scene set for future glories.

1 NARMER
EGYPT'S FIRST KING

Who is the first ancient Egyptian known to us by name? The origins of hieroglyphic writing have now been pushed back, beyond the beginning of the 1st Dynasty, into an era when Egypt was still a collection of competing kingdoms, not yet unified into a single nation-state. There are combinations of signs from this early period which may be names, but we cannot be sure, and in any case they are difficult to read. The rulers of Egypt's predynastic period must, for the moment, remain anonymous. The first king whose 'name' is readable, and consistently written on objects ranging from simple sherds of pottery to a decorated stone macehead, belongs at the very start of the dynastic sequence. His most famous artifact, a ceremonial palette from the temple at Hierakonpolis (ancient Nekhen, modern Kom el-Ahmar), stands in the entrance hall of the Egyptian Museum in Cairo, welcoming visitors at the start of their tour through 3,000 years of pharaonic culture (fig. 1). It has become an icon of the foundation of a great civilization; the king for whom it was made is recognized as the first in Egyptian history.

His name is Narmer – except that the reading 'Narmer' is almost certainly wrong. The two signs used to write the name, a catfish and a chisel, did indeed have the respective phonetic values 'nar' and 'mer' in later phases of hieroglyphic writing, but there are compelling reasons to think that they represented different sounds in this early period. Indeed, the 'name' Narmer may not be a name at all, rather, a combination of symbols associating the king with the fierce forces of nature (catfish) and their striking power (chisel). As such, it would belong within the dominant mode of expression found in prehistoric royal iconography. This explanation of Narmer's name would support his identification as a transitional figure, whose reign spanned the predynastic past and the dynastic future, and whose lasting achievement was to recast the ideology and iconography of royal power into new, lasting forms that would endure for the next three millennia.

What do we know about Narmer the man? He became king around 3000 BC and was almost certainly from the Upper Egyptian city of This; this was one of the early centres of Egyptian civilization and the capital of a kingdom which, by the closing years of the predynastic period, encompassed the northern part of Upper Egypt, most of Middle Egypt and parts of the Delta. Whether by diplomacy or force, Narmer extended his rule over the whole of Egypt, from the First Cataract to the fringes of the Delta. A key step in this process of territorial consolidation may have been Narmer's marriage to a woman named Neithhotep. Judging from the location of her tomb, she was descended from the old royal family of Nagada (ancient Nubt), one of This's rival centres in Upper Egypt which it may have conquered some years earlier. A strategic alliance between these two royal families would have been a good basis for building a wider political consensus. In this same vein, Narmer took pains to venerate the shrine of Horus at Hierakonpolis, the third major centre of Upper Egyptian power. Horus was not only the city's local god, but was also the god of kingship. So paying homage to his cult served the dual purpose of reinforcing Narmer's royal credentials while satisfying the elite of Hierakonpolis that their new ruler, if not a local man, intended to respect their traditions.

The two most impressive objects donated by Narmer to the temple of Horus were consummate examples of royal iconography, and powerful statements about the extent of royal power. The ceremonial macehead showed the king, enthroned beneath a canopy, watching a parade of prisoners and tribute, and observing rituals associated with the two localities – Buto (ancient Djebaut) in the northwestern Delta and Hierakonpolis itself in southern Upper Egypt – that symbolized the geographical extremes of his new realm. The decorated palette carried scenes of a similarly symbolic nature: the king smiting a bound captive, inspecting ranks of slain and decapitated enemies, tearing down the walls of a rebel stronghold. Whether the enemy was intended to represent a Delta chieftain or a foreign tribesman, the message was the same and crystal clear: as king of all Egypt, Narmer would brook no opposition. He would defend Egypt's borders, but the quid pro quo was the unswerving loyalty of the entire populace. This uncompromising message was reinforced at Egypt's southern frontier by the construction of a massive fortress on the island of Elephantine (ancient Abu) which both guarded the river approach from Nubia and towered over the local community. The authoritarian character of divine kingship had already been firmly established.

The xenophobia of state propaganda – on a cylinder seal from Hierakonpolis, Narmer is shown beating a group of Libyans, while an ivory fragment from his tomb shows a bearded Asiatic stooping in homage to the king – masked a more pragmatic attitude to foreign relations. The discovery of Egyptian pottery from the reign of Narmer at sites throughout the northern Delta and southern Palestine suggests active trade between the two regions. The royal court went to great lengths to obtain the valuable commodities it required to maintain its economic and political dominance. A series of inscriptions carved on an isolated rock outcrop in the heart of Egypt's eastern desert bear witness to an expedition sent by Narmer to this remote region, probably in search of gold or high-quality stone.

Objects bearing Narmer's name have been found at sites the length and breadth of Egypt, indicating a king whose authority was recognized over a greater area than any of his predecessors. Modern scholars have debated whether he or his immediate successor, Aha, should be accorded the position at the head of the 1st Dynasty. For the kings who came after them, there was no such debate. The necropolis seals of both Den (no. 3) and Qaa, from the middle and end of the 1st Dynasty respectively, put Narmer first in the list of Egypt's rulers. To them, Narmer was the undoubted founder figure. Five thousand years later, it seems churlish to disagree.

2 MERNEITH
THE FIRST WOMAN TO HOLD THE REINS OF POWER

The king was a unique figure in ancient Egypt. Ideologically, he was above the rest of humanity and was considered the earthly incarnation of the celestial god Horus. Politically, he was head of state and government; he ruled by decree, and all departments of government were answerable to him. Without a king, Egypt – in both ideological and political terms – would founder. This created a problem when, as happened on occasions, a new monarch came to the throne as a child. Although religious tenets could accommodate a minor as a channel between human and divine spheres, the business of government needed direction by an adult individual. The solution was a regency. In practical terms, it was dangerous to entrust such power to one of the young king's male relatives, since such a figure might then go one step further and usurp the throne. It was far safer to appoint as regent the person who could have no such ambitions and who, in any case, symbolized the transition between the old and new reigns: the king's mother.

The earliest attested regency in Egypt took place in the middle of the 1st Dynasty. The old king, Djet, had died, leaving the throne to his successor Den (no. 3). Since the new monarch was still a child, his mother Merneith governed in his place. She was the wife and mother of a king and may also have been a king's daughter, born to the third ruler of the dynasty, Djer. Merneith's period of office is the first certain instance of a woman holding the reins of power in Egypt. Of course, all official documents bore the name of the reigning king, despite his minority, so she is only sparsely attested by name: on three vessel fragments and a small ivory vessel from the Saqqara region. However, as *de facto* ruler of Egypt, Merneith was granted the privilege of a full mortuary complex in the ancestral royal burial-ground at Abydos (ancient Abdju). Her tomb was marked on the surface in the traditional manner, with a pair of large funerary stelae bearing the owner's name in raised relief.

This architectural acknowledgment of Merneith's regency seems to have been a decision taken personally by her son, Den, when he reached adulthood. His name features prominently on objects from Merneith's burial and his recently discovered necropolis seal lists 'the king's mother Merneith' alongside the previous rulers of the 1st Dynasty, starting with Narmer (no. 1). By contrast, the seal of Qaa, the last king of the dynasty, omits Merneith, indicating that, after her son's reign, she was no longer accorded equal status with the *de jure* rulers of the period. But during her regency and for the remainder of her life as king's mother, Merneith and Den clearly developed a strong bond. The son repaid his mother's loyalty and support in the most suitable manner, with a tomb fit for a king.

3 DEN
REFORMING RULER OF THE 1ST DYNASTY

Den is the best-attested king of the 1st Dynasty. Even taking into account his accession as a child, he enjoyed a lengthy reign: a recently discovered fragment of a limestone vessel from the southwest annex of his tomb mentions 'the second occasion of the *sed*(-festival)'; the *sed*-festival was the royal jubilee, usually celebrated after thirty years of a reign and thereafter at more frequent intervals. Of course, a long tenure as king is not noteworthy in itself; but Den's time on the throne was a period of exceptional innovation, of major cultural and material developments in almost every sphere, that helped Egypt take a further, decisive step on the path from nascent state to great civilization.

He declared his reforming agenda from the outset, starting with the royal titulary. Kings had previously been designated as being the incarnations of Horus and ruling under the protection of the Two Ladies, the patron goddesses of Upper and Lower Egypt. To these two established titles, Den added a third, *nesut-bity*, literally 'he of the reed and bee'. Best translated as Dual King, it signified the many dualities over which the monarch presided – divine and human, sacred and secular, Nile Valley and Delta, floodplain and desert, east and west – emphasizing that the harmony of opposites inherent in created order depended upon the person of the king for its continuation. This elaboration of the ideology of kingship was further reflected in the adoption of a new crown combining the white headdress of Upper Egypt and the red of Lower Egypt. Den signalled that he was going to be a king of both, of all.

Looking beyond the borders of Egypt, Den also inaugurated a new policy with regard to neighbouring lands. One of his secondary names, Zemti, means 'of the desert', and he seems to have taken a special interest in Egypt's arid, northeastern frontier zone. There is evidence from his reign for military activity in southern Palestine (whether actual or ritual) and trade expeditions using the coastal route from the Delta. The fruits of such sustained contact can be seen in the large number of Syro-Palestinian vessels – presumably containing valuable oils and unguents – imported into Egypt during Den's reign.

An intensification of foreign activity was matched by administrative reforms at home. An apparent increase in the number of high officials at Den's court may reflect changes in the structure of government. Tighter royal control over the affairs of state required not just able administrators but also an accurate assessment of the country's population and resources. Den saw to this as well: an entry from the middle of his reign, in the royal annals compiled in the late Old Kingdom (the so-called Palermo Stone), records a 'census of all the people of the north, west and east'. To be of use, all this information had to be recorded and archived. It may be no coincidence that the earliest roll of papyrus from Egypt was found among the grave goods of Den's Chancellor, Hemaka.

The end result of all this effort – increasing foreign trade, streamlining government, and improving the management of the economy – was the ability to devote greater resources to promoting kingship by fulfilling the sovereign's traditional duties. Hence, the Palermo Stone records Den's foundation of a new temple called 'thrones of the gods', while the king also engaged in other religious activities such as visiting important shrines, dedicating new cult images, and promoting rituals such as the running of the Apis bull. An overflowing royal treasury also allowed Den to commission new, more impressive royal monuments. At Abydos, his architects built a magnificent royal tomb with an important innovation: an entrance stairway giving access to the burial chamber. This greatly facilitated the provisioning of the tomb, and was swiftly adopted throughout Egypt. As for Den's funerary equipment, his craftsmen surpassed themselves. Stone vessels in a bewildering variety of forms – from imitation reed baskets to flowers – were a particularly fashionable product of the royal workshops. Under Den, Egyptian civilization reached a new level of sophistication.

4 KHASEKHEMWY
HARBINGER OF THE PYRAMID AGE

The 2nd Dynasty is one of the most obscure periods of ancient Egyptian history. Not only are its monuments fewer, and less well known, than those of the preceding or succeeding dynasties, its kings are also mostly shadowy figures, barely attested in the written or archaeological records. A notable exception is the last king of the 2nd Dynasty, whose reign marked a crucial turning-point in the development of Egyptian civilization.

At the beginning of his reign, the king adopted the Horus-name Khasekhem, 'the power has appeared'; it was a prophetic statement, since he would be the most influential monarch for a century or more. He showed a particular interest in the city of Hierakonpolis, one of the early centres of the Egyptian monarchy, and in its local temple, dedicated to Horus, the god of kingship. Here, Khasekhem donated a range of votive offerings, including vessels of travertine and granite and two seated statues of himself, one in limestone and the other in siltstone. All these objects bore inscriptions, not merely naming their royal donor, but also making reference to military action against a northern foe. Each of the vessels is decorated with a representation of the vulture-goddess Nekhbet, protector-deity of Upper Egypt, standing on a ring containing the word 'rebel'; an accompanying text describes the scene as 'the year of fighting the northern enemy'. In a similar vein, the bases of Khasekhem's statues carry inscriptions which show defeated enemies in contorted positions, labelled as 'northern enemies 47,209'. Although these allusions to military action against Lower Egypt could represent a ritual act, it seems more likely that they refer to an actual historical event: a civil war with the north in which Khasekhem fought to regain control over the whole country.

Khasekhem's battle for supremacy was not confined to confrontation with a northern enemy. A fragmentary stela from Hierakonpolis shows a defeated Nubian enemy, part of a scene of triumph labelled 'humbling the foreign land'. It seems that the king had to contend with rivals to his throne from two directions. The struggle with Lower Egypt was eventually resolved in Khasekhem's favour, and he marked his victory by changing his name to the dual form Khasekhemwy, 'the two powers have appeared'; it was consciously modelled on the name of the 2nd Dynasty's founder, Hetepsekhemwy, and thus announced a programme of national renewal. Khasekhemwy reinforced the message by adding to his name the epithet 'the two lords are at peace in him'. It was a clear indication that the troubles of the early part of his reign were over. The country could now look forward to renewed peace and prosperity.

One of the immediate consequences of a return to domestic stability was an upsurge in Egypt's international contacts. Trading links resumed with Byblos on the Lebanese coast, presumably to procure supplies of cedar-wood for ship-building. Sea-going craft allowed Egypt to engage in trade with its Mediterranean neighbours, and also to increase its political influence in the region. A stone block from the temple at Hierakonpolis, listing foreign countries, probably recorded tribute or enemies slain in battle; while a seal-impression preserves the earliest occurrence of the title 'Overseer of Foreign Lands'. Both suggest that Egypt under Khasekhemwy began a policy of conquering and annexing territory beyond its borders.

The increased revenue entering the royal treasury funded an upsurge in state construction projects. Khasekhemwy became a major patron of temple-building in Upper Egypt, at sites from Elkab (ancient Nekheb) to Gebelein (ancient Inerty). At Hierakonpolis, in addition to extending the temple, he commissioned an enormous cult enclosure (now known as the Fort) to be built near the town. It was constructed from mudbrick, with walls several metres thick, and was decorated around the entrance gateway with reliefs in pink granite showing the king taking part in royal rituals. Highly visible from the surrounding area, the building acted as a focus for the celebration of the royal cult.

In a break with recent practice, Khasekhemwy decided to opt for the traditional, hallowed royal necropolis at Abydos when planning his own funerary provision. His vast tomb made a greater use of dressed limestone – for the lining of the burial chamber – than any previous monument, pointing the way to the extensive use of stone in his successor's reign. The grave goods were no less impressive, bearing witness to the skill and sophistication of the royal work-shops: dolomite limestone vases with sheet-gold covers, a royal sceptre made from gold and the precious stone sard, and a bronze ewer and basin. These final items are the earliest bronze objects known from Egypt; the tin required for their manufacture must have come from Anatolia, and its procurement demonstrates the effectiveness of renewed trade with the eastern Mediterranean in Khasekhemwy's reign.

Like his predecessors of the 1st Dynasty, Khasekhemwy chose to complement his tomb (designed for security) with a funerary enclosure (designed for publicity) situated on the low desert, facing the town of Abydos. It is known today as the Shunet el-Zebib ('storehouse of raisins' in Arabic, reflecting its more recent use) and is a truly impressive structure. More than 4,500 years after it was built, it still towers over the surrounding landscape. Its eastern wall, closest to the town, was decorated with alternating recesses and buttresses, to resemble the façade of the royal compound at Memphis (ancient Ineb-hedj, 'white wall') and hence to proclaim its kingly associations. In this and other respects, Khasekhemwy's enclosure paved the way for the funerary monument built by his successor, Djoser (no. 5).

Hence, in its ambition and grandeur, the reign of Khasekhemwy foreshadows the Pyramid Age. His political achievements re-established the internal stability and prosperity needed for the great cultural achievements of his successors.

5 DJOSER
BUILDER OF THE STEP PYRAMID

Pyramids are the quintessential, iconic monuments of ancient Egypt. In their architectural sophistication, and the extraordinary organizational and logistical achievement they represent, they underline the age in which they were built as the first, great period of Egyptian civilization, when the resources of the country were harnessed and directed, as never before, towards state construction projects. In the annals of ancient Egypt, a special place is reserved, therefore, for the king whose reign witnessed the inauguration of this tradition of monumental stone architecture. Attested on contemporary monuments only by his Horus-name Netjerikhet – '(Horus is) the most divine (member) of the corporation (of gods)' – he is better known by the name that appears in later sources, Djoser ('holy').

Djoser was a member of the same royal family as his immediate predecessor, Khasekhemwy (no. 4). The latter's wife and the mother of his children, Nimaathap, was known in the reign of Djoser as 'the king's mother'. No inscription explicitly states that Djoser was Khasekhemwy's son, but the circumstantial evidence makes it very likely. Where Djoser did make a break with previous royal tradition was in the geographical focus of his activities – his surviving buildings are concentrated in the north rather than in the south of the country – and in the location and design of his mortuary complex. The Step Pyramid dominates modern accounts of Djoser's reign as it does the Saqqara plateau where it was built. It represented a turning-point: in architecture, being the first monument in Egypt to be finished entirely in dressed limestone; in construction techniques, giving engineers the opportunity to begin exploiting the full potential of stone as a building material; and in organization, necessitating and prompting the development of systematic regional government and a professional bureaucracy.

The rise of an official class, represented in large-scale statuary, is a key characteristic of Djoser's reign. The leading men of his court are the earliest group of high-ranking dignitaries whose identities are known. Besides the king's chief minister Imhotep (no. 7), there were the district administrators, Ankh and Sepa, who also held a number of important priestly offices between them; the Controller of the Royal Bark (the king's state boat), Ankhwa; the Chief Dentist, Hesira (no. 6); and Khabausokar, the controller of the royal workshops in which the statues of all these individuals were made. His artisans also created representations of Djoser's female relatives: his wife Hetephernebty (who may also have been a daughter of the previous king Khasekhemwy), known by the sobriquet 'she who sees Horus (i.e. the king)'; his daughter, Intkaes, and another princess, 'the king's daughter of his body', Redji, whose face shows clear similarities with relief representations of Djoser. The fine, seated basalt figure of Redji is the earliest surviving example of a statue depicting a named, female member of the Egyptian royal family.

The only surviving three-dimensional sculpture of the king himself is a seated, life-size statue from the *serdab* (statue chamber) of his pyramid, showing him as he wished to be remembered: dressed in the long, tight-fitting robe associated with the *sed*-festival; wearing the royal *nemes* headdress over a heavy wig; his face characterized by prominent, all-hearing ears; high cheekbones, thick lips and a wide mouth giving him a look of grim determination.

Djoser's reign witnessed an upsurge in creativity which extended to royal iconography. Statue bases from the Step Pyramid complex show the heads of Asiatics and Libyans, the traditional enemies of Egypt; by having himself depicted standing on his foes, Djoser showed that he was performing the primary duty of the Egyptian king – to defend the country – and made a powerful point to other would-be opponents. The innovative architecture of the Step Pyramid complex put particular emphasis on royal ideology, by providing eternal settings for important royal rituals. The great court in front of the pyramid formed a backdrop for the king's formal appearances and an arena for the ceremony of 'encompassing the field', where he strode around symbolic territorial markers to reassert his claim to Egypt. To the south of the pyramid, a separate court was designed as an eternal stage-set for the *sed*-festival (royal jubilee), at which the king would receive the homage of people and gods before being crowned again to mark the rejuvenation of his reign. Djoser's *sed*-festival was probably the occasion which prompted the construction of a shrine to the ennead (group of nine gods) at Heliopolis (ancient Iunu). The king's patronage of this site reflected the growing importance of its local cult, that of the sun-god Ra, and its associated priesthood.

Aside from construction projects at Saqqara and Heliopolis, Djoser also sent mining expeditions to the Wadi Maghara in southwestern Sinai, to bring back precious turquoise and perhaps copper for the royal workshops. At Beit Khallaf in Upper Egypt, the largest private tombs yet seen were built during his reign; one of them may have been the funerary monument of his own mother, Nimaathap. Other than these isolated glimpses, the events of Djoser's reign are attested only from much later inscriptions, such as the Famine Stela carved in the reign of Ptolemy V. At a remove of 2,500 years, it can scarcely be used as a reliable source, but it does demonstrate the longevity of Djoser's legacy.

More than a millennium after his death, the Ramesside court compiled the king list known as the Turin Canon, dividing the rulers of Egypt into major historical groupings. When the scribe came to the name of Djoser, he changed the ink in his pen and wrote in red rather than the usual black. He was in no doubt that the accession of Djoser marked the beginning of a new era: the age of the pyramids.

6 HESIRA
CHIEF DENTIST AT THE COURT OF DJOSER

Health care, at least for the governing elite, was surprisingly advanced in ancient Egypt, and was developed at an early period. A medical treatment manual addressing a wide variety of conditions is thought to date back to the Old Kingdom; while Merka, a high official at the end of the 1st Dynasty, held the title of 'scorpion doctor', among many others. Medical knowledge seems to have been acquired in the course of more general scholarship, and healthcare practitioners were seldom narrow specialists; rather, they exercised their skills as part of a portfolio of activities, in keeping with the broadly based nature of ancient Egyptian authority. A good example is Hesira, an official at the court of King Djoser and the first recorded dentist in history.

Hesira – also known by the short form of his name, Hesi – was not merely a dentist: he was Chief of Dentists, suggesting an already established profession. He was a member of the king's inner circle and owed his seniority, not so much to his knowledge of dentistry, as to his literacy: at a time when the scribal class (from which the bureaucracy was drawn) was still small, Hesira was Master of the Royal Scribes, and hence one of the leading administrators in government. To be a scribe was to have access to the levers of power. Little wonder, then, that Hesira always had himself depicted with his insignia of office, the scribal equipment of ink-palette, pen-holder and pigment bag. Within the administration, one of his major duties was overseeing the recruitment of corvée labour for state construction projects, in his capacity as 'greatest of tens of Upper Egypt'.

A feature of ancient Egypt throughout its history was the combination of civil and religious office in a single individual. Hesira was no exception. Although a man of essentially secular learning, he none the less held posts in the priesthoods of three important early cults: the fertility god Min; the lioness-goddess Mehit; and the falcon-god of Pe (Greek Buto, modern Tell el-Fara'in), Horus the Harpooner. This last office brought Hesira the added honour of being a Great One of Pe.

Of course, having achieved status and wealth, he did what any Egyptian would have done in a similar position: he commissioned a large and splendid tomb to guarantee his affluence throughout eternity. Hesira's tomb was built to the north of his monarch's Step Pyramid complex. It was decorated with wall paintings of funerary equipment – vases, chests and board games – and eleven recessed niches, each of which originally held an intricately sculpted wooden panel (fig. 2). Six of these panels have survived, and are among the finest reliefs from ancient Egypt in any medium; the modelling of anatomical details is especially notable. The panels show Hesira, surrounded by texts giving his titles and epithets, at various stages of his life. Even as a young man, he wore a rather sullen expression with a downturned mouth and narrow eyes. As an older man, his face was creased and wrinkled, but maintained the same sour look. He was evidently a follower of the latest court fashions, which included sporting a thin moustache and wearing a short, round wig with straight locks. Particularly characteristic of the Egyptian ruling class is his strong, aquiline nose. Finally, Hesira had a distinctly raised chin, suggesting a certain arrogance: although he lived more than 4,500 years ago, Djoser's Chief Dentist and Master of the Royal Scribes seems to have displayed the attitude of senior bureaucrats throughout history.

7 IMHOTEP
ARCHITECT AND SAGE WHO BECAME A GOD

The radical idea of taking the single-stepped royal tomb of the 1st and 2nd Dynasties and transforming it into a far more imposing structure, by placing one step on top of another, and so upwards to the apex – in short, the concept of the pyramid – was a defining moment in the long course of pharaonic civilization. Tradition has ascribed this remarkable innovation to an individual who has been called 'the greatest intellect of the Early Dynastic Period' and who was to become synonymous with knowledge, both practical and magical. His name echoes down the forty-six centuries since his architectural creation first took shape on the Saqqara plateau, and has come to stand in popular culture for ancient Egypt itself: Imhotep.

Given the early period at which he lived and worked, it is not surprising that the contemporary evidence for Imhotep is rather meagre. Indeed, he is named only twice in 3rd Dynasty contexts: once on the base of a statue of King Djoser from the Step Pyramid complex, and again in a graffito on the enclosure wall of the pyramid complex of Djoser's successor, Sekhemkhet. None the less, these two attestations tell us a great deal about Imhotep's position at court and his career. The statue base of Djoser which names Imhotep was originally set up in a small room on the south side of the entrance colonnade leading to the Great Court of the Step Pyramid complex. It would thus have been passed by all those entering or leaving the monument. This very public location, combined with the naming of a private individual on the base of a royal statue, demonstrates Imhotep's pre-eminent rank at Djoser's court. The statue base gives his titles as Royal Seal-Bearer, First Under the King, Ruler of the Great Estate, member of the elite, Greatest of Seers, and Overseer of Sculptors and Painters; with the possible exception of the last title, there is nothing explicit to link him with the design or construction of the king's funerary monument. But who else, except the architect and inspiration behind the Step Pyramid, would have been given such a prominent place in its final set-up? The graffito from the principal monument of the next reign suggests that Imhotep's skills as an architect were prized by Djoser's successor, too; and that the great man, late in life, had a hand in designing Egypt's second pyramid, thus developing the tradition that he himself had started.

According to much later sources, Imhotep's wife was called Renpetnefret, his mother Khereduankh and his father Kanefer. In the absence of further 3rd Dynasty texts there is no way of verifying this information; but the suggestion that Kanefer was himself a Superintendent of Royal Works certainly makes sense, as it explains how a man such as Imhotep could have become so well acquainted with the architectural, technological and organizational aspects of major construction projects. These skills were stretched to the limit in creating an entirely novel monument for Djoser. The world's first large-scale stone building involved, among other things, the quarrying, transportation, setting, dressing and decorating of nearly a million tons of limestone: an unprecedented feat of engineering and logistics.

It is little wonder, therefore, that, after his death at the end of the 3rd Dynasty, a host of myths and legends grew up around the great Imhotep. Wisdom literature was ascribed to him: one of the *Songs of the Harper* (a series of songs written in the Middle and New Kingdoms) contained the lines: 'I have heard the sayings of Imhotep... which we quoted in proverbs so much.' By the 18th Dynasty, Imhotep had become the focus of popular veneration; libations were offered to him, and he was regarded as the patron of scribes. In the Late Period, with tourists visiting the Step Pyramid in greater numbers, Imhotep's reputation grew, and he was recognized as the son of the god Ptah; indeed he was himself deified as a god of writing, architecture, wisdom and medicine (fig. 3). In the 30th Dynasty, the cult of Imhotep was one of the most important in the Memphite area, receiving royal patronage. The last native-born ruler of Egypt, Nakhthorheb (no. 95), called himself 'beloved of Imhotep son of Ptah', while the king's subjects worshipped Imhotep as 'the august god who gives life to the people'. In common with other popular deities, he was seen as a healer, and it was in this context that he subsequently became closely identified with the Greek god of medicine, Asklepius.

The cult of Imhotep reached its apogee under the Ptolemies. The main centres of worship and pilgrimage were the temple of Ptah at

Memphis and the Asklepion at Saqqara (believed to be Imhotep's burial-place), but other shrines were built throughout the country, for example at Deir el-Medina in western Thebes, at Heliopolis at the base of the Delta and at Xoïs in the north-central Delta. A Ptolemaic stela, purporting to date to the reign of Djoser, was carved on the island of Sehel in the First Cataract; it told of how the king consulted Imhotep over how best to bring to an end seven years of famine. Nearby, on the island of Philae, Ptolemy V built a small temple to Imhotep from where his cult spread southwards into Nubia, even as far as Meroë. At Edfu, an inscription credited Imhotep with inventing the principles of temple architecture, thus remembering the origins of his fame. At the various shrines dedicated to Imhotep, devotees paid for images of the sage to be presented as votive offerings; almost 400 bronze statues are known, mostly from Memphis and Saqqara. They depicted him as a scribe, with an unrolled papyrus; as a priest, with a long apron; or as the son of Ptah, wearing a skull-cap.

As a god of healing and medicine, Imhotep continued to be venerated into the Roman Period; in the temple of Dendera, he was credited with arcane knowledge of astronomy and astrology. Thus began the final, bizarre chapter in the posthumous life of the 3rd Dynasty official. He became a figure in popular romances, while an Arabic text of the tenth century AD mentioned him as an alchemist. Magician, healer, sage, scribe: the many incarnations in which Imhotep was venerated all reflect the monumental achievement of the Step Pyramid complex which changed Egypt and the ancient Egyptians forever. It is indeed fitting that the reputation of the man who created the defining symbol of Egyptian civilization should have survived longer than that of any other of his countrymen.

8 METJEN
CAREER CIVIL SERVANT

In the 3rd Dynasty, perhaps for the first time, it became possible for individuals of humble origins to rise by their own talents through the ranks of the administration to the highest echelons of government. The opening up of the bureaucracy to men of non-royal background was probably an inevitable result of the greater professionalization required for pyramid-building. It also had the effect, naturally, of widening the pool of talent available to the king in the allocation of important responsibilities. Metjen, a career civil servant whose life spanned virtually the entire 3rd Dynasty, exemplified this new meritocracy.

Metjen's tomb at Saqqara contains the earliest extensive auto-biographical inscription from ancient Egypt. It charts his career from its unspectacular beginning to its impressive conclusion. Given the Lower Egyptian geographical focus of his career, it seems likely that Metjen was born somewhere in the Delta. His father Inpuemankh was a judge and scribe, so Metjen would have been brought up to read and write, a prerequisite for government office. His first job was as a scribe, too, with responsibility for a storehouse of provisions and its contents: in other words, a small cog in the great machine of the Egyptian redistributive economy.

His aptitude for accountancy must have come to the attention of his superiors in the central government, for he was duly promoted to be Under Field-Judge – responsible for determining field boundaries, a crucial role in an agricultural economy – and local governor of Xoïs, a town in the north-central Delta which may have been Metjen's birthplace. A further promotion, to Judge of All Land Disputes, followed, his first government-level post. From there, his talents swiftly brought him new and greater responsibilities, including overseeing the national flax-harvest, a key crop, essential for the manufacture of linen.

At the height of his career, Metjen returned to his background of local government, as regional administrator, on behalf of the king, in a host of Delta nomes (provinces). At one time or another, he controlled the 2nd (Letopolite), 5th (Saite), 6th (Xoite), 7th (Harpoon) and 16th (Mendesian) nomes of Lower Egypt, comprising a great swathe of the northern Delta; he was also Palace-Ruler (administrator appointed by the king) of two townships, and the governor of a fortress. Outside the Delta, he administered 'the cow stronghold', perhaps one of the western oases, and held the associated positions of Desert Governor and Master of the Hunt. In the eastern Fayum, he was a district administrator and 'ruler of the palace towns of the southern lake', in other words the pleasure-palaces established by Egyptian kings on the shores of Lake Fayum. A slight anomaly, given the Lower Egyptian focus of his other responsibilities, was the post of administrator, nomarch (provincial governor) and Overseer of Commissions in the 17th (Jackal) nome of Upper Egypt.

To add to the 50 arouras (13.5 ha, 33 acres) of land he inherited from his mother Nebsenet under the terms of her will, Metjen was liberally rewarded for his loyal service with further, substantial grants of land and provisions from the state. In addition, an extensive estate was established to provide income in perpetuity for his mortuary cult. Perhaps the gift from the state of which he was proudest, however, was his house. Metjen's description conjures up the image of an ideal home, with all the features a person of wealth and status would have expected: 'An estate 200 cubits (105 m, 343 ft) long by 200 cubits wide, with a wall equipped and set with good wood, a very big pool made in it, and planted with figs and grapes.' The Delta had been the centre of Egyptian wine-making since at least the 1st Dynasty, and Metjen was clearly an enthusiastic grower since, in addition to the vines planted around his house, he also had a separate, walled vineyard. Metjen thus lived out the remainder of his days in considerable comfort, surrounded by the luxuries that were the reward, not of birth, but of merit.

PART 2

The Pyramid Age
Old Kingdom

The pyramids are the quintessential symbols of ancient Egyptian civilization. Their antiquity, monumentality, perfection and mystery sum up all those things about pharaonic culture that have enthralled the western mind since Napoleon's expedition at the end of the eighteenth century. The Great Pyramid of Khufu (no. 10) and its two companions at Giza are the best known, and together constitute the only surviving wonder of the ancient world. But the vast necropolis of Memphis, ancient Egypt's traditional capital, is littered with pyramids stretching over a distance of 33 km (21 miles), from Abu Rawash in the north to Dahshur in the south. The era that saw the construction of these extraordinary buildings is known to Egyptologists as the Old Kingdom. It is the first great period of strong, centralized rule, when the state used its new-found wealth in tandem with its absolute political and economic control to promote its own pre-eminence. If the government's motive for pyramid-building is clear enough, what did the population at large gain from the enterprise?

The answer goes to the heart of the Egyptian world-view, and the contract between the ruler and those he ruled. Under this contract, the people were expected to give a percentage of their agricultural production in tax; the state used some of this to fund itself and its grandiose projects, but stored the rest in granaries, as 'buffer stocks' to alleviate the effects of famine in lean years. The people gave their labour on a seasonal basis to state projects; in return they received permission to farm their land – which in theory belonged to the king – the rest of the year, and rations from the state while they were engaged on government work. By means of these reciprocal arrangements, the Egyptians were able to build vast monuments like the pyramids. At the same time, it can be said that the pyramids built Egypt: as a structured, organized and highly efficient command economy. However, the administrative effort and expenditure of resources required for truly massive pyramids could not be sustained over the long term; after the 4th Dynasty, royal funerary monuments returned to a more modest scale, as illustrated by the pyramids of Unas (no. 15) and Pepi II (no. 20).

If royal tombs dominated cultural expression in the Old Kingdom, the royal family held an equally central place in the power-politics of the period. The lavish tomb equipment given to the king's mother Hetepheres (no. 9) by her son Khufu remains one of the finest collections of grave goods ever found in Egypt, and illustrates the artistic patronage exercised by the monarch's inner circle. Despite the increasing professionalization of the administration, which allowed talented individuals like Weni (no. 18) to rise in the hierarchy, most of the really senior positions of authority were still held by the king's male relatives. Men such as Hemiunu in the 4th Dynasty (no. 11), Ptahshepses in the 5th (no. 13) and Mereruka in the 6th (no. 17) all owed their influence to their royal connections. The king's patronage could bring not only power and wealth but also the privilege of a tomb in the court necropolis at Saqqara (the burial-ground for the capital city of Memphis). In a society as concerned with mortuary provision as it was with status, it was hardly surprising that the construction of one's tomb should have been regarded as a key indicator of success. High officials like Metjetji (no. 16) displayed their exalted rank and worldly wealth by means of large and elaborately decorated tomb-chapels. Even lesser members of the royal court, such as the dwarf Perniankhu (no. 12), were able to secure a burial close to their monarch's own funerary monument; they hoped, by this means, to continue receiving royal favour for eternity.

The scenes and texts in the private tombs of the Old Kingdom provide valuable insights into many aspects of contemporary culture, from craftsmanship to farming practices, from the structure of the administration to the lifestyle of the elite. The location of tombs, too, points to an important development in ancient Egyptian society.

As the Pyramid Age progressed, an increasing number of high officials opted to be buried, not in the great court cemetery of Memphis, but in their own home regions. The rise of local identity went hand-in-hand with an upsurge in provincial autonomy, particularly in the 6th Dynasty, as the central government began to devolve more power to the regions. For a dignitary like Pepiankh (no. 14), there was no doubt that his status derived from his seniority in his home town, even if he expressed it through the usual plethora of courtly epithets and titles. One locality with an especially strong sense of its own identity was Elephantine (ancient Abu). The reasons for this were partly geographical – the town was 800 km (500 miles) by river from the capital and royal residence at Memphis – and partly cultural, the inhabitants of the First Cataract region tending to look as much towards Nubia as towards Egypt. Indeed, the local officials of Abu were valuable to the central government for their knowledge and understanding of Nubia, a land which supplied the court with a range of exotic and prestigious products, from ebony to panther-skins. In the 6th Dynasty, individuals such as Harkhuf (no. 19) and Pepinakht-Heqaib (no. 21) grew rich and famous as a result of distinguished government service in the foreign lands beyond Egypt's southern border.

Just as the centralization of power characterized the apogee of pyramid-building in the 4th Dynasty, so the process of decentralization marked the decline of royal authority towards the end of the Old Kingdom. In the end, the decentralizing forces inherent within Egyptian society proved uncontainable, exacerbated by dynastic squabbles and conflicts over the succession in the wake of Pepi II's extraordinarily long reign. Royal authority faded as regional autonomy grew in strength, ushering in a period of political fragmentation that was to have a profound and long-lasting effect on Egyptian society and the Egyptian psyche.

9 HETEPHERES
MOTHER OF KING KHUFU

The equipment from the tomb of Hetepheres is one of the treasures of Cairo's Egyptian Museum (figs 5 and 6). In its purity and elegance of design, exemplary craftsmanship and sumptuous materials, it encapsulates the self-confidence and restrained opulence of the Pyramid Age. But what about the woman for whom it was made? Who was Hetepheres and what would her life have been like?

The bare facts of her background are clear enough. She was the wife of a king (Sneferu), the mother of a king (Khufu) and very probably the daughter of a king (Huni), too. Indeed, her status derived entirely from her relationships with the men in her family. The Egyptian language had no word for 'queen', only terms for 'king's wife' or 'king's mother'. Nevertheless, as the powerful mother of an all-powerful king, Hetepheres would have been by far the most influential woman, and probably one of the most influential people of either sex, at Khufu's court. The titles on her chair, in gold hieroglyphs inlaid on ebony panels, suggest as much: Mother of the Dual King, Follower of Horus, Director of the Ruler, the Gracious One, whose every utterance is done for her. The third of these epithets is particularly telling, for it suggests that Khufu, like so many despotic rulers through history, took orders from only one person, and that was his mother.

Although Hetepheres lived during one of the greatest periods of ancient Egyptian civilization, witnessing at first hand the construction of the first true pyramids – from Meidum and Dahshur under her father and husband to the Great Pyramid of Giza under her son – surprisingly little is known about her life. However, thanks to her remarkable burial goods, rather more can be said about her lifestyle, and by extension, that of the Old Kingdom nobility in general. Among her items of furniture was a carrying-chair, and this seems to have been a favoured method of transport for high-status individuals of the time – impressive, perhaps, but not particularly comfortable. The occupant would have sat on the wooden seat board (perhaps softened by a cushion) with their knees drawn up against their chest. In Hetepheres' case, the spectacle would have been made more dazzling by the lavish use of gold on her carrying-chair.

The impression of a peripatetic existence, moving from one royal residence to another, is reinforced by the other items in her tomb equipment. These included a bed with a separate canopy, two low chairs, and several jewelry boxes. The furniture, though embellished with feet in the shape of lions' paws and decorated with inlays and gold foil, was relatively simple, lightweight and highly portable. It would have been easily dismantled and re-erected as Hetepheres and her entourage travelled around the country. In keeping with such a mobile lifestyle, a woman's wealth was carried largely on or about her person. A representation of Hetepheres on her carrying-chair shows her wearing no fewer than fourteen bracelets on her right arm. These she kept in a specially made jewelry box, itself covered in gold leaf inside and out, which could accommodate twenty bracelets in two rows of ten. The bracelets themselves were of exceptional quality, and would have outshone anything worn by her contemporaries both in terms of their design and their materials. They were made from silver, at a time when it was far more precious than gold (Egypt had gold in abundance, whereas silver had to be imported from overseas); each bracelet was decorated with four stylized butterflies inlaid in turquoise, lapis lazuli and carnelian, separated by small carnelian discs. Similar animal and floral elements featured in the decoration of her furniture, while the footboard of the bed carried a feather pattern in faience.

The overall impression given by Hetepheres' belongings is of luxury and magnificence appropriate to a king's mother. As she travelled around in her carrying-chair, holding a lotus flower to her nose, her multiple silver bracelets glinting in the sun, she must have been a dazzling sight, even in a country and at a time when the greatest monument the world had ever seen was rising slowly on the Giza plateau.

10 KHUFU
LORD OF THE GREAT PYRAMID

'Man fears time, but Time fears the pyramids.' The well-known Arab proverb sums up the feelings of awe and wonder that visitors of countless generations have experienced when looking up at the pyramids of Giza and especially the most magnificent of the three, the Great Pyramid of Khufu. Icon of ancient Egyptian civilization, the Great Pyramid is both age-old and timeless. Its stupendous size and phenomenal precision are bewildering. The statistics of its construction are familiar, but bear repeating. The monument contains about 2,300,000 blocks of limestone, meaning that the builders would have had to set one block in place every two or three minutes during a ten-hour day, working seven days a week, fifty-two weeks a year for the duration of Khufu's reign. The Grand Gallery is a breathtaking architectural achievement, its corbelled roof rising to a height of 8.74 m (26 ft). Shafts leading from the burial chamber and a second chamber (probably intended to house the king's *ka*-statue) extend in a straight line through the solid masonry to the outer edge of the pyramid, and are perfectly aligned to the constellation Orion and the circumpolar stars. The pyramid itself has a base length of 230.33 m (756 ft), and would originally have risen to a height of 146.59 m (481 ft), yet its orientation is only one-twentieth of a degree (3'6" to be precise) off true north. If the architectural achievement is staggering, so too are the logistics. The administrative and organizational effort required to realize such an enormous building project must have tested the Egyptian state to an unprecedented degree; indeed, it has been said that, while the Egyptians built the pyramids, the pyramids also built Egypt.

Much has been written about the Great Pyramid, yet surprisingly little is known about the man for whom it was built, King Khufu. His name, in full, was Khnum-khufui, 'Khnum, he protects me', suggesting a special affinity with the creator-god Khnum who, according to Egyptian religion, fashioned men on his potter's wheel. Khufu certainly seems to have grown up with a sense of his own god-given status. His taste for gargantuan monuments did not, however, come out of the blue. His father Sneferu had inaugurated the era of colossal pyramid construction, and Khufu would have grown up seeing two huge pyramids rise above the sands of Dahshur. He succeeded his father when still a relatively young man, since he is known to have reigned for at least twenty-four years and probably achieved nearer thirty. Khufu's senior wife, 'great of sceptre', was Meritites, but he had at least one other consort. His eldest son and heir was Kawab, but he apparently predeceased his father, so instead the throne passed next to another son Djedefra and then to his younger brother Khafra. Khufu's remaining sons included princes named Khufukhaf, Minkhaf, Hordjedef, Bauefra and Babaef. With the notable exception of the king's mother, Hetepheres (no. 9), it seems to have been quite a male-dominated royal family. Many of Khufu's relatives were buried in mastabas (tombs with a bench-like, rectangular superstructure) in the extensive eastern cemetery laid out adjacent to the Great Pyramid. In death, as in life, the king intended to be surrounded by his inner circle.

To supply the mammoth building project taking shape on the Giza plateau, a huge limestone quarry was opened up nearby, and expeditions were sent by Khufu to secure smaller quantities of costlier stone from sites the length and breadth of Egypt: diorite from the southern Libyan desert near Toshka, calcite from Hatnub in Middle Egypt, turquoise from the Wadi Maghara in southwestern Sinai. In retrospect, it looks as if the entire economic and bureaucratic machinery of the state was directed to a single purpose: the construction of a monument to kingship, a 'resurrection machine' on an unprecedented scale. So, too, it must have appeared to Egyptians of Khufu's own time and to the generations who came after. The Great Pyramid gave its royal builder the posthumous reputation, perhaps richly deserved, of a megalomaniac tyrant. A series of stories composed several centuries later, at the end of the Middle Kingdom, cast him in a poor light, especially by comparison with his father Sneferu. In one of the so-called *Tales of Wonder*, set in Khufu's reign, the court is visited by a magician who is reputed to be able to reattach a severed head. Intrigued, Khufu orders him to demonstrate his powers on a human prisoner, but the magician manages to persuade the king to use a goose instead, deploring that such a thing should be done to one of 'god's cattle'.

By the fourth century BC, Khufu's reputation had reached an all-time low. The Greek historian Herodotus wrote: 'Cheops [i.e. Khufu] brought the country into all kinds of misery. He closed the temples, forbade his subjects to offer sacrifices, and compelled them without exception to labour upon his works.... The Egyptians can hardly bring themselves to mention... Cheops..., so great is their hatred.' In a civilization accustomed to – indeed, predicated upon – large-scale royal building projects, it seems that the biggest monument of all aroused more revulsion than wonder, and seemed somehow to overstep the normal standards of decency and decorum.

Another, more recent dictator, Napoleon Bonaparte, is reputed to have addressed his troops, camped on the Giza plateau, with the words: 'Soldiers of France, forty centuries gaze down upon you.' It is a delicious irony that the only known three-dimensional image of Khufu, builder of Egypt's greatest monument, is a tiny, ivory statuette, scarcely bigger than a man's thumb, measuring just 7.6 cm (3 in.) in height (fig. 4). Though the Great Pyramid itself looks likely to survive another four millennia, the vagaries of archaeological survival have certainly cut its original owner down to size.

11 HEMIUNU
OVERSEER OF WORKS

The Great Pyramid erected at Giza for King Khufu was not only the tallest building the world had ever seen (or would see for another 4,400 years); it was also the biggest construction project and the most complex feat of administration ever undertaken in ancient Egypt, a civilization characterized by grand monuments and an all-encompassing bureaucracy. The sheer logistics of the operation – provisioning and organizing the workforce, housed in its own 'pyramid city'; quarrying and transporting the stone; building and maintaining the ramps; marshalling the surveyors, architects and supervisors – were as impressive a feat as the pyramid itself. Yet in charge of the whole building site was one man: his name was Hemiunu.

In the early 4th Dynasty, nearly all senior officials were members of the royal family and Hemiunu was no exception. He was probably the son of Prince Nefermaat, and hence the grandson of Sneferu and nephew of Khufu. His position at court would certainly have opened up opportunities for rapid advancement, but Hemiunu must have possessed innate ability as well, for his rise through the ranks of the administration was impressive. His promotion is reflected in his tomb, which began as a substantial enough monument next to the Great Pyramid but was considerably enlarged to keep pace with Hemiunu's status. One of its reliefs shows him in his prime, his facial features suggesting a combination of self-confidence and determination: aquiline nose, rounded chin and strong jaw.

His many titles convey the same impression, of a man who knew himself to be one of the most important individuals in the country. In addition to his roles as courtier and Elder of the Palace, Hemiunu also held a number of significant religious offices, including priest of Bastet (cat-goddess), priest of Shesmetet (lioness-goddess), priest of the panther-goddess, priest of the Ram of Mendes, Keeper of the Apis (sacred bull of Memphis), Keeper of the White Bull, and High Priest of Thoth. This last was particularly appropriate since Thoth was the god of wisdom and writing, essential requirements for the Egyptian bureaucrat. We may perhaps glimpse one of Hemiunu's private interests in his unusual title Director of Music of the South and the North. But there is no doubting his principal offices, which were the reason for his exceptional prominence: Overseer of Royal Scribes (in other words, head of the civil service) and Overseer of All Construction Projects of the King.

The building of the Great Pyramid, and the subsequent clearance of the associated ramps and other project infrastructure, is thought to have been accomplished within a period of twenty years. It is therefore possible that Hemiunu saw the project through from inception to completion. The kudos and personal satisfaction which this undertaking of a lifetime must have brought him can be seen in the other remarkable piece of work which he directed, a sculpture of exceptional workmanship which was found in the statue chamber of his tomb. Originally painted, with inlaid eyes made from gold and rock-crystal, and hieroglyphic inscriptions on the base rendered in coloured paste, the statue shows Hemiunu seated, wearing a short kilt tied at the waist with a knot. The most striking feature of the sculpture is Hemiunu's corpulence. His breasts and chest sag under their own weight, while his enormous belly crushes his navel. By comparison with his obese frame, his head looks strangely small. In a country where most of the population survived on subsistence rations, to be fat was a marker of wealth and privilege, for it demonstrated the ability to indulge, to eat more than was absolutely necessary, and to avoid hard manual labour. Hemiunu's masterful direction of the greatest construction project in history brought him commensurately great personal rewards.

12 PERNIANKHU
COURT DWARF

Throughout history, royal courts have had their jesters, individuals tasked with entertaining the king and members of his family. In ancient Egypt, the favoured candidates for these entertainers were 'little people', either pygmies from sub-Saharan Africa or native Egyptians with dwarfism. Perniankhu was one such court dwarf who lived during the 4th Dynasty.

The Egyptians showed no obvious prejudice against people of restricted growth. Indeed, because the role of court dwarf involved unusually close and private access to the person of the king, such individuals were – like court jesters in medieval Europe – often highly respected and honoured members of the royal entourage, if not close confidants of the monarch. Seneb, perhaps a relative of Perniankhu, was a priest of Khufu and Djedefra as well as Director of Dwarfs in Charge of Dressing (the sovereign), and was appointed tutor to the king's son, reflecting the trust placed in him by the royal family. Perniankhu, 'the king's dwarf who delights his lord every day', likewise achieved prestige and wealth, reflected both in his burial in the great western cemetery at Giza and in his tomb statue.

The basalt sculpture of Perniankhu is a minor masterpiece of Old Kingdom art. It shows him wearing a short white kilt fastened with a black belt, and the short, curled, shoulder-length wig fashionable in the 4th Dynasty. His upper body is strong and muscular, but his lower body shows clear signs of deformity. His legs are short and bowed, his ankles exceptionally thick, and his feet flat. His left knee is also different from his right, suggesting either injury or congenital deformity. Nevertheless, Perniankhu is shown with two unambiguous symbols of authority: a sceptre in his right hand and a long staff in his left. These regalia, reserved for officials of high status, indicate that he must have been successful in his career, an early example of an enduring tradition of court dwarfs.

13 PTAHSHEPSES
ROYAL SON-IN-LAW

All power in ancient Egypt derived from the king. That was certainly the theory throughout pharaonic history; at the height of the Pyramid Age, it was also the practice. Although the highest ranks of the administration had been opened up to persons of non-royal birth in the 4th Dynasty, the most powerful offices of state were undoubtedly appointed by the king in person. Proximity to the monarch's inner circle therefore brought with it a far greater chance of preferment. This is illustrated particularly well by the life and career of Ptahshepses, whose tomb at Abusir is the largest private funerary monument of the Old Kingdom.

Little is known of Ptahshepses' origins, but his court career had evidently been successful enough at a relatively early stage for him to commission a tomb in the royal necropolis of the 5th Dynasty.

It was furnished with several decorated chambers inside the lime-stone superstructure, but was still relatively modest by the standards of the time. Ptahshepses may already have been employed in royal building projects – one of his subsequent appointments was Overseer of All the King's Works – and he clearly had knowledge of the building techniques used in the king's pyramid and its associated structures, for he employed some of them in his own monument. Hence, the roof of the burial chamber in his tomb was constructed from four pairs of huge stone slabs, just like those used to seal the burial chamber in a royal pyramid. This was an innovation in private tomb architecture, and Ptahshepses' monument marked a turning-point in the development of the Old Kingdom tomb.

A major turning-point in his own life occurred when he married the lady Khamerernebty, Sole King's Ornament, a priestess of Hathor Lady of the Sycamore, and, most significantly, daughter of the reigning king Niuserra. As the monarch's son-in-law, Ptahshepses now found himself in the innermost circle at court, with intimate access to the ultimate source of power. This is reflected in several of his titles, including Favourite of His Lord, Servant of the Throne, Director of the Palace, Keeper of the Diadem and the three related epithets 'privy to the secret of the House of Morning', 'privy to the secret of the god's word' and 'privy to his lord's secret in all his places'. His new status prompted a major enlargement of his funerary monument, with the addition of a chapel with niches for statues, fronted by a grand entrance with two limestone columns in the shape of lotus bundles.

At the same time, a change in the decoration inside the tomb may hint at an aspect of Ptahshepses' private life that is otherwise kept well hidden. The careful erasure throughout the tomb of the figure and name of his eldest son seems to indicate a deliberate act of disinheritance. This may have been because the eldest son was the offspring of an earlier marriage and, following Ptahshepses' union with the king's daughter, his children from his new, royal wife were given precedence. He certainly portrays himself as a family man, surrounded by at least seven sons and two daughters.

As Ptahshepses' influence and authority grew, he began to surround himself with his own 'court' in miniature. This included companions, scribes, barbers, a steward and a hairdresser; a particularly favoured attendant was his doctor. Ptahshepses must have struck an imposing figure in his long skirt and broad beaded collar, holding a staff of office, particularly when he was carried from place to place in his shaded palanquin, borne by sixteen men, with his other retainers following on behind. His wife Khamerernebty was adorned with a glittering array of jewelry about her neck, wrists and ankles, her status emphasized by her long, heavy wig reaching down to the middle of her back.

The culmination of Ptahshepses' career came with his appointment as vizier, an office combining the duties of Chief Justice as well as Prime Minister. This promotion to the head of the Egyptian government was marked by a second, even grander, programme of enlargements to his tomb at Abusir. His finished monument measured a staggering 80 by 107 m (262 by 351 ft), and required yet another new entrance: a portico with two lotiform columns reaching 6 m (20 ft) in height. With its gleaming walls of white limestone, Ptahshepses' monument must have dominated the burial-ground at Abusir, as it still does today: a permanent and fitting memorial to the grandest of nobles.

14 PEPIANKH
CENTENARIAN OFFICIAL

Not many people live to see their 100th birthday, even in modern, affluent, medically advanced societies. In ancient Egypt, where the average life expectancy was probably between thirty and thirty-six, it would have been highly unusual to reach the age of sixty. Only two kings, Pepi II (no. 20) and Ramesses II (no. 70), are known to have reached their eighties. But one man, Pepiankh-the-Middle, surpassed them all: for, if we are to believe his autobiographical inscription, he was ancient Egypt's only attested centenarian.

Pepiankh must have been born in the early 6th Dynasty, at Cusae (ancient Qus, modern el-Qusiya) in Middle Egypt, to a powerful local family. His record-breaking longevity was, it seems, matched by his plethora of titles and epithets, for by the end of his career, he had amassed a truly staggering collection, even by the status-obsessed and bombastic standards of the time. Pepiankh was a member of the elite, high official, councillor, Keeper of Nekhen and Headman of Nekheb (all purely honorary titles, denoting rank); his administrative titles included Chief Justice and Vizier, Chief Scribe of the Royal Tablet, Royal Seal-Bearer, Attendant of the Apis, Spokesman of Every Resident of Pe, Overseer of the Two Granaries, Overseer of the Two Purification Rooms, Overseer of the Storehouse, Senior Administrator, Scribe of the Royal Tablet of the Court, God's Seal-Bearer, and, curiously, draughtsman; in the religious sphere he was Chief Priest of Hathor Lady of Qus, Chief Lector-Priest (responsible for composing and guarding sacred texts) and Sem-Priest (officiant at funerary rites); while at court, he gloried in the status of Sole Companion, Lector-Priest, Overseer of Upper Egypt in the Middle Nomes, Royal Chamberlain, Staff of Commoners, Pillar of Kenmut, Priest of Maat, 'privy to the secret of every royal command' and 'favourite of the king in every place of his'.

Clearly, not all these titles can have translated into executive roles, and Pepiankh himself indicated which of them were his principal offices: 'I passed all the time that I spent in the function of a magistrate, while doing good and saying what is wished, in order to gain good repute with the god.' Like all successful individuals in ancient Egypt, Pepiankh knew only too well which palms to grease, since promotion depended as much on keeping in with the powerful as it did upon ability. In his administration of justice, keeping the parties happy was evidently his primary concern – 'I have judged two parties so as to content them, for I knew that is what the god wants' – but equally important was protecting his own reputation: 'As for anything said against me before the magistrates, I came out of it safely, while it fell on the accusers; I was cleared of it before the magistrates, for they had spoken against me in slander.' Here we see the real motivation of men like Pepiankh with moderately influential positions: to retain their power and defend their privileges against those who sought to supplant them.

Like most provincial officials of the time, Pepiankh combined administrative duties with service in the local temple: 'I spent a great part of this time as Chief Priest of Hathor Lady of Qus, entering unto Hathor Lady of Qus, to see her and to perform her ceremonial with my hands.' He clearly attributed his long life to the benevolence of his goddess: 'All things succeeded with me because I was a priest of Hathor Lady of Qus, and because I protected the goddess to her satisfaction.'

For the successful Egyptian, it was important to make proper preparations for burial since there was always the hope that life's rewards would be continued in the afterlife. Hence, Pepiankh gave careful consideration to his funeral arrangements and had his tomb constructed on virgin ground, 'in a clean place, in a good place, wherein no work had been done [previously]'. Obsession with rank and status; piety to one's local god; concern for the afterlife: Pepiankh embodied the typical preoccupations of an ancient Egyptian, but did so in the course of a wholly atypical lifespan.

15 UNAS
THE ENIGMATIC MONARCH

'Unas is he who eats men, feeds on gods...
Unas eats their magic, swallows their spirits:
Their big ones are for his morning meal,
Their middle ones for his evening meal,
Their little ones for his night meal,
And the oldest males and females for his fuel.'

These chilling verses are among several hundred inscribed on the walls of the inner chambers of the pyramid of Unas at Saqqara. Collectively, they are known as the Pyramid Texts, the oldest surviving body of religious literature from ancient Egypt. The language and imagery of some utterances suggest that they date back many centuries, perhaps even to the dawn of Egyptian history. Others were surely composed anew at the end of the 5th Dynasty. We may assume that spells, incantations and prayers played a part at all royal funerals and in all royal mortuary cults. Yet the idea of inscribing them permanently on the walls of the king's tomb, to stand for eternity, was an innovation of the reign of Unas.

Like the underlying meaning of the so-called Cannibal Hymn, quoted above, Unas remains an enigma and a paradox. He called his pyramid 'The Places of Unas are Perfection', yet it fell into such decay that it attracted the attention of Prince Khaemwaset (no. 72), who restored it in the 19th Dynasty. Unas was revered long after his death, yet during his lifetime he seems to have been sensitive to his own uncertain ancestry, taking pains to associate himself with some of his most illustrious forebears by building his pyramid directly above the tomb of Hetepsekhemwy, founder of the 2nd Dynasty, and in a diagonal line with the pyramids of Djoser (founder of the 3rd) and Userkaf (founder of the 5th).

Moreover, Unas's reign is poorly documented, and even its length is uncertain. At least three viziers held office under him, suggesting a lengthy period as monarch. Later historians allotted him between thirty and thirty-three years, and he seems to have been on the throne long enough to celebrate a *sed*-festival (jubilee), since the decorative programme of his pyramid temple includes scenes of Unas enthroned, receiving gifts from the gods and the personifications of Egypt's nomes (districts), quintessential elements of a *sed*-festival. An excerpt from the Pyramid Texts in Unas's pyramid gives a vivid description of how the king would have appeared at such important occasions:

'His panther skin is on him,
His staff in his arm, his sceptre in his hand.'

Despite the lack of historical inscriptions from his reign, the decoration of his pyramid causeway includes a wealth of scenes, at least some of which must relate to actual events. But here, too, it is difficult to disentangle illusion and reality. A scene of Unas slaying a defeated

Libyan chief turns out to have been copied, detail by detail, from an earlier monument of the 5th Dynasty. It probably represents a standardized scene, part of the ritual of kingship. By contrast, an isolated block showing a battle between Egyptian troops and an army of Asiatics appears for the first time, suggesting that it may record a real military encounter. It may be confirmed by isolated figures of bearded Asiatics that occur elsewhere on the Unas causeway; and two stone vase fragments inscribed with the king's name have been found at the port of Byblos, on the Lebanese coast, which served as Egypt's gateway to the natural resources of the Levant.

More straightforward are the scenes depicting human activities or the natural world, such as a marketplace busy with customers and merchants, workshops of metalworkers, farm labourers gathering figs and honey or harvesting grain, and a hunt in the desert. Perhaps the most famous scenes from the causeway are, fittingly for Unas and his reign, also the most enigmatic. These are the harrowing images of famine: a man on the verge of death is supported by his emaciated wife, while a male friend grips his arm; a woman desperate for food eats the lice from her own head; a little boy with the distended belly of starvation begs a woman for food. There can be little doubt that these record the mental and physical anguish of famine victims, yet there are no inscriptions to identify the starving people. It is scarcely conceivable that they are native Egyptians, since the whole purpose of art in a funerary context was to immortalize the desired state of affairs. Perhaps they are desert tribespeople, their parlous state shown in order to emphasize the wretchedness of those living beyond the rule of the Egyptian king. The mystery of these haunting scenes remains.

The site chosen by Unas for his pyramid was not only symbolically aligned with the monuments of earlier dynastic founders. It also made use of existing natural features, the causeway following the route of a long wadi and the valley temple sited on the shore of a lake at the foot of the escarpment. The embellishment of the causeway walls certainly broke new ground, and so did the treatment of the chambers beneath the pyramid, which were the first since the reign of Djoser to be decorated. Around the sarcophagus, the walls of the burial chamber were lined with white alabaster, grooved and painted to resemble an enclosure made from a wooden frame and reed matting, representing the archetypal shrine in ancient Egyptian religious thought. With the coffin painted black to symbolize the earth and the ceiling studded with golden stars against a dark blue background to mimic the night sky, Unas had conceived his final resting-place as a microcosm of the universe. Around him, the texts carved and painted blue – the colour of the watery abyss of the underworld – were designed to assist his resurrection from the earth and his safe passage into the heavens to live forever as 'an indestructible spirit'.

The carving of the utterances in stone was designed, above all, to obviate reliance on mortuary priests; yet, Unas's mortuary cult lasted well into the Middle Kingdom: a final contradiction in the life of this most enigmatic of kings. It is just possible that all the paradoxes were intentional, a veil behind which the man of mysterious origins could hide. As one of his Pyramid Texts succinctly put it: 'Unas is the master of cunning.'

16 METJETJI
COURTIER, PATRON, AESTHETE

The Old Kingdom private tombs at Saqqara are some of the most beautiful monuments to have survived from ancient Egypt. Their detailed, lively decoration bears witness to the skill and sophistication of Egyptian artists, and to the discernment and patronage of those high officials granted the privilege of a burial in the necropolis of the capital city, Memphis. One such official was Metjetji, who served at court at the end of the 5th Dynasty. Although his career was neither unusual nor particularly remarkable, the quality of the decoration from his tomb is exceptionally fine. He thus serves as an exemplar of the bureaucrat-patron at the height of the Pyramid Age.

Metjetji was a family man, with four sons – Ptahhotep, Khuensobek, Sabuptah and Ihy – and a daughter, Iretsobek. Not unexpectedly, two of their names honour Ptah, patron deity of Memphis, the city where Metjetji lived and worked. However, the fact that he named one son and one daughter in honour of Sobek, crocodile god of the Fayum, suggests a family connection with this region. As well as being a proud father, he was also a loyal son to his parents. According to Egyptian custom, he oversaw their burial and requested a coffin for them from the royal workshops. His request was granted, a sign of his standing at court where he had risen to the rank of Overseer of the Office of the Palace Tenants. He also held the rank of Liege of the King of the Great Palace, member of the elite, high official and district administrator. Put more simply, he was 'honoured by Unas [king at the time], his master'.

A man of means, Metjetji had his own estates, and would go out to receive the produce from them wearing sandals and a feline pelt partly covering his kilt and apron. Indeed, one of his additional duties at court was Chief Keeper of Fabrics, and he seems to have had something of a penchant for fine clothing. In his tomb, he is shown wearing a kilt with a pleated apron, bracelets, a broad bead collar and a long wig with fine locks partly covering his ears. He had a fashionably short beard and must have been quite the model of a well-dressed noble. His other leisure pursuits, as befitted a person of his rank and status, included playing board games and listening to musical concerts. He also had a spotted greyhound as a pet, which his son Ihy looked after while Metjetji was on official business.

An elegant tomb with well-executed decoration was an essential accoutrement for a high official, not only proclaiming his status during his lifetime but, crucially, guaranteeing that it would continue into the afterlife. Metjetji's tomb was adorned with mural paintings as well as reliefs, and it must have been a costly affair; but he was at pains to stress that he had been a good and generous employer to the workers, and had paid them from his own wealth: 'As for all those who built for me this tomb, I paid them after they had performed the work here, with the copper that was an endowment from my personal property. I gave them clothes and provided their nourishment with the bread and beer from my personal property, and they praised God for me because of it.'

Modesty was not a quality valued by ancient Egyptian officialdom. On his false door – in front of which priests and visitors would present the offerings in the mortuary cult – Metjetji had himself depicted eight times, more often than not holding a long staff emblematic of authority. Among the offerings listed on the false door are the usual bread, beer, meat, fowl, alabaster and linen, but also green and black eye-paint. Once again, we catch a glimpse of Metjetji the aesthete. His appreciation of sophistication is summed up in his wish for the afterlife: 'to walk on the beautiful roads of the West and enjoy a perfect burial in the necropolis.' He certainly achieved the latter and, it may be hoped, the former as well.

17 MERERUKA
GRAND VIZIER

'I was a great one of the king' says the high official Mereruka at the beginning of his autobiographical inscription; and there could be no better summary of his privileged position. For Mereruka owed his wealth and status entirely to his sovereign, Teti, having married the king's eldest daughter, Watetkhethor, also known as Seshseshet. When another of Teti's sons-in-law, Kagemni, retired as vizier, it was Mereruka who assumed this most important office at the head of the Egyptian government. The vizierate combined courtly, administrative and judicial functions in a single person. Moreover, it brought with it a host of other responsibilities and dignities, ranging from honorary governorships of important localities to responsibility for the king's pyramid complex and mortuary estate. Mereruka thus found himself with a central role in almost every sphere of Egyptian life. In religious affairs, he was a lector-priest, responsible for reciting spells and incantations during acts of worship. In government, he headed all departments as vizier while also holding his own portfolio as Overseer of All the King's Works. He was Overseer of the Six Great Mansions (Chief Justice) and honorary administrator of Dep (Greek Buto, modern Tell el-Fara'in), an ancient, northwestern Delta town of great sacred significance. As Teti's most trusted official, Mereruka was also in charge of the most important royal project of all, the king's mortuary complex. This involved overseeing both the estate that would supply Teti's mortuary cult in perpetuity and supervising the priests and tenants of the pyramid town, together with the construction of the pyramid itself, called 'Teti is enduring of places'.

Despite a heavy raft of responsibilities, life as a high official was not without its compensations. A host of servants tended to Mereruka's every need. Rather than having to walk, he was borne in a carrying-chair while attendants looked after his pets (two dogs and a monkey). In his leisure time, he enjoyed playing the board game *senet* ('passing') and painting. A scene in Mereruka's tomb shows him seated at an easel, painting a representation of the seasons, depicted in human form. He was evidently a man of cultured and refined tastes. These are reflected not just in the decoration of his tomb, but in the structure itself. As befitted the most powerful commoner in the land, it was the largest private tomb of its time, and, indeed, was destined to remain the largest in the Saqqara necropolis. Comprising thirty-two rooms, it included separate annexes for Mereruka's wife and eldest son (the latter given the loyal name Meri-Teti, 'beloved of Teti'). At the centre of the tomb was a magnificent hall of six columns, with a funerary statue of Mereruka standing before an offering table.

The customary scenes of craftsmen at work were accompanied by other, more bizarre, images of life in 6th Dynasty Egypt. It was common enough to include depictions of animal husbandry in a tomb, since these decorations magically guaranteed supplies of meat in the afterlife, should the actual offerings deposited with the grave goods be destroyed. In Mereruka's tomb, however, we gain unexpected insights into the short-lived attempts by 6th Dynasty farmers to domesticate exotic animals: scenes show attendants force-feeding hyenas to fatten them for the table, while semi-tame antelopes feed from mangers. The cuisine of Teti's court was apparently rather rarified.

Away from all this sophistication, Mereruka was a proud son, husband, brother and father. Known to his closest relatives and friends as plain Meri, he took pride in his extended family: his mother Nedjetemipet, his princess wife, his nine brothers and at least four sons. All found a place in the decoration of his great monument for eternity, the tomb he had built right next to the pyramid of his father-in-law and monarch. Having achieved high office, Mereruka was determined to remain within the king's inner circle forever. He may have been a commoner by birth, but by marrying well, he had ensured a glorious afterlife for himself and his entire family.

18 WENI
ROYAL FACTOTUM

The exercise of power was a highly flexible affair in ancient Egypt. Authority was rarely if ever wielded in a single defined post in the modern sense of a 'job'. Rather, an individual might be expected to carry out a wide range of responsibilities within a single career. Royal authority to act was what mattered, not relevant experience in a specific area. Few individuals illustrate this flexibility better than Weni, whose long and distinguished career, described in detail in the autobiographical inscription on his tomb at Abydos, spanned the first three reigns of the 6th Dynasty.

Under King Teti, Weni was, in his own words, 'a headband-wearing youth'. His father was Vizier, and already he was marked out for a career in the administration, holding the junior post of storehouse custodian. He then received his first promotion, to Inspector of Palace Tenants, another office connected with economic matters. Significantly, this new appointment brought Weni closer to the day-to-day running of the royal palace. He was being groomed for the king's personal service.

With the death of Teti and the accession of Pepi I, Weni might have feared that his career would stall, but the outcome was quite the reverse. He was promoted again, and this time to the office of Overseer of the Robing Room, a position which gave him regular and intimate access to the king. Weni's enhanced status at court was recognized with the rank of companion, and he was also made Inspector of Priests of Pepi I's pyramid town. Soon, his loyal service to the monarch was rewarded with further responsibility of a sensitive judicial nature: hearing legal cases 'alone with the Chief Judge and Vizier, concerning all kinds of secrets'. In particular, Weni was appointed to represent the king in cases concerning the royal harem. This was to stand him in good stead later in his career.

Weni's rapid rise through the ranks of the administration brought with it substantial material benefits. Like all successful Egyptians in mid-career, he was already making provision for his burial and mortuary cult. Using his special access to the king, he successfully petitioned for the privilege of a stone sarcophagus, usually reserved for members of the royal family. It was transported 'in a royal barge together with its lid, a doorway, a lintel, two jambs and a libation-table by a company of sailors under the command of a royal seal-bearer'. This show of royal favour must have been a signal honour.

Promotion followed promotion, as Weni was appointed Overseer, rather than merely Inspector, of Palace Tenants, and raised to the rank of sole companion. His main duties were connected with royal ceremonial, and involved guarding, escorting and attending the king on the occasion of audiences and visits. Like monarchs throughout the ages, Egyptian kings were susceptible to plots and palace coups, very often hatched in the harem which housed the women and children of the royal family. Indeed, it was in this institution that one of Pepi I's wives plotted against him. When the conspiracy was uncovered, Weni was deputed to hear and try the charge, alone and in secret: a powerful demonstration of the great trust placed in him by the king.

Weni's next commission was altogether different. The 'sand-dwellers' of western Asia – the nomadic tribespeople of the Sinai – were rebelling against Egyptian authority and threatening security on the country's northeastern border. So Weni was sent to put down the insurgency, with an army of Egyptian conscripts, bolstered by mercenaries from Nubia and the bordering desert regions under his command. He led the army through the Delta to engage the sand-dwellers in their desert homeland. In a classic pincer movement, half of the Egyptian army was ferried by boat, landing in the enemy's rear, while the other half travelled overland to launch a frontal attack. Weni's strategic skill resulted in a famous victory, but it was not to last: he boasted – somewhat shallowly – of being sent on four more occasions to attack the sand-dwellers, each time they rebelled.

After a string of onerous military postings, Weni could perhaps have looked forward to a quieter end to his career. But the death of Pepi I changed everything. As a tried and trusted courtier, Weni was appointed Chamberlain of the Palace and Sandal-Bearer to the new king, Merenra. He was also made Governor of Upper Egypt.

Weni's strategic abilities, honed in battle against the sand-dwellers, were now deployed in a civilian context, to transport large stone blocks for Merenra's pyramid from the quarries at Ibhat (a site in Lower Nubia) and Elephantine. A single expedition to both quarry sites was unprecedented, but with the aid of six barges and three tow-boats, Weni brought it to a successful conclusion. His reward was to be sent on another similar assignment: transporting an alabaster altar for the king's pyramid from the quarries at Hatnub, in a specially constructed barge of acacia wood, measuring 60 cubits long by 30 cubits wide (31.4 by 15.7 m, 103 by 51½ ft). What made the undertaking even more difficult was that it took place in the summer season, when the river level was low. None the less, Weni boasts of having accomplished the entire operation in a matter of seventeen days.

For the final mission of his career, he was able to deploy the skills he had acquired in some of his previous military and operational roles. His task was two-fold. First, he had to supervise the construction of three barges and four tow-boats, to bring more granite for the king's pyramid from Elephantine. Second, he was put in charge of digging five canals in Upper Egypt, perhaps to aid the passage of the huge boats and their heavy cargo. Not only was the work finished satisfactorily, Weni also adds: 'Indeed, I made a saving for the Palace with all these five canals.'

His comment is telling, and more revealing of his inner nature than the preceding description of his half-century-long career. For, despite his illustrious succession of senior judicial, military and civilian appointments, something of the young storehouse custodian still shines through this bean-counting remark.

19 HARKHUF
EXPLORER OF DISTANT LANDS

Egypt's oldest narrative of foreign travel is inscribed on the façade of a rock-cut tomb, high in the cliffs overlooking the Nile at Aswan. The tomb's owner, Harkhuf, ranks as one of the greatest explorers of the ancient world.

Like most high-ranking officials in the Old Kingdom, he bore a string of titles denoting his status in court circles. He was also Governor of Upper Egypt and 'of all mountain-lands belonging to the southern region'. However, his substantive office was that of Chief of Scouts, which gave him responsibility for maintaining security on Egypt's southern border, and for ensuring that the peoples of Nubia and beyond delivered a steady supply of exotic products – whether as trade or tribute – to the royal treasury. In Harkhuf's own words, he was the person 'who brings the produce of all foreign lands to his lord'.

It was on just such a mission to secure trade routes and bring back prestige commodities that Harkhuf undertook his first expedition to the distant land of Yam. Beyond the limits of Egypt's control, though still within its sphere of influence, Yam lay in present-day Sudan, perhaps along the Shendi reach of the Upper Nile. On the orders of the king, Merenra, Harkhuf and his father left on their 1,000-mile return trip, returning again just seven months later, laden with exotic goods for their sovereign.

Such was the success of this endeavour that Harkhuf was sent to Yam a second time, on this occasion as expedition leader in his own right. He left from Elephantine on the road leading due south, but the interest on this journey lay in the political geography of Lower Nubia that Harkhuf made a point of noting on his return trip: 'I came down through the region of the house of the chief of Satju and Irtjet, I explored those foreign lands. I have not found it done by any companion and Chief of Scouts who went to Yam previously.' In particular, the enumeration of districts within the territory of Irtjet constitutes our best evidence for the administration of Lower Nubia at this period. Indeed, it is possible that on this second journey, the trip to Yam, ostensibly to bring back produce, was in fact a pretext: the real purpose may have been to gather intelligence about the state of Lower Nubia. For many centuries, the peoples of the Upper Nile Valley had been subject to Egyptian control; but they were now showing signs of wishing to reassert their political autonomy. The coalescence of districts into larger territorial units was a warning sign that Egypt could not afford to ignore, and accurate information about the level of the threat was vital. Harkhuf returned to Egypt, mission accomplished, after eight months away.

Perhaps in response to the new political realities in Lower Nubia, Harkhuf's third expedition to Yam followed a different route. He left the Nile Valley in the district of This (ancient Tjeni, near modern Girga), and took the Oasis Road which led via the Kharga Oasis through the eastern Sahara to the Darfur region of Sudan. This route is still used by camel-trains today, and is called in Arabic the Darb el-Arba'in, 'the road of 40 (days)'. In order to reach Yam, Harkhuf must have left the road at some point, turning eastwards back towards the Nile. However, when he arrived at his destination, Harkhuf met with an unexpected turn of events, again the result of a changing political situation. The ruler of Yam, with whom Harkhuf wished to trade, had left his own country to wage a military campaign against the Tjemeh of southeastern Libya. Evidently Yam, too, was concerned to defend itself against possible adversaries. Undeterred by this complication, Harkhuf set out immediately in pursuit of the ruler of Yam, following him to Tjemeh-land. The two men met and concluded their negotiations to mutual satisfaction. For his part, Harkhuf proudly set out on his journey back to Egypt with a caravan of 300 donkeys, laden with all the most valuable products of Africa: incense, ebony, precious oil, throwsticks, panther-skins and elephant tusks.

With Lower Nubian chiefs now openly flouting Egyptian suprem-acy, Harkhuf might have expected a difficult return trip. He was not wrong. Travelling as before along the Nile Valley, he discovered that the chief of Satju and Irtjet had added the whole of Wawat (Nubia north of the Second Cataract) to his growing lands. This enlarged state saw itself as the equal of Egypt, and the chief was not about to allow such a rich booty as Harkhuf's to pass unhindered through his territory. Only the presence of an armed escort provided by the ruler of Yam won the day for Harkhuf. Having negotiated safe passage, he hurried home to Egypt. We can imagine his relief when, as he neared the royal residence at Memphis, he was welcomed by a convoy of ships laden with supplies of food and drink: not only the staples of bread and beer, but cakes and wine as well.

After three expeditions to Yam on the orders of Merenra, Harkhuf now found himself answerable to a new sovereign, in the form of the boy-king Pepi II (no. 20). In the young monarch's first year on the throne, Harkhuf departed on his fourth and final journey to Yam. He does not record the route he took, but we may assume that he carefully avoided passing through the restive statelets of Lower Nubia, opting instead for the safer Oasis Road. On arrival in Yam, he sent a dispatch to Pepi saying that he was returning with 'all kinds of great and beautiful gifts'. Pre-eminent among them was 'a pygmy of the god's dances from the land of the horizon-dwellers', in other words from the ends of the earth. Harkhuf compared his prize to the pygmy brought from Punt (modern Sudan or Eritrea) in the reign of the 5th Dynasty king Isesi, but noted that never before had a pygmy been brought back to Egypt from Yam. In reply, the king sent Harkhuf a letter full of excitement and anticipation, urging him to 'Come north to the residence at once! Hurry and bring with you this pygmy... to delight the heart of King Neferkara [the throne-name of Pepi II].'

Receiving this personal correspondence from the king was the high-point of Harkhuf's career. He had the complete text of the royal letter inscribed on the façade of his tomb, in pride of place next to the account of his four epic expeditions. For the old explorer, the eagerness of a six-year-old monarch eclipsed all the wonders of Africa.

20 PEPI II
EGYPT'S LONGEST-REIGNING KING

A magnificent alabaster statue, now in the Brooklyn Museum of Art, New York, shows a tiny royal figure, wearing the *nemes* headdress of kingship, sitting on his mother's lap (fig. 9). The composition is striking for, although the child is represented as a miniature adult to conform to the decorum of monarchy, his scale and posture emphasize his infancy and vulnerability. The boy king in question is Neferkara Pepi II, last ruler of the 6th Dynasty. According to later historians, notably Manetho (no. 99), Pepi II came to the throne at the age of six and, since he lived to be one hundred, reigned for longer than any other monarch in Egyptian history.

Of this unusually long reign, surprisingly little is known, with the exception of the king's early years. Pepi succeeded his elder brother Merenra, who seems to have died unexpectedly early. Because the new king was still only a child, power was exercised on his behalf by his mother, Ankhenesmerira (who may have commissioned the aforementioned statue to underline her relationship to the monarch), aided by her brother Djau, who had been appointed southern vizier by Pepi I. Egyptian artists were evidently rather unused to expressing the concept of a child king, and the results, produced for Pepi II, are unusual experiments in royal iconography. For example, a statue from Pepi II's pyramid complex shows him as a naked child, squatting with his hands on his knees, yet wearing the royal uraeus (cobra) on his brow.

The most famous event from the first decade of Pepi's reign is the journey made by Harkhuf (no. 19) to Yam which brought back a dancing pygmy as a trophy for the young king. As soon as Pepi heard about the pygmy, he was unable to contain his excitement and wrote to Harkhuf, urging him to take great care of his precious charge: 'When he goes down with you into the ship, get worthy men to be around him on deck, lest he fall into the water! When he lies down at night, get worthy men to lie around him in his tent. Inspect ten times at night! My Person desires to see this pygmy more than the gifts of the Sinai and of Punt!' The combination of childlike enthusiasm and royal authority has made this one of the most memorable extracts from the ancient Egyptian textual record.

Despite his lengthy reign, Pepi II did not depart from the standard 6th Dynasty model in planning his pyramid complex at south Saqqara. The main monument was 150 cubits (78.6 m, 258 ft) square at its base and 100 cubits (52.4 m, 172 ft) high. Appropriately for a king whose extraordinary longevity must have seemed to many of his countrymen more like immortality, the pyramid was named 'Neferkara is established and living'. It was inscribed inside with extracts from the Pyramid Texts, while much of the decoration of the pyramid temple was slavishly copied from the 5th Dynasty complex of Sahura at Abusir. It is as if artistic creativity had stalled, symptom of a wider malaise in the country at large, which would lead to the breakdown of royal authority and of a dominant court culture after Pepi's death. Outside the Nile Valley, too, conditions were worsening. In Nubia, the coalition of states reported by Harkhuf began to grow more powerful and threaten Egyptian dominance. One of Pepi's senior officials, the Chancellor Mehu, was killed by hostile locals while on an expedition to Nubia, and his body had to be retrieved by his son Sabni in the course of a difficult mission.

Back in the capital, however, Pepi seems to have enjoyed a relatively peaceful reign, surrounded by his growing family. He had at least four wives, including two half-sisters Neith and Iput, his niece Ankhesenpepi, and another woman, perhaps a distant cousin, Wedjebten. All were granted their own burials around the king's pyramid. The burial chamber of Neith's pyramid was decorated with Pyramid Texts, for the first time in a non-kingly context. The distinctions between royal and non-royal burial customs and funerary beliefs had already begun to blur, presaging the full-scale 'democratization of the afterlife' of the ensuing First Intermediate Period.

Pepi's great age at his death – he saw ten viziers come and go – caused major problems for the succession: he had outlived so many of his heirs that the royal family struggled to find a single candidate who could command widespread support. A son named Nemtiemsaf II, mentioned as Crown Prince on a stela from Neith's pyramid complex, emerged as the next king, but did not last long. He was followed by a series of equally ephemeral rulers as Egypt headed towards political fragmentation. As for Pepi's posthumous reputation, history was decidedly unkind. A folklore story, perhaps composed in the late Middle Kingdom and popular for many centuries, told of a homosexual relationship between a king Neferkara and his general Sasenet. The tale presents the king's behaviour in a salacious and unfavourable light:

> 'Then he noticed the Person of the Dual King Neferkara going out at night.... Then he threw a brick and kicked [the wall], so that a ladder was let down for him. Then he ascended.... Now after His Person had done what he desired with him [Sasenet], he returned to the palace...'

It was an ignominious fate for the last significant ruler of the Pyramid Age.

21 PEPINAKHT-HEQAIB
LOCAL HERO

Like his predecessor Harkhuf (no. 19), Pepinakht, the Chief of Scouts in the latter part of the reign of Pepi II (no. 20), also undertook several challenging expeditions to foreign lands. However, for Pepinakht ('Pepi is victorious'), named in honour of his monarch, fame was to result in more than a mere rock-cut tomb in the cliffs above Aswan.

As nomarch (provincial governor) of the southernmost province of Egypt, in charge of expeditions to Lower Nubia and the security of Egypt's Nubian frontier, Pepinakht's loyalty to the crown was rewarded during his career with the sobriquet Heqaib, 'ruler of the heart', and with appointments to the mortuary cults of Pepi II and his two predecessors. But Pepinakht's real skill lay in the twin arms of foreign policy: trade and war. In his own words, it was he 'who brings the produce of foreign lands to his lord' and he 'who casts the terror of Horus into foreign lands'.

Since the beginning of Pepi II's reign Lower Nubia had continued to coalesce politically and now posed a real threat to Egypt. Hence, Pepinakht's first royal mission was to deliver a military blow that would reassert Egyptian hegemony – 'to hack up Wawat and Irtjet'. His own account conveys the essence of the bloody encounter in stark and uncompromising fashion:

'I acted to the satisfaction of my lord. I slew a large number of them.... I brought a large number of them to the Residence as captives, while I was at the head of numerous, strong and bold troops. My lord trusted me fully in every mission on which he sent me.'

Despite Pepinakht's confidence in his own abilities, the confederacy of Wawat, Irtjet and Satju – later to flower culturally as the so-called C-Group – was not going to be defeated so easily. A second mission 'to pacify these lands' was required a few years later, and this time Pepinakht took out an insurance policy against any future insurgency. In addition to the long-horned and short-horned cattle which he conveyed to the royal residence as campaign booty, he also brought human trophies: the sons of the rebellious rulers. This was standard Egyptian practice, and it accomplished two key objectives at once. Not only were the young princes hostages at the Egyptian court, guaranteeing the obedience of their relatives back in Nubia, it was also the hope and intention that they would become culturally Egyptianized through growing up at court with young Egyptian princes. Hence, when they eventually succeeded to their Nubian lands, they might prove more loyal than their fathers. As Pepinakht immodestly remarks of his achievements: 'I performed the tasks of Headman of the South through my excellent vigilance in doing my lord's wish.'

Having shown his skill and fortitude in difficult circumstances, Pepinakht was duly sent on a far more dangerous and complex mission. The scenario is worthy of a spy novel, and it sheds a fascinating light on the unpleasant realities of Egyptian foreign policy at the end of the Old Kingdom. Some years earlier, another Overseer of Scouts and ship's captain named Anankhet had travelled to the Lebanese coast to build a ship for a voyage to the fabled land of Punt. While engaged in this task, he and the company of soldiers with him had been ambushed and killed by a group of 'sand-dwellers', those persistent troublemakers on Egypt's northeastern border who had been the target of at least five campaigns earlier in the 6th Dynasty (see Weni, no. 18). For an Egyptian, not to receive a proper burial at home was an appalling prospect, since it spelled utter oblivion. For the Egyptian authorities, to lose an important official to insurgents and not to recover his body was an unbearable injury to national pride. So Pepinakht, the seasoned operator in foreign conflict zones, was sent by the king to retrieve and repatriate Anankhet's body. That Pepinakht accomplished his mission successfully, driving the rebels to flight and killing some of them in the process, says much about his personal qualities. It also helps to explain his later reputation as a local hero.

Pepinakht was succeeded as Overseer of Scouts by his son Sabni, whose own mission to Wawat was to bring back a pair of obelisks for the temple of Ra at Heliopolis. This was, however, one of the last gasps of royal power, not only in Lower Nubia but also in Egypt itself. For the death of Pepi II was followed by a succession of ephemeral reigns, a weakening of royal authority and the eventual collapse of the Old Kingdom state. But for Pepinakht, the future was altogether brighter. His remarkable career had won him fame in his local community, and his memory continued to be revered long after his death. A shrine was built on the island of Elephantine, dedicated to 'Heqaib', where worshippers came and prayed to their hero to intercede on their behalf with the divine powers. The cult of Heqaib grew in popularity and, for generations, visitors to the sanctuary left votive objects and statues as tokens of their belief in his supernatural powers. During the First Intermediate Period and early Middle Kingdom, the cult was even patronized by several kings, in an extraordinary reversal of the usual pattern of Egyptian religion.

Today, more than 4,000 years after his life and death, Heqaib's shrine has been excavated and once again receives a steady stream of visitors who come to pay tribute to the place and the man who inspired it.

PART 3

Civil War and Restoration
First Intermediate Period
and Middle Kingdom

Following the collapse of central authority at the end of the Old Kingdom, Egypt fragmented along traditional territorial lines. The eventual successors of Pepi II saw the extent of their authority reduced to the Delta and northern Nile Valley, while other, local potentates governed their own home regions in Upper Egypt. Prominent among the latter were Ankhtifi (no. 23), who controlled the three southern-most provinces, and his great rival, the ruler of Thebes. As the various would-be monarchs jostled for power, certain localities and routes of communication became strategically important, notably the desert tracks behind Thebes. Recent discoveries of inscriptions carved here by a local official named Tjauti (no. 22) have greatly expanded our picture of geo-political relations during the First Intermediate Period, as the era following the Old Kingdom is termed.

Within a few generations, however, the ruler of Thebes, named Intef, emerged as the most powerful man in Upper Egypt, and the prime mover behind a strategy to reunify the whole country by mili-tary means. The adoption of a royal titulary by Intef I threw down a direct challenge to the king of the 9th/10th Dynasty based at the city of Herakleopolis (ancient Hnes) in Middle Egypt, and a full-scale civil war ensued. Major advances were made by Intef II (no. 25) while his second successor, Mentuhotep II (no. 27), achieved ultimate victory, inaugurating a new period of strong, central government known as the Middle Kingdom.

Egypt, however, was a changed country. The weakening of royal authority during the First Intermediate Period had not only been accompanied by a corresponding rise in provincial autonomy; it had also brought about a blurring of the previously sharp distinctions between royal and private in many spheres, not least religion. In the Old Kingdom, the promise of an afterlife in the company of the gods had been reserved for the king. However, once the monarch no longer held a place at the apex of society, the hope of rebirth and an eternal existence gradually filtered down to other strata of the population as well. The 'democratization of the afterlife' had a profound effect on Egyptian philosophy and religion, as reflected in the lives of state officials like Tjetji (no. 26) and relatively humble individuals such as the priestess Hemira (no. 24). Changes in belief also influenced mortuary practices; the tomb models characteristic of Middle Kingdom private burials – exemplified, most famously, by those of Meketra (no. 28) – were intended to ensure eternal provision of all the necessities of life. Thanks to their detailed representations, such models have yielded much evidence for the technology of the period.

Other insights into ordinary life are provided by the written word. More widespread use of documents combined with the vagaries of archaeological preservation mean that texts, on papyrus and other media, are much better attested from the Middle Kingdom than from previous periods. They range from the private correspondence of a farmer named Hekanakht (no. 30) to the legal contracts of Hapdjefa (no. 32) and literary works composed for King Amenemhat I (no. 29). Alongside a flowering of great literature, the 12th Dynasty, inaugurated by Amenemhat, witnessed a new sophistication in craft production. The royal workshops achieved a level of technical skill and artistic creativity not seen since the Old Kingdom. To provide the artisans with the finest materials, expeditions were sent to distant lands in search of precious stones; the hardships involved are eloquently conveyed by the inscription of one such expedition leader, Horwerra (no. 36).

In political terms, the Middle Kingdom is a conundrum. On the one hand, the 12th Dynasty was perhaps the most stable royal line ever to rule Egypt. By a combination of ruthlessness and guile, powerfully expressed in the statuary of Senusret III (no. 35), the kings kept a lid on internal dissent and presided over a glittering court. The traditional duties of kingship were scrupulously observed, such as the refurbishing of cult images for use in important festivals – as described in the inscription of Ikhernofret (no. 34). The institution of co-regency protected the monarchy, ensuring a smooth succession between kings, while massive defensive fortifications in the Delta and Lower Nubia protected the country against foreign aggression. On the other hand, and set against this picture of totalitarian rule, considerable authority was exercised at a regional level by the leaders of Egypt's provinces. The 12th Dynasty was 'the age of the nomarchs'; men like Sarenput of Elephantine (no. 31) and Khnumhotep of Beni Hasan (no. 33) ruled their local areas in the manner of princes, and built themselves decorated tombs on an equally lavish scale. The power of the nomarchs seems to have been reduced under Senusret III, but the genie was out of the bottle: having tasted a high level of autonomy, the provinces would not be so easily reabsorbed into a centralized state.

In the latter years of the Middle Kingdom, the combination of dynastic crisis and internal pressures once again led to a weakening of royal authority. A degree of stability was provided by families of high officials passing their offices down from father to son; by contrast, the throne passed from one faction to another, to the extent that one king, Sobekhotep III (no. 37), even made a virtue of his non-royal ancestry. In the end, however, it was not so much domestic divisions as external forces that brought the Middle Kingdom state to its knees. The massive fortresses built by the 12th Dynasty kings throughout Lower Nubia had been a response to a perceived threat from the Kingdom of Kush. The Walls of the Ruler, constructed along the northeastern edge of the Delta, were supposed to protect Egypt against Asiatic infiltration. But without decisive leadership from the centre, neither proved effective. Immigrants from Syria-Palestine (ancient Retjenu) not only settled in the Delta in increasing numbers, they even set up their own mini-states and eventually claimed the kingship of Egypt itself. From the south, the Kushites invaded the Nile Valley, laid waste to its towns and carried off its treasures. Egypt was once again a land divided; history had come full circle.

22 TJAUTI
CONTROLLER OF DESERT ROUTES

There is more to Egypt, ancient and modern, than the Valley and Delta of the River Nile. The broad expanses of desert to the east and west, though inhospitable and largely unknown to the modern visitor, have always been important economically and strategically. This was never more so than in the First Intermediate Period, when Egypt was racked by civil war. On one side were the kings of the 9th/10th Dynasty based at Herakleopolis, who saw themselves as the legitimate heirs of the Old Kingdom monarchs. Ranged against them were the princes of Thebes, who were seeking to expand their control ever further in pursuit of the kingship of the whole country. The front line in the conflict lay at the border between Waset and Netjerwy (the provinces of Thebes and Coptos). The latter was governed by a nomarch (provincial governor) loyal to the Herakleopolitans. His name was Tjauti and his exploits, which have recently come to light through discoveries in the western desert, illuminate the progress of the civil war and the means by which it was waged.

As well as being governor of the Coptite province, Tjauti was also God's Father, 'beloved of the god', member of the elite and Overseer of Upper Egypt. The first title may indicate that he was related to the Herakleopolitan royal family; he was certainly their loyal servant. Perhaps his most important role was as 'confidant of the king in the door of the desert of Upper Egypt', in other words the man responsible for maintaining and patrolling the desert routes and passes that criss-crossed the arid lands either side of the Nile Valley. These routes were extensively used by trade caravans and messengers; they formed a vital communication network linking the Herakleopolitan realm with areas further south. In particular, the routes crossing the giant Qena bend in the course of the Nile reduced journey times between northern and southern Upper Egypt by several days. Keeping control of them was thus a key strategic objective, for if they fell into enemy hands, the Thebans would be able to outflank and isolate the nome (province) of Coptos and its two northern neighbours. Thebes would then have unimpeded access to the holy and symbolic site of Abydos (ancient Abdju), jewel in the Herakleopolitans' crown.

Tjauti, like his predecessors, governed his nome from the town of Khozam which lay directly opposite the point where the desert routes met the Nile Valley – such was their importance. It was thus a severe setback to him and the entire Herakleopolitan cause when the Thebans succeeded in closing one of the desert roads. Tjauti fought back, engaging the enemy in combat and building a new road to guarantee continued Herakleopolitan control of the Qena bend. He summed up his efforts in an inscription carved on a rocky outcrop by the side of the road: 'I have made this for crossing the mountain which the ruler of another nome had closed. I fought with his nome.'

Ironically, Tjauti's great achievement was also to be his downfall. His new road, one of the best in the western desert, unwittingly hastened the conquest of the Coptite nome by the Thebans, and allowed them in due course to attack Abydos, desecrating its holy places and thus fatally weakening Herakleopolitan rule. The desert routes that had kept the Theban expansion at bay ultimately secured them their prize, the reunification of Egypt and the lordship of the Two Lands.

23 ANKHTIFI
PROVINCIAL LEADER IN A TIME OF CIVIL WAR

While the Thebans were extending their power northwards, conquering and adding the province of Coptos (ancient Netjerwy) to their growing territory, one man was building a rival power-base in the deep south of Egypt. Ankhtifi held the usual string of honours associated with a provincial leader – member of the elite, high official, Royal Seal-Bearer, sole companion and lector priest – but combined these with military titles – General, Chief of Scouts and Chief of Desert Regions – reflecting the martial character of the age. We know relatively little of his family life, other than the name of his wife, Nebi, and the fact that they had four sons, the eldest called Idy.

Ankhtifi's home and administrative capital was the town of Moalla (ancient Hefat), from which he governed the nome of Hierakonpolis (ancient Nekhen). Through a combination of skilled political tactics and wise administration, he succeeded in bringing two further provinces under his effective control, putting him in a position to challenge Thebes for supremacy in Upper Egypt. The first, decisive move came in response to mismanagement in the neighbouring province of Edfu (ruled by a man named Khuu). As Ankhtifi himself recounted: 'I found the domain of Khuu flooded... and neglected by the one who was in charge... and ruined.' He lost no time in annexing the nome to his own territory, restructuring its governance and re-establishing order. With two provinces under his leadership, he next made an alliance with the Elephantine nome (ancient Ta-Sety), thus creating a political union of the three southernmost nomes of Egypt. The Theban princes to the north, fresh from their conquest of Coptos, must have looked southwards with a mixture of fear and loathing: here, on their southern doorstep, was a serious rival who could thwart their high ambitions to unify the whole country under their sway.

The inevitable conflict was not long in coming. The Thebes–Coptos alliance stormed and captured Ankhtifi's fortresses to the west of Armant, evidently intending to use them as a bridgehead for an all-out assault on Hierakonpolis. Ankhtifi retaliated, recapturing his bases and pressing on into enemy territory. But the Thebans had decided to save their fire for another occasion and refused to fight. Ankhtifi took this as cowardice, but it must have made him uneasy. For him, fighting the Thebans was not civil war so much as self-interest; he knew that his confederation of three nomes was a thorn in the Theban side, and in the circumstances, attack was the best form of defence. Ultimately, however, Theban expansionism proved unstoppable. Ankhtifi's rival confederation did not survive his own passing, and his heirs were forced to submit to Theban domination.

Aside from the battlefield, Ankhtifi was particularly proud of his administrative abilities. He boasted: 'I am the vanguard of men and the rearguard of men..., a leader of the land through active conduct, strong in speech, collected in thought.' His leadership skills were tested to the limit when a major famine hit the whole region: 'Upper Egypt was dying of hunger; every man was eating his children.' Ankhtifi took immediate steps to deal with the situation, releasing emergency stockpiles of food. After checking that his own nome had sufficient – 'nobody died of hunger in this nome' – he sent food aid to Elephantine and other major towns, including even Nagada (ancient Nubt) and Dendera within the Theban realm: a remarkably philanthropic act in the middle of a war. Thanks to his actions, serious loss of life was averted in southern Upper Egypt.

The final act of Ankhtifi's drama-filled career was the construction of a resting-place for eternity. Though his tomb on the outskirts of Moalla was a rock-cut structure, following the provincial tradition established in the 5th Dynasty, the particular choice of location gave it an added significance. For it was cut into a hill that closely resembled... a pyramid. A mere provincial leader in life, Ankhtifi had secured for himself a royal afterlife.

24 HEMIRA
HUMBLE PRIESTESS FROM THE DELTA

We see ancient Egypt almost exclusively through men's eyes. All the highest offices of state were reserved for men; tombs and temples were built, decorated and dedicated by men for men. Even on the rare occasions when a woman gained the throne, ideology and tradition required her to be presented, in texts and images, as male. Those women about whom something is known are mostly royal and are defined by their relationship to a man: King's Mother, King's Wife or King's Daughter. A rare exception to this rule is the priestess Hemira, who affords us a fleeting glimpse into the world of the Egyptian woman.

Hemira's sole surviving monument is the false door from her tomb. Its slightly awkward decoration betrays its provincial origins – the town of Busiris (ancient Djedu) in the central Delta – and its date. For Hemira lived in the early First Intermediate Period, when royal authority had become fractured and artists in different parts of the country, freed from the constraints of a powerful court tradition, worked in their own, distinctive local or regional styles. The texts on Hemira's false door are sparse, and mostly concerned with the provision of supplies for the afterlife. Yet small details shine through to illuminate the woman herself.

While her birth name was Hemira, her friends knew her by her 'good name' (nickname), Hemi. No mention is made of any husband, children or parents. Hemira seems to have been her own woman: perhaps unmarried, certainly confident of her own place in society. Her occupation was priestess in the cult of Hathor Lady of Djedu. The main temple at Busiris was dedicated to the god Osiris (god of the underworld), and was an important centre of pilgrimage in ancient Egypt. Hemira, however, evidently served in a smaller, subsidiary temple, dedicated to a goddess and perhaps staffed mainly by women.

Whether because of her provincial background, or by her nature, she seems to have been rather old-fashioned in her tastes. On one side of her monument, she is shown as a girl with her hair in a long pigtail ending in a disc; this style was already out of fashion by the early First Intermediate Period. Nevertheless, the inclusion of this image suggests a twinge of nostalgia on the part of the mature Hemira for the carefree days of her childhood. On the other side of the false door, she is depicted at the end of her life, as an old woman with sagging breasts. The monument thus reflects the span of her life, centred around a picture of her in middle age, seated before an offering table. As she looked forward to the next life, she appealed to those who might visit her tomb and pray for her eternal sustenance: 'As for all people who will say "bread for Hemi in this, her tomb", I am an effective spirit and will not allow it to go ill with them.'

25 INTEF II
THEBAN WARRIOR-KING

Intef II, known by his Horus-name Wahankh, was born into a world of conflict, and the civil war of reunification between the Herakleopolitan 9th/10th Dynasty and the Theban 11th would dominate his whole life. He came to the throne as a young man and lost no time in pursuing the battles that his predecessor, Intef I, had begun. Theban authority already held sway in the seven southern-most nomes (provinces) of Upper Egypt, but this was not enough. The great prize was the sacred site of Abydos (ancient Abdju), which lay just to the north of Theban territory. Here, the kings of Egypt's 1st Dynasty were interred, in a holy spot believed to be one of the entrances to the underworld. For a would-be king of all Egypt, control of Abydos and its surrounding province, the nome of This (ancient Tjeni), was essential. But This, like the rest of the northern Nile Valley, was still loyal to the Herakleopolitan kings. Direct confron-tation between the two opposing sides was therefore inevitable. An inscription carved for one of Intef's loyal followers, Djari, records the beginning of the conflict: the Thebans had finally broken out of their southern heartland and had begun in earnest the battle for the rest of Egypt.

The first Theban attack on This was only partially successful, and provoked a violent response from the enemy. Intef realized that the province would be difficult to capture, so decided instead to outflank his opponents. In a brilliant piece of military strategy, he used the desert routes to circumvent This and occupy the area to the north. By setting his new border at Wadi Hesy in Middle Egypt, he managed to cut This off from direct Herakleopolitan aid. Its fate was sealed. He sent a message to the Herakleopolitan king Khety, setting out the new state of affairs, but the outcome was never in doubt: 'I landed in the sacred valley, captured Tjeni in its entirety, and laid open all her fortresses. I made it the Gate of the North.' Intef's first-hand account is full of passion and determination. He presented his conquest of This as a deliverance, suggesting that the Herakleopolitan rulers had previously desecrated the cemeteries of Abydos. This was probably war propaganda, showing that Intef was master of psychological as well as military tactics.

The effects of civil war were beginning to tell in the country at large, with famine stalking the land. With so many men now conscripted to fight for one side or the other, the vital work of maintaining irrigation channels and tending the crops seems to have been neglected. But Intef was not to be deflected from his ultimate goal. He boasted of having ravaged the Herakleopolitan realm as far north as the apex of the Delta. While this may have overstated the real situation, there is no doubt that he had significantly enlarged the Theban area of control.

The latter part of his reign may have been marked by a truce, allowing Thebes to trade with both north and south, and building work to be undertaken – after all, one of the key duties of kingship was to beautify the temples of the gods. Intef's most significant project was on the east bank of Thebes, at a site called Ipet-sut, 'the most select of places' (Karnak). Here he inaugurated a temple to 'his father' Amun-Ra. Although the pre-eminent deity of the Theban region was the warlike god Montu (personal god of Intef's grand-father, Mentuhotep), the priests of Karnak had begun to elevate their local god Amun to greater prominence. An ancient creator god, he was now identified with the sun, and hence given the dual name Amun-Ra. All that remains from Intef's temple is a small octagonal pillar, inscribed down one side with rather crudely cut hieroglyphs; but his patronage of the cult of Amun-Ra began the long history of Egypt's most splendid temple, that was eventually to become the world's largest religious building.

Opposite Karnak, on the western bank of the Nile, and next to the tomb of his predecessor, Intef began his own funerary monument. It was fronted by a great courtyard surrounded by the tomb-chapels of his most loyal followers. In the king's own chapel, he erected a stela inscribed with a moving hymn to Ra, the sun god, and Hathor, the protector goddess who resided in the Theban hills. The verse hints at a human frailty lying behind the visage of a great conqueror:

'Commend me to early dawn:
May he put his guard about me;

I am the nursling of early dawn,
I am the nursling of night's early hours.'

For all his superhuman achievements, Intef still regarded death and the afterlife with a mixture of awe and trepidation. Another touching indication of his humanity was immortalized on a second, more informal stela, where the king was shown in the company of his beloved pet dogs. Their names are Berber – suggesting imported, pedigree animals – with Egyptian translations: Behkai ('gazelle'), Abaqer ('hound'), Pehtes ('blackie') and Teqru ('kettle'). The king who ruled for fifty years and set Thebes on the road to national domination still found time for the simple pleasures of life.

26 TJETJI
HIGH OFFICIAL WHO SERVED TWO MONARCHS

Intef II's military victories greatly expanded his area of control and marked a turning-point in the civil war. They created a sense, for perhaps the first time, that the Theban rulers were true kings-in-waiting, rather than mere provincial leaders jockeying for position and influence. This shift in direction and mindset was marked by the establishment of a fully fledged royal court at Thebes, complete with its functionaries, artists and craftsmen. The emergence of the fledgling Middle Kingdom state is exemplified by the career of Tjetji, who served as Chamberlain and Treasurer under Intef II and his successor Intef III.

Tjetji's funerary stela, a rectangular slab of limestone with finely executed hieroglyphs and reliefs, shows the development of a new courtly style under the Intefs, replacing the sub-standard work of the local workshops during the preceding decades. The figure of Tjetji himself is elegant and ornate, wearing a calf-length kilt with starched apron, and a broad bead collar around his neck. In the hierarchy so typical of ancient Egyptian government, he is accompanied by two lesser officials, shown on a smaller scale: his seal-bearer and favourite Magegi, and his follower Tjeru.

As well as being the king's chamberlain, with private access to the monarch, Tjetji held the important post of Chancellor, responsible for all economic matters within the Theban realm. He tells us that Intef ruled an area 'from Abu to Tjeni', comprising the eight southernmost provinces of Egypt. Although representing less than one-quarter of the country, this territory included some of Egypt's most productive agricultural land, as well as its holiest site, Abydos. It was therefore a major responsibility to account for all the income and expenditure of the royal treasury, but Tjetji boasted of fulfilling his duties in an exemplary fashion:

> 'The treasure was in my hand, under my seal, being the best of every good thing brought to The Person of my lord from Upper Egypt, from Lower Egypt... and what was brought to The Person of my lord by the chiefs who rule the Red Land, owing to the fear of him throughout the hill countries... I accounted for them to him without any punishable fault ever happening, because my competence was great... I was thus His Person's true intimate.'

At the heart of the economy was the assessment and collection of taxes, and Tjetji saw to it that a new boat was built to carry treasury officials up and down the Nile to perform their duties.

Nothing was more characteristic of ancient Egyptian administrators than an obsession with correct procedure, and Tjetji was proud of his record in improving the performance of the departments under his control. He also took satisfaction in being a self-made man who had risen to the top through his own achievements: 'I am wealthy, I am great, I furnished myself from my own property, given me by The Person of my lord, because of his great love for me.' This contentment is reflected in Tjetji's portly figure, with a rotund chest and rolls of fat at his waist.

The key historical interest in Tjetji's inscription lies in its reference to the death of Intef II – 'he went in peace to his horizon' – and the accession of his son and heir, Intef III. These moments of transition were dangerous and uncertain, especially for members of the outgoing regime, but Tjetji's qualities were too valuable for the new king to do without, so Intef III 'gave me every function that had been mine in the time of his father'. At the end of a long and successful career, Tjetji looked forward to his own passing, and his stela included a moving prayer for a blessed afterlife:

> '*May he cross the firmament, traverse the sky,*
> *Ascend to the great god, land in peace in the good west...*
> *May he stride in good peace to the horizon,*
> *To the place where Osiris dwells.*'

This is an eloquent demonstration that the promise of life after death had already spread beyond the king and his immediate family to other sections of the population. The turbulent years of the First Intermediate Period had changed Egyptian society forever, and Tjetji had been in the middle of those changes. In his hopes for an eternal life, as in the manner of his earthly existence, he pointed the way to a new order.

27 MENTUHOTEP II
REUNIFIER OF EGYPT

The reign of Intef III was brief, lasting no more than a few years at most. He was succeeded on the throne by his son. The new king, rather than bearing the same name as his three predecessors, was instead named after the 11th Dynasty's founder, Mentuhotep ('Montu is satisfied'). This signalled the new ruler's devotion, not only to his illustrious forebear, but also to the Theban war-god, Montu. Indeed, the young king was to fulfil both promises, proving himself a great war-leader and completing the work of the dynasty by bringing the whole of Egypt together again, under Theban control. In the annals of later generations, Mentuhotep II would be listed alongside the legendary Menes (Narmer), first king of the 1st Dynasty, as one of Egypt's great founder rulers: the man who reunified the Two Lands and brought to an end the shame of political disunity.

Mentuhotep can scarcely have been older than a teenager when he acceded to the throne. Inspired by his association with the Theban god of war, the young king must also have been acutely conscious of the military successes of his grandfather Intef II. With a double descent from the great king, through his father and mother (both of whom were children of Intef II), Mentuhotep must have felt a special sense of responsibility for defending and widening his grandfather's hard-won victories. There is little evidence pertaining to the first decade of his reign, but he probably spent it learning and honing his skills as a military strategist and leader of men. His opportunity to put these into practice came in his fourteenth regnal year, when the nome of This – which included the sacred site of Abydos – rose in rebellion against Theban rule. If the Herakleopolitan kings of the 9th/10th Dynasty could win back control of such a symbolic region, the tide of the civil war might turn in their favour. The long-term repercussions of allowing the Thinite nome to secede from the Theban confederation and join with the enemy would not have been lost on Mentuhotep. The battle for This would be the crucial encounter of the whole, decades-long struggle for reunification.

Not only did the Thinite rebellion draw a swift and crushing response from Mentuhotep's forces, but the king was also careful to ensure that the momentum of victory was maintained. Having dealt with the insurgents, the Theban troops marched steadily northwards, capturing the key Herakleopolitan stronghold of Asyut (ancient Sawty) before eventually taking the enemy capital itself, the fortified town of Herakleopolis. If he had proved his tactical capabilities in war, Mentuhotep showed himself equally adept at using psychology to stir patriotic feelings in the minds of his people: in a remarkable example of national myth-making, he had sixty Theban soldiers, slain in battle, interred in state in a mass tomb at Deir el-Bahri in western Thebes. It was one of the world's first 'war cemeteries', a reminder to the Thebans of their collective sacrifice in the cause of national reunification. Moreover, to mark his decisive victory over the old adversary, Mentuhotep adopted a new throne-name and added a Horus-name to his royal titulary. As the undisputed king of all Egypt, he was now the true and worthy incarnation of the supreme celestial deity.

Kingship in the traditional Egyptian mould required more than nomenclature to project itself: it also required grand buildings. In his unusually long reign of fifty years – equalling that of his grandfather, Intef II – Mentuhotep commissioned construction projects throughout his Theban heartland, at Gebelein, el-Tod and Deir el-Ballas; and further afield at Elkab, Dendera and Abydos. But by far his most ambitious undertaking was his own mortuary temple, in a spectacular embayment in the cliffs at Deir el-Bahri. Not only did the site afford a magnificent natural backdrop for a building; it also lay directly opposite – and within view of – Karnak, where Intef II had begun a temple to the local Theban god, Amun. Perhaps most important for Mentuhotep, however, was Deir el-Bahri's long association with the mother-goddess and royal protectress, Hathor, who was believed to dwell in bovine form within the Western Mountain of Thebes. By choosing to build his tomb and temple for eternity at Deir el-Bahri, Mentuhotep was symbolically enfolding himself in Hathor's protecting embrace.

As the monument of a unifying king, it was only fitting that Mentuhotep's mortuary temple should combine aspects of the distinctive 11th Dynasty Theban style with elements typical of Old Kingdom, Memphite architecture. The building rose from the ground towards the cliff in great terraces, linked by ramps. The façade of the lowest terrace comprised a long series of pillars, and this theme was continued on the upper level with porticoes surrounding a central massif. Behind lay yet more pillars, laid out in the form of a hypostyle (columned) hall. The overall impression would have been startlingly different from anything that had been built before, yet undeniably regal in its scale, decoration and bold symmetry. The king's tomb itself lay deep inside the cliff, in an alabaster shrine nestling at the end of a passageway 150 m (492 ft) long, hewn into the rock. Balancing this, at the entrance of the temple, another long tunnel led to a chamber for the king's *ka*-statue, representing him with the black skin of the god-king Osiris.

Some of Mentuhotep's key officials chose to be buried within the sacred precincts of their monarch's architectural masterpiece: the Chief Steward Henenu, the Chancellor Khety, and the Viziers Ipi and Dagi; the limestone sarcophagus of the last-named was inscribed on the inside with a full complement of Coffin Texts, showing that religious concepts previously reserved for the king had fully percolated down to other echelons of society. Khety also seems to have played a key role in Mentuhotep's military campaigns following the reunification of Egypt. These were targeted against Nubia. In the thirty-ninth year of the king's reign, an expedition was launched to Abisko, south of the First Cataract, probably to regain Egyptian control of trade routes. The success of this action was marked by Mentuhotep's adoption of the epithet 'unifier of the Two Lands'. Two years later, Khety was able to sail at the head of a large fleet from Lower Nubia to Aswan. Mentuhotep's policies in Nubia, though carried out on a relatively small scale, none the less laid the foundations for the more aggressive military operations of the succeeding 12th Dynasty.

Nor were Mentuhotep's conquests confined to the battlefield, for he had at least seven wives. Indeed, unusually for a ruler of the Middle Kingdom, his family life is remarkably well attested. His chief consort, Neferu, was also his full sister. A secondary wife, Tem, bore him his only known child, the son who was to succeed him as Mentuhotep III. Three other women, Ashayet, Henhenet (who died in childbirth) and Sadeh, were all named in inscriptions as 'king's wives', while two further concubines, Kawit and Kemsit, were buried within the king's mortuary temple at Deir el-Bahri. The scenes on their fine limestone sarcophagi and in their burial chamber – Ashayet is shown smelling a fragrant lotus flower, Kemsit a jar of perfumed ointment, while Kawit is shown having her hair braided – conjure up an image of relaxed sophistication, of a court enjoying the fruits of peace in the aftermath of a brutal civil war (figs 7 and 8). Such was the lasting achievement of Mentuhotep II: to restore Egypt to her former glory, dispelling the divisions of the past and ushering in a new golden age of high culture.

28 MEKETRA
CHANCELLOR UNDER MENTUHOTEP II

With the wars of reunification over, the administration of Egypt under Mentuhotep II returned to its primary task of overseeing the economy: recording the country's wealth, collecting taxes, and supervising the manufacture of secondary products to pay government employees and finance the court's building projects. At the centre of operations, in charge of the treasury, was the chancellor, one of the most important officials in the country. Mentuhotep's chancellor, however, is famous not so much for his career as for the contents of his Theban tomb.

His name was Meketra and he was buried in an impressive resting-place, cut into the hillside near Deir el-Bahri. The tomb was built according to the latest fashion, with an approach ramp sloping steeply up the cliff face, and a broad court giving access to a passageway leading to the burial chamber. Most of the tomb and its contents were robbed in antiquity, but the thieves overlooked a small, concealed chamber near the entrance. When archaeologists opened it in the 1930s, they found a unique collection of wooden models, numbering twenty-five in total. Their size, quality and attention to detail are remarkable; together, they provide fascinating snapshots of the life of a high official in 11th Dynasty Egypt.

The most complex of the models depicts the census of cattle. As well as being a practical necessity, allowing the state to keep a count of the nation's livestock, this was also a highly symbolic act, since 'cattle' signified agricultural wealth in general. As the herds of cattle were driven past, Meketra sat on a stool under an awning, accompanied by scribes and other officials. His other duties would have required frequent travel the length and breadth of Egypt, and we may reasonably assume that Meketra's fleet of thirteen model boats replicated the full-size craft at his daily disposal. They included four boats for river travel, two kitchen tenders, four faster yachts, a lightweight sporting boat and two fishing boats.

Like all Egyptians, Meketra was concerned to ensure an eternal supply of commodities for his afterlife. His tomb models therefore included two female offering-bearers, and scale models of food and craft production, each activity contained within a walled room. They provide our best source of evidence for Middle Kingdom technology, embracing spinning and weaving, carpentry, butchery, the baking of bread and brewing of beer, and the storage of grain. In daily life, such activities may have taken place in workshops surrounding Meketra's house in Thebes.

The house itself is represented by two models which give us an indication of the sophistication and comfort enjoyed by a government official under Mentuhotep II. The street façade of Meketra's house presented a tall, plastered wall; at its centre was the main entrance, comprising a decorative fretwork or moulded panel above double doors. A single door to the right may have been the entrance for servants and deliveries. A tall, latticed window on the other side would have allowed ventilation into the house, while minimizing the influx of dust and dirt from the street. In Meketra's models, the inner rooms of the residence have been reduced to a single thickness of wood, in order to emphasize the house's finest feature: a walled garden with rows of sycamore-fig trees surrounding a rectangular pool. This would have provided Meketra and his family with shade throughout the day, while permanent water was particularly desirable in the dry heat of an Egyptian town. A portico of columns shaded the garden front of the house, offering a gentle transition between interior and exterior spaces. Life in 11th Dynasty Thebes didn't come much better than this. For Meketra, the material rewards of high office were considerable.

29 AMENEMHAT I
VICTIM OF A COURT CONSPIRACY

Mentuhotep II had changed the course of Egyptian history, bringing an end to the fragmentation of the First Intermediate Period and inaugurating a new era of strong, central government, the Middle Kingdom. But his own descendants were not to enjoy the fruits of reunification for very long. Both Mentuhotep II's successors had brief reigns; with the death of his second successor, Mentuhotep IV, the 11th Dynasty royal line came to an end. The family that had ruled Thebes since the dying days of the Old Kingdom found itself without a male heir. To whom would the throne now pass?

There were always powerful men at the Egyptian court, and the most influential in the brief reign of Mentuhotep IV was the member of the elite, Mayor of the City, Vizier, Overseer of the King's Works and royal favourite Amenemhat. His early career is known primarily from a series of four inscriptions carved deep in the eastern desert, on the rock face of the siltstone quarries in the Wadi Hammamat. Amenemhat led an expedition in the second year of Mentuhotep IV's reign, to quarry and bring back a block of the precious green-black stone for the king's sarcophagus. And Amenemhat made sure that the entire undertaking was recorded in unusual detail at the quarry site, giving himself full credit for the mission's success.

The next time a powerful man called Amenemhat is encountered, he is king of Egypt in succession to Mentuhotep IV. Although court documents never equated the two Amenemhats as one and the same person, there can be little doubt that the Vizier and royal favourite exploited his position at court to seize the throne when it fell vacant. But that was merely the first hurdle in the path to power. The problem with usurpation was that it tore the veil of divinity and mystery that normally protected the office of kingship, revealing it for what it was: a source of unrivalled authority and wealth that occasionally, and often in unpredictable circumstances, came within the grasp of ambitious men. Amenemhat clearly had both ambition and resolution to act; but having seized power, he had to move swiftly and decisively to impose his personal authority on Egypt, and legitimize his new dynasty.

His most explicit statement to this effect was the establishment of a new capital city for his government, named – to prove a point – Amenemhat-Itj-Tawy, 'Amenemhat seizes the Two Lands'. Probably located close to the modern settlement of Lisht, it was to remain the principal royal residence for the next four centuries. By relocating the centre of administration from Thebes to the apex of the Delta, where it had been throughout the Old Kingdom, the new king was deliberately associating himself with his illustrious forebears of the Pyramid Age: here was a renaissance ruler intent upon restoring Egypt to its former glory. To reinforce this message, he ordered work to commence on his funerary monument, the first full-scale royal pyramid to be built in Egypt for 300 years. Moreover, Amenemhat took unusual steps to give his own complex legitimacy and potency by embedding within its structure blocks taken from the Giza monuments of Khufu, greatest of all pyramid-builders (no. 10).

The other great construction project of Amenemhat's reign marked a decisive shift, not in domestic affairs, but in foreign policy. Since the late Old Kingdom, Egypt had faced a persistent irritant on its northeastern border in the shape of the 'sand-dwellers'. These semi-nomadic tribespeople of the Sinai peninsula and southern Palestine launched periodic attacks on Egyptian trade caravans, disrupting the economic activity that kept the royal court supplied with prestige commodities such as timber, oil and wine. Occasional military campaigns, such as those led by Weni (no. 18) in the 6th Dynasty, served to reassert Egyptian hegemony. But now, the nature of the threat was changing. The fertile fields of the Nile Delta were attracting a steady flow of those same tribespeople from the harsher environments of the Levant. If allowed to continue unchecked, large-scale migration of foreigners into Egypt would threaten the country's stability. So Amenemhat commanded a great defensive fortification, known as 'the Walls of the Ruler', to be built the entire length of Egypt's northeastern frontier. For 200 years, it succeeded in its purpose, keeping the Two Lands relatively secure from undue foreign influence.

This combination – of confidence in a new age, coupled with insecurity about threats from within and without – is the paradox at the heart of Amenemhat and his reign. He inaugurated the greatest flowering of literature in ancient Egypt's long history, the true mark of a renaissance ruler; but the newly composed texts were largely propagandistic in nature, designed above all to legitimize the dynasty. Amenemhat's desire to establish himself as rightful king even extended to rewriting history. Hence, one of the greatest compositions of his reign was the Prophecy of Neferti, a mythical work in which social upheaval and widespread disorder were banished by a 'saviour' called Ameny (a shortened form of the king's own name). In promoting Amenemhat as reunifier of his country, this account conveniently passed over Mentuhotep II and his two successors.

The literature of the 12th Dynasty has become famous for its concentration on the theme of 'national distress', in which the proper disposition of society is disrupted or reversed. This reflected not so much an abiding memory of the First Intermediate Period and the civil war between south and north as a deep-seated unease within the court of Amenemhat and his successors. Despite the fiction expounded in texts and monuments, Egypt had changed irrevocably since the end of the Old Kingdom. The previous certainties had gone forever. Royal authority now depended as much on coercion and political manoeuvering as it did on the concept of divinity. To bolster the chances of his new royal line remaining on the throne, Amenemhat instituted a radical new policy to mark the twentieth anniversary of his accession: he had his son and heir, Senusret, crowned king to reign alongside him.

Yet, in the end, after a reign of thirty years the dubious manner of Amenemhat's accession came back to haunt him. Those closest to the king, who had seen him gain power through naked ambition rather than royal kinship thought they might try something similar. A band of assassins attacked Amenemhat while he was asleep in the royal apartments. He awoke to find swords brandished against him. Helpless without his palace guard, he succumbed to the attackers. But his shrewd policy of co-regency worked as intended, ensuring a relatively trouble-free assumption of sole power by his son Senusret I.

Amenemhat's greatest legacy was thus to give his descendants the security of office that he himself had so earnestly desired, but which eluded him to the last.

30 HEKANAKHT
FARMER AND LETTER-WRITER

Occasionally, very occasionally, we catch glimpses – through the barrage of official propaganda and religious texts that dominate the ancient Egyptian written record – of unadorned reality, of raw feelings and the complexities of human relationships. Perhaps the most famous examples of texts 'from daily life' are the letters written home by a farmer, Hekanakht, in the early years of the Middle Kingdom.

At the time he wrote, Hekanakht was probably in his mid to late thirties, distinctly middle-aged in ancient Egyptian terms. He was already married for the second time (of which, more below) and was master of a large household of relatives and dependants. He must have been fairly well educated by the standards of the age, certainly literate enough to write some or all of his own letters; he resorted to employing a professional scribe only when something more formal was required.

Although his chief occupation – and preoccupation – was farming, Hekanakht had an important role as *ka*-servant (mortuary priest) in the cult of Ipi, a vizier under Mentuhotep II. Ipi's tomb was at Thebes, and Hekanakht's duties required him to spend extended periods of time in 'the southern city', a long way from his home in the settlement of Nebsyt ('sidder grove'), close to the Fayum region and Memphis. To judge from the name of Hekanakht's youngest son, (Mer-)Sneferu, the family may have lived in the vicinity of the 4th Dynasty pyramids of King Sneferu at Dahshur.

It was during one of his sojourns in Thebes, between the autumn of year 5 (of Amenemhat I?) and the summer of year 7, that Hekanakht wrote many of his letters home. They are dominated by economic matters, ranging from the collection of debts to the distribution of grain, reflecting his worries about leaving his farming interests in the hands of others. His tone is concerned, but also impatient and hectoring: 'Take great care! Watch over my seed-corn! Look after all my property! Look, I count you responsible for it. Take great care with all my property!' In particular, Hekanakht, a man with a keen business sense, was anxious to ensure that his steward, Merisu, made the necessary and timely preparations for the coming agricultural year: not siphoning off any of the grain held in reserve to pay the rent on a parcel of farm land; investigating the possibility of renting additional land if the circumstances looked favourable; and so forth. Despite his relatively humble status in the ancient Egyptian social hierarchy, Hekanakht was evidently quite a successful farmer. Indeed, he had financial dealings with at least twenty-eight different individuals. Sixteen of them farmed land in the same region, called Perhaa. One of these, Herunefer, was a moderately high-ranking employee of the state, and by far the most exalted of Hekanakht's acquaintances.

Besides interactions with business colleagues and neighbours, Hekanakht's personal relationships were dominated by the members of his large household. In addition to three unnamed servants, his relatives and dependants numbered eighteen. They included his foreman, Nakht; the household steward, Merisu; the household scribe, Sihathor; a fieldhand in charge of the family's cattle, Sinebniut; Hekanakht's mother, Ipi; a senior female relative, Hetepet; a younger brother, Inpu; a son by a previous marriage, Sneferu; a younger sister or daughter by a previous marriage, Sitniut; two daughters by Hekanakht's second marriage, Nefret and Sitwerut; and the new wife herself, Iutenhab, also known as Hetepet. Hekanakht demonstrated the typically reverent attitude of an Egyptian man to his mother, sending her particular greetings and reassuring her 'Don't worry about me. Look, I'm well and alive.' He also betrayed more than a touch of favouritism towards his son Sneferu, telling his other relatives: 'Whatever he wants, you shall make him content with what he wants.'

Most of the household members were probably in their teens or twenties, and the atmosphere seems to have been both competitive and febrile. With such a large number of people living under one roof, it is not surprising that tensions came to the surface from time to time. Their principal cause was the attitude of Hekanakht's other relatives to his new wife, herself only in her twenties. He clearly felt that, in his absence, the others were ganging up on the new arrival. Believing that one of his female servants, Senen, had behaved particularly badly towards Iutenhab, Hekanakht had the unfortunate girl promptly dismissed. He then threw this back at his family, accusing them of not protecting the wife against the maid's malice because they regarded the former as a slut and a parvenu: 'Shall you not respect my new wife?!' he wrote, in a tone of exasperation.

There was clearly more to Hekanakht's domestic arrangements than meets the eye, even reading between the lines of his numerous letters home. So intriguing is the relationship between his new wife, the servant girl and the other family members that Agatha Christie took it as the basis of her murder mystery novel, *Death Comes As The End*. Whether the simmering resentment in a small farmstead in Nebsyt in the twentieth century BC led to parricide we shall never know; but it certainly sheds a fascinating and curiously familiar light on ordinary family life in ancient Egypt.

31 SARENPUT
PRINCE OF ELEPHANTINE

The rise of a new dynasty provided opportunities for men of humble origins but possessing talent and ambition to achieve high office. The accession to sole power of Senusret I, in the dramatic circumstances of his father's assassination, gave particular impetus to the promotion of outsiders, since the best way for the king to ensure the loyalty of his officials was to surround himself with men who owed him everything. One such man was Sarenput (I), appointed nomarch (provincial governor) and prince of Elephantine (ancient Abu) early in Senusret I's reign.

Of Sarenput's father we know nothing, but the name shared by his mother and wife, Sat-tjeni, suggests that one or both women may have come from the town of This in northern Upper Egypt. Like most couples of the time, Sarenput and Sat-tjeni had a large family: three sons, all named Heqaib, and two daughters, one named Satethetep in honour of the local goddess of Elephantine and the younger named Sat-tjeni after her mother and grandmother. In the account of his life, Sarenput is silent about his early career, but shows no such reticence about the honours bestowed on him by Senusret I. His promotion was as striking as it was swift: from nowhere, he became at once a member of the elite, high official, Royal Seal-Bearer, sole companion, and Overseer of Priests of Satet Lady of Elephantine. He also held the office of Overseer of Priests of Khnum, the principal god of the First Cataract region, and boasted of officiating in the temple on the great festival day.

As regional governor of Ta-Sety, the southernmost province of Egypt, Sarenput had significant economic duties. He was responsible for the supervision of settlements and the collection of taxes in Egyptian-controlled Lower Nubia: he was, in his own words, 'the one to whom the produce of the Medjay is reported, namely the tribute of the princes of the deserts'. He was also closely involved in any military expeditions sent from Egypt into Nubia, since Elephantine was the point of departure for such campaigns. Sarenput was therefore, without hyperbole, 'a possessor of the king's secrets in the army, hearing what is heard, who(se name) is upon the signet-rings in all matters of foreign countries in the royal apartments'. As prince of Elephantine, he also had special responsibility for all shipping through the First Cataract in his capacity as 'great overseer of ships in the palace'. It was probably no overstatement to say that 'he who sails and he who lands are under his control'. Much of the traffic from Nubia to Egypt and vice-versa was trade-related, and Sarenput boasted of 'furnishing the treasuries through the towns of Ta-Sety'.

Loyalty to the king was Sarenput's guiding principle in life: 'I was one straightforward in the royal presence, void of falsehood... I was his servant near to his heart, doing what his lord loves.' Such devoted service – 'guiding the god to all that is good' – was rewarded with a shower of gifts from the palace: 'When His Person proceeded to overthrow vile Kush, His Person caused to be brought to me a bull, uncooked. As for all that was done in Elephantine, His Person caused to be brought to me the flank or the hind-quarters of a bull, and a dish filled with all kinds of good things, with five geese uncooked upon it; and four men carried it to me.'

It may have been a paltry gift by the standards of the Egyptian court, but Sarenput evidently took rather exaggerated pride in this token of royal favour, as only someone newly promoted to high office could.

A far more significant gift was a magnificent tomb cut into the cliff-face overlooking the River Nile and the island of Elephantine. As Sarenput explained, 'His Person exalted me in the land: I was distinguished beyond the (other) princes of the nomes. I (reversed) the customs of antiquity; it was caused that I should reach heaven in a moment.' The tomb in question was destined to be the most sumptuous built in the area to date: 'I appointed craftsmen to the work in my tomb, and His Person praised me on account of it very greatly and very often in the presence of the courtiers and of the Lady of the Land.'

A spacious rock-cut forecourt gave access to the tomb chambers through a doorway of white marble. The burial itself was furnished with 'every requisite' from the royal workshops as a further reward for loyal service. The walls were decorated with fine reliefs, and dominating everything were Sarenput's autobiographical inscriptions – the same text, repeated twice, word for word – just in case posterity should forget his meteoric rise from obscurity. As for the hereafter, Sarenput confidently looked forward to an eternal afterlife in the celestial realm: 'My head pierced the sky, I grazed the bodies of the stars, I danced like the planets.'

Not a bad ending for a self-made man.

32 HAPDJEFA
PROVINCIAL GOVERNOR WITH A LEGAL MINDSET

Ancient Egyptians went to great lengths to ensure that the basic necessities of life would be provided to them, unhindered, in an eternal afterlife. Tomb paintings of offering-bearers, or, more fundamentally, of bakers and brewers at work, served this purpose; so did tomb models, in three dimensions; so, too, did the offering formula itself, inscribed on the false door or funerary stela, promising bread, beer and other supplies for the spirit of the deceased, should the actual commodities, buried in the tomb, be exhausted or destroyed. These multiple insurance policies were built into the very fabric of Egyptian funerary practices, because the worst fate of all was to die another death. Failure to survive the afterlife through lack of proper provision would result in total annihilation.

Hapdjefa, nomarch of Asyut in the reign of Senusret I, took preparations for his afterlife to a new extreme. Inscribed in pride of place on the east wall (facing the sunrise) of the great hall of his rock-cut tomb at Asyut are a series of ten contracts. With legalistic precision, they specify the arrangements that, Hapdjefa hoped, would ensure regular supplies for his mortuary cult after his death. As well as detailing a complex web of interrelated transactions, they also shed fascinating light on the political and social conditions of the period, and on what it meant to be a nomarch in early 12th Dynasty Egypt.

During the civil war between the Herakleopolitan 9th/10th Dynasty and the Theban 11th, Asyut had been on the northern side. Once the Thebans emerged victorious, they set about appointing new governors in those regions that had been loyal to their enemies. Hapdjefa was a direct successor, and perhaps a descendant, of the pro-Theban nomarch installed to govern Asyut at the end of the First Intermediate Period. He was certainly a high-ranking member of the royal administration, with the usual titles: member of the elite, high official, Royal Seal-Bearer, and sole companion. He also had economic responsibilities as Overseer of the Two Granaries, and in typical Egyptian fashion combined civil office with religious duties in his local temples: he was a priest of Hor-Anubis as well as Overseer of Priests of Wepwawet Lord of Sawty. He was married twice, to women called Senu and Wepa, and had a daughter whom he named Idny after his mother.

As nomarch, Hapdjefa owned two types of property and had three sources of income. There was the land (and its revenue) which he had inherited in a private capacity from his father – his paternal estate. This he could use and bequeath, in turn, as he wished. There was also the land which he owned by virtue of his office – his 'nomarch's estate'. He could not dispose of this since it was not his personal property; any arrangement which he made concerning this land and its income was valid only so long as his successors chose to recognize it. Finally, as a senior priest in the local cult, Hapdjefa was entitled to a certain proportion of the temple revenue and offerings, calculated as a number of days per year. His mortuary contracts involve both types of land, all three sources of income, and four distinct sections of Egyptian society: the nomarch himself, his subordinate officials, citizens, and the serfs who toiled in the fields.

The first contract stipulates that the local priests will provide white bread in return for a share of a bull from the temple. In the second contract, the priests' recompense for providing bread is grain from the nomarch's estate. The third contract involves the temple itself providing bread and beer in exchange for a portion of Hapdjefa's temple revenue: a curiously self-cancelling arrangement. The fourth contract binds the priests to provide yet more white bread in return for fuel, beer and bread of their own. And so the arrangements continue, with temple officials and priests, to guarantee the provision of bread, beer, meat and candle-wicks in exchange for temple revenue, land and grain. In the ninth and tenth contracts, Hapdjefa intended to ensure not only the provisions for his mortuary cult, but also their delivery to his tomb-chapel: the overseers of the necropolis and another necropolis official would guarantee both, in exchange for land and meat, two of the most valuable commodities at the nomarch's disposal.

Seldom can an Egyptian have made such elaborate preparation for his afterlife, but it was ultimately to no avail. When Hapdjefa's

1 Siltstone commemorative palette of Narmer (no. 1), from Hierakonpolis, beginning of the 1st Dynasty. In what was to become the quintessential iconography of Egyptian kingship, Narmer is shown holding a mace in his upraised arm, to smite a defeated enemy. The small figure behind the king is his sandal-bearer.

2 BELOW Wooden relief panel of Hesira (no. 6), 3rd Dynasty. He is shown in the prime of life with a young, muscular body and confident expression. The hieroglyphs above his head give a selection of his courtly titles, while the sceptre in his left hand signifies his position of authority.

3 OPPOSITE Bronze votive statue of the deified Imhotep (no. 7), Late Period. Credited with designing the Step Pyramid of Djoser, Imhotep's posthumous reputation was transformed into that of a sage and healer. In the Ptolemaic Period he was associated with the Greek god of medicine, Asklepius, and his shrine at Saqqara became a place of pilgrimage.

4 Ivory statuette of Khufu (no. 10), 4th Dynasty. This tiny figurine is the
only certain representation of the king who built the Great Pyramid.
It shows him enthroned, carrying the flail and wearing the red crown
associated with Lower Egypt. Despite the statuette's small size, the king's
expression of ruthless determination is unmistakable.

5 Detail of gold leaf from the funerary equipment of
Hetepheres (no. 9), 4th Dynasty. The band of hieroglyphs gives the
names and titles of Hetepheres' late husband, King Sneferu.

6 Silver bracelets from the tomb equipment of Hetepheres (no. 9),
4th Dynasty. At this period of Egyptian history, silver was more
precious than gold. So these bracelets, inlaid with carnelian, turquoise
and lapis lazuli in a butterfly design, would have been extremely rare
and costly objects, indicative of Hetepheres' royal status.

7 Painted limestone relief of Kemsit from her tomb-chapel in the mortuary complex of Mentuhotep II (no. 27) at Deir el-Bahri, western Thebes, 11th Dynasty. One of the king's seven wives, Kemsit wears an elaborate feathered dress and holds a vessel of perfumed ointment to her nose.

8 Painted limestone relief of Mentuhotep II (no. 27) and his wife Kemsit, from the king's mortuary complex at Deir el-Bahri, western Thebes, 11th Dynasty. The elongated limbs and fish-tail cosmetic line around the eye are typical of the Theban style of representation which developed during the First Intermediate Period.

9 Calcite statue showing the infant king Pepi II (no. 20) sitting on the lap of his mother, Ankhenesmerira II, late 6th Dynasty. Although a baby, Pepi is shown as a miniature adult complete with royal regalia, in order to emphasize his full kingly status.

tomb was excavated in the 1880s, it was found plundered, like those of his less obsessive contemporaries. Its (useless) mortuary contracts were the only point of interest.

33 KHNUMHOTEP
HEREDITARY NOBLE

The First Intermediate Period witnessed the emergence of strong, local identities and cultural traditions which survived into the early Middle Kingdom. Politically, too, the 11th and early 12th Dynasties were characterized by powerful provincial governors, the nomarchs, who surrounded themselves with miniature courts and ruled their districts often without overt reference to the king. The 'era of the nomarchs' is most spectacularly attested at the site of Beni Hasan in the central Nile Valley, where the governors of the Oryx-nome (the sixteenth province of Upper Egypt) built their lavish rock-cut tombs in an arresting location overlooking the river. One of these tomb owners, Khnumhotep, has left us a particularly detailed picture of the relations between the central monarchy and the nomarchs over four generations during the first half of the 12th Dynasty.

Khnumhotep reached adulthood and enjoyed the pinnacle of his career during the reigns of Amenemhat II and Senusret II, but his family's involvement in local politics went back much further, to the beginning of the dynasty. His grandfather, the first Khnumhotep, had been appointed governor of the Oryx-nome by Amenemhat I as part of the new dynasty's programme to consolidate its power throughout Egypt. The nomarch's authority extended over both banks of the Nile and included the important regional centre of Menat-Khufu. Khnumhotep-the-first was able to strengthen the family's influence still further by marrying off his daughter to Nehri, vizier and governor of the royal residence city of Itj-tawy. As for Khnumhotep's two sons, each inherited in due course a portion of their father's domain. The elder son Amenemhat succeeded as nomarch while the younger son Nakht received the town governorship of Menat-Khufu. When Nakht died without issue, in the nineteenth year of the reign of Amenemhat II, the governorship of Menat-Khufu duly passed to his sister's son, Khnumhotep-the-second.

The second Khnumhotep acknowledged the importance of his descent, on his mother's and his father's side: 'This my chief nobility is my birth.' He secured the family position by making a strategic alliance of his own, marrying the eldest daughter of the neighbouring nomarch. By this means, Khnumhotep's own sons, Nakht and Khnumhotep-the-third, stood to inherit the governorship of the Jackal and Oryx-nomes respectively.

The highlight of Khnumhotep's two-decades-long career as governor of Menat-Khufu and of the adjoining eastern highlands was the visit, in the sixth year of the reign of Senusret II, of a trading party of Asiatics from the land of Shu (in present-day Israel/Palestine). Led by their chief, Abisha, the visitors included women and children as well as men; the main commodity they brought to the Nile Valley for exchange was galena, the lead sulphide ore much prized by the ancient Egyptians as the principal ingredient in *mesdemet* (black eye-paint). What they took back to their own land in return is not recorded, but the peaceful nature of their reception at Menat-Khufu indicates a two-way trading arrangement between equal parties.

Khnumhotep's other notable achievement – and one for which Egyptologists have cause to be especially thankful – was to leave behind a lavish architectural legacy. In Menat-Khufu he carried out several projects:

'I made a monument in the midst of my city; I built a colonnaded hall which I found in ruins; I erected it with columns anew; inscribed with my own name. I perpetuated the name of my father upon them. I recorded my deeds upon every monument.'

At Beni Hasan, he built his own rock-cut tomb 'that he might perpetuate his name forever, that he might perpetuate the name of his official staff, the excellent ones who were in his household'. Khnumhotep's magnanimity towards his employees extended to giving credit (in the form of an inscription) to the architect who built the tomb. It is thus one of very few monuments from ancient Egypt whose builder is known by name. Khnumhotep also took great pains to restore the tombs of earlier nomarchs: 'I kept alive the name of my fathers which I found obliterated upon the doorways, making them legible in form, accurate in reading....Behold it is an excellent son who restores the name of the ancestors.' Of course, Khnumhotep's motive was not entirely altruistic: his entire career and social position had depended upon his inheritance as 'Nehri's son, born of a nomarch's daughter'; and his continued standing in the eyes of posterity would depend on preserving his ancestor's monuments as much as on his own achievements. In ancient Egypt, inherited status made demands as well as conferring benefits.

34 IKHERNOFRET
WITNESS OF THE OSIRIS MYSTERIES

During the Middle Kingdom, Abydos (ancient Abdju) was the most important religious site in Egypt and a place of pilgrimage for thousands of worshippers. They came to pay homage to Osiris, god of the underworld, whose own resurrection offered the promise of rebirth to his followers. Abdju was the site of an important temple of Osiris (where he was associated with the local jackal god Khentiamentiu) and of a tomb believed to be the god's own burial-place. The sacred spaces and buildings of Abdju thus mirrored the central elements of the Osiris myth: his kingship on earth, his death, and his rebirth to eternal life.

· Once a year, Abdju was the stage for a lavish festival which re-enacted these mythical events: the 'mysteries of Osiris'. But the Osiris story was so potent, and its annual performance so laden with symbolism, that the mysteries were rarely described. Fortunately, however, one account, albeit veiled, has survived. It is doubly fortuitous that its author, Ikhernofret, was probably the individual best placed to provide a description.

Ikhernofret lived in the Memphite region during the reign of Senusret III. In common with other sons of the nobility, he grew up in the royal palace as a foster-child of the king (presumably Senusret II), and attended lessons with the heir to the throne. His close relationship with the royal family was reflected in his early promotion: he received the courtly rank of companion when he was only twenty-six years old. When his childhood friend and playmate became king as Senusret III, Ikhernofret found himself one of his sovereign's most trusted officials. He garnered titles and responsibilities, rising swiftly to become a member of the elite, high official, Royal Seal-Bearer, sole companion, Overseer of the Two Gold Houses, Overseer of the Two Silver Houses, and Chief Seal-Bearer to the King. His career was based predominantly in the royal treasury, looking after the income which supported the court and its projects, and administering economic affairs on behalf of the king. But of this work we know little.

By contrast, one brief episode in Ikhernofret's life occupied a central place in his autobiographical inscription. The trust placed in him by Senusret III led to a unique commission, one that was to take Ikhernofret to the very heart of Egyptian religious life. The king had just returned from a victorious campaign in Nubia, and brought back with him considerable quantities of gold as booty. As part of his continuing contract with the gods, Senusret III decided to allocate some of this treasure to the cult of Osiris; more specifically, he ordered that the god's sacred image, housed in the temple at Abydos, should be adorned anew with gold. Ikhernofret was charged with carrying out this special assignment. The king's words were clear: 'Now My Person sends you to do this because My Person knows that no one could do it but you.'

Ikhernofret therefore set sail from the royal residence at Itj-tawy, bound for Abydos, to act in the king's place as 'his beloved son'. On arrival at the sacred site, he set to work diligently. The annual Osiris mysteries were about to take place, and there was much to do. First, he supervised the construction and decoration of the god's bark-shrine, the portable boat which conveyed the cult image. The materials employed were the costliest available: gold, silver, lapis lazuli, bronze, cedar and another precious aromatic timber known as *sesenedjem*. Second, Ikhernofret saw to it that the shrines of the various gods attending upon Osiris-Khentiamentiu during the festival were renewed and refurbished. Third – and here the punctiliousness of the treasury official shines through – he led a thorough appraisal and re-training of the priests themselves: 'I made the hour-priests diligent at their tasks... I made them know the ritual of every day and of the feasts of the beginnings of the seasons.' Fourth, he oversaw the adornment of the *neshmet*-bark, the boat that would play a central role in the ceremonies to come. All that remained was to prepare the cult statue of the god himself. Under Ikhernofret's watchful eye, it was decked out with lapis lazuli, turquoise, electrum and 'all costly stones'. Finally, in his office as stolist and 'master of secrets' (in other words, one permitted access to the divine presence), he clothed the image of Osiris with the god's royal regalia.

Everything was set for the celebrations to begin. To reflect the three elements of the Osiris myth (kingship, death and rebirth), the mysteries comprised three separate processions in which the god's statue was transported between his temple and tomb amid staged scenes of fighting. In the first act, the god appeared as a living ruler. As master of ceremonies, Ikhernofret took the role of Wepwawet ('the opener of the ways'), the jackal god who went before Osiris as his herald. The central part of the drama re-enacted the death, rebirth and funeral of Osiris. A 'Great Procession' escorted the god's image, enclosed in a special boat-shrine to the holy place called Peqer. This was the site of the 'tomb of Osiris' (in fact the burial-place of the 1st Dynasty king Djer). The final act was the procession back to the temple, in which the reborn god returned to his 'house'. Ikhernofret followed the image back into the sanctuary and purified it: the Osiris mysteries had been brought to a successful conclusion for another year.

He was understandably proud of his achievements, and determined – like all pious Egyptians of the time – to gain permanent favour from Osiris. So Ikhernofret built a small chapel on the 'Terrace of the Great

God', the banks lining the main processional route from the temple to Peqer. A presence here would allow him to participate vicariously in the sacred rites, each and every year. Inside his chapel, Ikhernofret erected a stela, showing him seated at an offering table with members of his family; the accompanying text gave a lengthy account of his involvement in the Osiris mysteries. But his piety did not end there. In a gesture of solidarity, he also allowed his close friends and work colleagues to put up their own stelae in his chapel: the promise of resurrection offered by Osiris was for everyone.

35 SENUSRET III
LORD OF NUBIA

In the Classical world that followed the demise of the pharaohs, a popular legend was told about 'high Sesostris', an heroic and archetypal Egyptian ruler who built great monuments, won decisive military victories and gave his country new laws. On one level, it simply reflected the ideal of Egyptian kingship, projected onto a single figure. But there was also a real man behind the myth: Senusret III (Sesostris in Greek), fifth king of the 12th Dynasty. He was, indeed, a ruler who imposed his will on the country more effectively than most of its monarchs.

The fourth-century BC historian Manetho noted that Senusret III was unusually and impressively tall: four cubits, three palms and two fingers, to be precise (1.98 m, 6 ft 6 in.). If true, he would have cut an imposing figure that would have given him a natural air of authority. Whatever his physical stature, Senusret certainly displayed a commanding personality. Early in his reign, he set about reforming the administration of Egypt. The result was to recentralize power in the hands of the king and his closest advisers. Senusret reorganized his realm into three large administrative units (the Delta, Upper Egypt as far south as Hierakonpolis, and Elephantine together with Lower Nubia), each governed by a council of elders reporting to a vizier.

This effectively ended the regional autonomy that had characterized the early 12th Dynasty.

The decline of the nomarchs and the corresponding elevation of the king was eloquently expressed in a cycle of hymns, probably composed to be sung in front of statues of Senusret III:

> 'Hail to you, Khakaura, our Horus, Divine of Form!
> Land's protector who widens its borders,
> Who smites foreign countries with his crown,
> Who holds the Two Lands in his arms' embrace.'

This same monarchical authority was to be reflected in Senusret III's pyramid complex at Dahshur which was surrounded by a large court cemetery, so that the king's closest officials might accompany him in death as they had in life.

If Senusret III's domestic programme was ambitious, it paled into insignificance by comparison with his military and territorial achievements in Nubia. Early in his reign, he signalled his intention towards Egypt's southern dependencies by reopening the channel around the First Cataract at Aswan that had originally been excavated by Pepi I and Merenra in the 6th Dynasty. Senusret dredged it to remove the accumulated silt of centuries, widened and deepened it: all to allow his warships swift and unimpeded access to Nubia. Further repairs to the channel in his eighth year on the throne were the prelude to a devastating campaign, the first of four that the king unleashed over the next decade. They were planned with military precision: temporary campaign palaces were built for Senusret and his commanders, at the well-defended sites of Kor and Uronarti in the Second Cataract region. The army's supply chain from Egypt was reinforced by a series of fortified granaries, the largest at Askut sited on a virtually impregnable island in the middle of the Nile. The campaigns themselves were prosecuted with unyielding ferocity. Senusret showed no mercy to his adversaries: 'I carried off their women, I carried off their subjects, went forth to their wells, smote their bulls; I reaped their grain and set fire to it.' Resistance was futile in the face of such overwhelming force.

The underlying reason for these campaigns was to safeguard Egypt's access to trade routes and the valuable mineral resources of the Nubian deserts. To this end, conquest was backed up by a comprehensive programme of military occupation via a series of fortresses in the Second Cataract region. Senusret III's forts fulfilled the practical objective of border and customs control, marking Egypt's new southern frontier and regulating the movement of people and commodities. At the same time, the forts had a psychological purpose: they were a deliberate show of force, a display of Egyptian military and administrative power, directed at the land that lay beyond the Second Cataract, the Kingdom of Kush. This new power on the Upper Nile was a growing danger to Egypt and Egyptian interests in Nubia. Despite the belittling tone directed towards Kush in official Egyptian texts, it is clear that the threat was keenly felt. The massive fortifications were Senusret III's decisive response, and were designed as a defensive grouping.

In his domination of Lower Nubia, as in his imposition of royal authority throughout Egypt, Senusret invoked his own personality as an inspiration and a rallying-point. On a stela erected at Semna in the sixteenth year of his reign, he exhorted his descendants to defend Egypt's southern border – not for the country's sake, but for his: 'As for every son of mine who shall maintain this boundary which My Person has made: he is my son, he is born of My Person, the likeness of a son who champions his father, who maintains the boundary of him that begat him. But as for whoever shall abandon it, who will not fight for it, he is no son of mine, and was not born to me.' Senusret went one step further, ensuring that he had a permanent presence at Semna to encourage the appropriate behaviour: 'My Person has had a statue of My Person set up on this boundary which My Person has made, so that you might be inspired by it, and fight on behalf of it.'

Indeed, statuary was something of an obsession where Senusret III was concerned. Statues were erected throughout Egypt to symbolize the ubiquity of the king's power. Moreover, the pieces were not the usual idealized representations, but remarkably distinctive 'portraits'. Their facial features departed so markedly from previous custom that they must have been ordered by the king himself. Senusret was shown with bulging eyes under heavy eyelids, a furrowed brow, hollow cheeks and a downturned mouth. The significance of this brooding and sullen expression is hotly debated: was it chosen to emphasize the burden of kingship or, rather, the grim determination of a ruthless autocrat? It may be noted that the king's body was always shown as vigorous and youthful, and his ears were deliberately exaggerated, to denote an all-hearing monarch.

There is no doubt that Senusret was adept at using texts and images to assert his authority. Despite decisive reforms, he none the less saw himself as the inheritor of a mantle of kingship that stretched back to the greatest rulers of the Old Kingdom. Hence, he consciously took the 3rd Dynasty Step Pyramid complex of Djoser as the model for his own funerary monument at Dahshur. He also built a tomb complex at Abydos, a site for which he showed special reverence.

Whichever was his final resting-place, Senusret had assured his immortality by his own actions. The king who had imposed himself on Nubia was later deified in the region. In Egypt, too, memories would live on of the ruler who had raised royal authority to new heights, ending provincial autonomy and promoting kingship in a sustained barrage of propaganda. Through the force of his own personality, Senusret had not merely acted as an ideal Egyptian king: he had cast himself as the new model ruler, the pattern for future generations. The legend of 'high Sesostris' was born.

36 HORWERRA
EXPEDITION LEADER

Middle Kingdom jewelry is among the finest and most sophisticated from the ancient world. The royal workshops of the 12th Dynasty took the art of cloisonné decoration to new heights, inlaying complex designs in gold with a distinctive combination of three semi-precious stones: red carnelian, dark blue lapis lazuli and pale blue turquoise. To keep the jewelry-makers supplied, regular mining expeditions were launched to some of the most remote parts of Egypt. The late 12th Dynasty, in particular, witnessed a frenzy of such activity, and the focus of much of it was the region known as the Turquoise Terraces (modern Serabit el-Khadim), in the southwest of the mountainous Sinai peninsula. The most vivid picture of life on a mining expedition is provided by a remarkable inscription left for us by Horwerra.

Horwerra was the Director of Gangs, and was evidently a frequent visitor to the Turquoise Terraces. His success had brought him promotion within the court, to the office and rank of God's Seal-Bearer, Overseer of the Chamber, royal acquaintance, and Friend of the Great House. Perhaps because of his experience and trustworthiness, he was engaged in the sixth year of the reign of Amenemhat III to lead yet another expedition to the turquoise mines. However, this was no ordinary undertaking: it had been scheduled to arrive in the Sinai on the threshold of summer, 'when it was not the proper season for coming to this mining region'.

The expedition set out from Egypt with its full complement of twenty-three members. Besides Horwerra, the group comprised three keepers of the chamber and the keeper of the treasury; an overseer of stone-cutters and his team of eleven quarrymen; three cup-bearers, for bringing water to the work-place; a domestic servant attached to the treasury, the appropriately named Ip ('counter'); a priest to look after the spiritual well-being of the expedition; and, last but not least, a scorpion-doctor. Threats to the men's safety came as much from venomous bites and stings as from the sun, heat, dust and rock-falls.

Horwerra soon faced dissent in the ranks. His men gave full vent to their doubts about the wisdom of going to the mining region at the wrong time of year. Not only was the weather unbearably hot, but they believed this would affect the quality of the turquoise itself: 'the mineral comes at this time, but it is the colour which is lacking at this painful time of summer.' Horwerra had to agree, admitting: 'Finding the colour seemed difficult to me, while the hill-country was hot in summer, the mountains were scorching and skins were troubled.' Realizing that he had to show leadership, he rallied his men at dawn.

He told them that the power of the king was his inspiration, and that the expedition should press on despite the conditions.

For several weeks, Horwerra's workmen toiled in hot and uncomfortable conditions to extract seams of turquoise from the surrounding bedrock. The work was dusty and dangerous, and the pace was unrelenting. Finally, on the first day of *shemu*, the month of summer, he ordered a halt to the work. They had mined enough of the precious turquoise and could return home. No losses had occurred under Horwerra's command and he could later boast: 'Very well did I make my expedition. There were no raised voices against my labour, and what I did was successful.'

Before returning home to the green of the Nile Valley, Horwerra decided to leave a permanent record of his work at the Turquoise Terraces, as an inspiration to subsequent expeditions and a permanent memorial to his own accomplishments. He had chosen his spot well: he set up his tall, sandstone stela on the approach to the sanctuary of the goddess Hathor. On the front, reliefs showed the king worshipping the goddess and Horwerra worshipping the king: a perfect reflection of the proper, hierarchical, Egyptian world-view. But on the back, visible by pilgrims as they entered the temple, Horwerra carved his own inscription: a testament to his resolve and determination in the deserts of the Sinai.

37 SOBEKHOTEP III
COMMONER WHO BECAME KING

For a period of two hundred years in the 12th Dynasty, the succession passed smoothly and without interruption from one generation to another, aided by the institution of co-regency. Egypt was secure at home, strong in Nubia, prosperous and confident. Few, therefore, could have foreseen that within a few years of Amenemhat III's death, Egypt's stability would be dealt a serious blow by pressures inside and outside the royal court. First, there were dynastic issues.

The accession of a female king, Sobekneferu, strongly suggests that the royal line itself had come to an end, causing a crisis in the succession. A further strain was the infiltration of migrants from the Levant into the eastern Delta. This had begun much earlier, but as the Middle Kingdom progressed, the trickle had turned into a flood. Taking advantage of a weakened monarchy, a rival dynasty of Canaanite origin seized power in the region.

The result was a further diminution of royal authority and a rapid succession of rulers, as one prominent family after another sought to put its favoured candidate on the throne. At first, it seems that the kings were still the lineal descendants of the great 12th Dynasty rulers. The accession of Sekhemrasewadjtawy Sobekhotep – Sobekhotep III – changed all that. For he had no royal blood whatsoever. Indeed, he openly flaunted his non-royal origins on a series of scarabs, an altar, a rock inscription and a stela. His father was a commoner, albeit with the rank of a member of the elite and high official. He may have been a military officer. Sobekhotep himself had certainly forged his early career in the army, and was eventually appointed to serve in 'the ruler's crew', the king's personal bodyguard. This must have given him an intimate knowledge of the court, and of royal security – an ideal springboard from which to launch a *coup d'état*. The self-confidence with which he publicized his commoner relatives (his father Mentuhotep; his mother Iuhetibu; his two brothers Khakau and Seneb; his sister Reniseneb; and his two daughters Iuhetibu Fendy and Dedetanuq) suggests that his immediate predecessors, despite their royal blood, had become seriously discredited in the eyes of their subordinates. Sobekhotep's appeal may have been precisely the fact that he offered something different: a natural leader of men untainted by the misdoings of earlier 13th Dynasty kings.

He did not disappoint his backers. He ushered in a new era in Egyptian politics, one that was to restore a measure of stability in the administration and thus one of national prosperity. A papyrus dated to his first and second years on the throne gives an insight into the day-to-day activities of workers in Upper Egypt. It is symptomatic of the changes that were being introduced at all levels. Numbers of key government officials were increased; royal building projects were once again put at the heart of the state's activities. As a result, Sobekhotep III is one of the best-attested kings of the 13th Dynasty, despite a brief reign of just four years.

Having only daughters, Sobekhotep did not inaugurate a new dynasty; after his demise, his family lost power just as quickly as it had gained it. Yet succeeding generations showed no ill-will towards the usurper king, the ultimate social climber who had seized a discredited throne and given it a much-needed injection of dynamism. Sobekhotep's successor was another man of humble parentage, Neferhotep I: Egypt's ruling class had evidently decided that non-royal blood could be a positive advantage when it came to restoring the country's tarnished dignity.

PART 4

A Golden Age
EARLY 18TH DYNASTY

The collapse of central government at the end of the Middle Kingdom was an even greater blow to Egyptian self-esteem than the same phenomenon had been five centuries before: the difference this time was that it ushered in not just a period of division but of subjugation. The rule of the Hyksos 15th Dynasty, exemplified by its most prominent king, Apepi (no. 38), constituted a gross affront to Egyptian ideology, since the Two Lands were supposed to be the focus and model of creation, intrinsically superior to all other countries. Hence, the motive for expelling the Hyksos was not merely national reunification but the re-establishment of created order. Once again, the impetus for reunification came from Upper Egypt, more specifically from the rulers of Thebes. Leading from the front, the kings of the 17th Dynasty were not afraid to engage the enemy in battle; one of them, Taa II (no. 39), seems to have been killed in action. After several decades of fighting, recounted by two soldiers who were in the thick of the action (nos 41 and 42), the Hyksos were driven out and Egypt's autonomy restored.

The character of the New Kingdom was greatly influenced by the events surrounding its birth. The Hyksos and Kushite invasions of the Second Intermediate Period had awoken Egypt to the new realities of international relations. Strong natural borders and a sense of patriotic superiority were no longer sufficiently good defence against well-armed, determined and envious neighbours. If Egypt were to maintain its independence, it would have to do so by force, conquering and annexing adjacent lands to create a militarized buffer zone against future attack. The kings of the early 18th Dynasty took up this challenge with gusto. They established a permanent, professional army, and launched a policy of extending Egypt's borders to create an empire in the Near East. This culminated in the extraordinary series of campaigns under Thutmose III (no. 45), the greatest of the warrior pharaohs. From now on, military iconography was a key element in the symbolism of kingship, while the army became a powerful bloc within Egyptian society.

To set against this militarism, the prominent role played by successive generations of royal women is another striking feature of the 18th Dynasty. The influence of kings' wives during the wars of liberation continued long after the expulsion of the Hyksos, in the wider arena of national politics. Women such as Ahmose-Nefertari (no. 40) and Tiye (no. 53) did not meekly stand beside their husbands in the performance of official royal duties, they actively participated in the business of government, maintaining their own households and influencing key decisions. Hatshepsut (no. 43), daughter of one king and wife of another, went a step further and proclaimed herself monarch. Despite the glories of her reign, her gender was contrary to the ideology of kingship and led to the desecration of her monuments and memory after her death – a fate in which her favourite and factotum, Senenmut (no. 44), seems to have shared.

The splendour of Egypt's Golden Age is best attested at Thebes, cult centre of the chief state god, Amun-Ra, and a religious capital to rival the administrative capital of Memphis. The rulers of the 18th Dynasty lavished attention on Thebes' temples, built their funerary monuments on its West Bank, and were interred in spectacular tombs cut into the hillside in the remote Valley of the Kings. Alongside the royal sepulchres, the ruling class built their own tombs in the Theban necropolis. As well as being architectural and artistic gems, the tombs also provide a wealth of information about the lives and careers of the men who ran Egypt (nos 46–51, 54–55) – from the vizier at the top of the bureaucratic ladder (no. 47) to a humble scribe on its bottom rung (no. 54). In the cosmopolitan and diverse society of the New Kingdom, it was truly possible for a man of modest means to rise to great prominence through his own abilities. Amenhotep son of Hapu (no. 55) did just that, winning exceptional royal favour during his lifetime and posthumous deification.

His career culminated in the reign of Amenhotep III (no. 52) which marked the zenith of 18th Dynasty grandeur and opulence. The king's elaborate jubilee celebrations, the first of which was stage-managed by Amenhotep son of Hapu, were designed to raise the institution of kingship to a new level; the king's building projects in Nubia were even more explicit, the temple at Soleb being dedicated to his deified self. The quasi-divine nature of the Egyptian monarchy had been a fundamental tenet of religion and government since the beginning of the 1st Dynasty, but Amenhotep III's policies steered a new course, in the direction of full-scale divinity during the king's own lifetime. It was a bold move, commensurate with the glories of the age; but it would spell disaster for Egypt when embraced, with even greater fervour, by Amenhotep's son and heir.

38 APEPI
AN ASIATIC ON THE THRONE OF EGYPT

Of all the dynasties to rule Egypt, perhaps the most enigmatic is the 15th: a line of six kings of Asiatic origin, known to posterity as the Hyksos (a Greek corruption of the Egyptian phrase *hekau-khasut*, 'the rulers of foreign lands'). Their precise geographical origin is uncertain, but was probably the Lebanese coastal plain around Byblos. What is clear is that they and their kin brought to Egypt a wholly alien culture; yet, within three generations, these foreign rulers had become sufficiently acculturated to adopt full Egyptian royal titles. The best known of these 'Asiatic kings' is the fifth Hyksos ruler, Apepi, who has come to exemplify this extraordinary chapter in the history of ancient Egypt. His long reign of forty years witnessed many of the key events leading to the foundation of the New Kingdom.

Apepi came to power as a young man, as the result of a coup, his predecessor, Khyan, having appointed his own son, Yanassi, as heir apparent. The usurper was clearly of non-royal birth, but little else is known about his family, save the names of his two sisters, Tani and

Ziway, and his daughter Harit. Apepi may also have had a son, another Apepi, but he is scarcely attested. Although the Hyksos capital and stronghold was at Avaris (ancient Hut-waret, modern Tell el-Dab'a) in the northeastern Delta, Apepi commissioned construction projects and carried out other royal activities throughout Egypt, from Thebes in the south to the Memphite region and southern Palestine in the north and east. He seems to have shown a particular interest in the area around Gebelein (ancient Inerty) in Upper Egypt, dedicating an adze to the nearby cult of Sobek Lord of Sumenu, and building a shrine at Gebelein itself, of which only the limestone architrave survives, inscribed with Apepi's royal names and titles.

However, it seems that relatively early in Apepi's reign, the Hyksos grip on Upper Egypt – always a stronghold of Egyptian nationalism – began to weaken. Perhaps sensing that territory was slipping from his grasp, Apepi may have ordered a scorched-earth policy, looting and destroying many of Thebes' temples and royal tombs. Certainly, he plundered a large number of royal statues, bringing them back to Avaris to be re-inscribed with his own name. Erected in his own palaces and temples, they would have served to proclaim his authority as king, even if his tactical retreat northwards told a different story. None the less, Apepi made the best of his situation by concluding a formal treaty with his opponents to set the official border at Cusae (ancient Qus). The next two decades of his reign seem to have been calm, with the two states sharing the Nile Valley and trading with each other in relative peace.

All that changed with the accession in Thebes of a young, dynamic and determined ruler, Taa II (no. 39). Taa moved swiftly to launch an attack on Hyksos-controlled territory. Although he was killed in battle before he had been able to make major gains, it was a Pyrrhic victory for Apepi. The next Theban king, Kamose, continued the relentless advance, within three years pushing Apepi's forces back to Atfih, just north of the entrance to the Fayum. In the face of these disastrous setbacks, Apepi tried to maintain his royal dignity by adopting new titles and epithets: 'he whose power brings about victorious frontiers: there is no country free from paying him tribute' and 'stout-hearted on the day of battle, he who is more famous than any other king;

how miserable are the foreign lands that do not recognize him'. His throne-name, Auserra, proclaimed 'great is the strength of Ra (i.e. the king)'. It was all wishful thinking.

While the machinery of government continued to function – for example, in the thirty-third year of Apepi's reign, scribes were commissioned to copy out a long and important mathematical papyrus – the Hyksos state was on a permanent war footing. Society was heavily militarized, as shown by a dagger belonging to one of Apepi's soldiers, Abed, which is decorated with an image of his follower Nehemen armed with a lance, short bow and dagger. Fighting dominated the last decade of Apepi's reign. When he died, probably in his late sixties, he must have known that the end of Hyksos rule in Egypt was near. His successor, another usurper, lasted barely a year before the Asiatics were finally driven out of the Delta by the forces of the Theban Ahmose, who thus inaugurated the 18th Dynasty.

Apepi's memory was reviled by subsequent generations of ancient Egyptians, not least because of his misfortune to have shared a name with the giant snake that embodied chaos in Egyptian mythology. True to this association, Apepi came to be seen as the epitome of evil, representing everything that was bad and shameful about Egypt's period of subjection to foreign rule. Yet, despite his alien background, he tried, in many ways, to rule as a model monarch. Hero or villain, the 'Asiatic king' remains a figure of fascination.

39 TAA II
KING SLAIN IN BATTLE AGAINST THE HYKSOS

After generations of political fragmentation and rule by foreigners, the Egyptians turned once again to Thebes for deliverance. In the darkest days of Hyksos rule, a military family had risen to prominence that seemed to offer the same hope of national rebirth as the Intefs and Mentuhotep II (no. 27) had delivered at the end of the First

Intermediate Period. While Apepi reigned from his Delta stronghold, a brave Theban called Taa succeeded his father as local ruler. His was a small territory, but it offered the only resistance to foreign domination and might therefore form the springboard for a wider liberation movement. Hence, Taa had the hopes and expectations of a people resting on his shoulders.

Fortunately, he was the right man in the right place at the right time. He was fairly tall for an ancient Egyptian, at 1.7 m (5 ft 7 in.), and he had the muscular body of a fit and active man. His large head was topped by thick, black, curly hair: he was every inch a potential hero in the making. Taa was the son of another Taa and a remarkable mother named Tetisheri, who was destined to be revered as a great ancestress of the 18th Dynasty kings. To judge from later records, she was a forceful and influential woman in her own right, and seems to have instilled in her son a determination that would carry him through difficult and dangerous situations. The younger Taa took as his principal wife his own full-sister, Ahhotep; like her mother, she was a feisty and strong-willed woman who did not hesitate to steel her husband's resolve for the war that lay ahead. Taa married at least two of his other siblings and by these various wives had a large family, including four sons and as many as seven daughters. Most of his children were named Ahmose, in honour of the moon-god; Ahmose-Nefertari (no. 40) was destined to equal her mother and grandmother in terms of influence.

The royal family, together with their closest advisers and generals, spent much of their time in the town of Deir el-Ballas, north of Thebes itself. The town was strategically located to control river traffic and caravan routes across the deserts. With two fortified palaces, it provided a secure forward position for the war against the Hyksos that all now expected to be launched. Shortly after his accession, Taa – still only in his late twenties or early thirties – decided that the time had come to begin the re-conquest of Egypt. He ordered the attack on the Hyksos to begin. The sense of anticipation and excitement in the Theban camp as the enemy was engaged must have been considerable. However, the liberators, as they now saw themselves, suffered a devastating blow early in the campaign when their leader,

Taa himself, was killed in action. He may have been struck from behind – taken by surprise – while riding his chariot. Felled by the initial blows, Taa was set upon by his attackers who inflicted further lethal wounds with their daggers, axes and spears.

In the thick of battle, there was neither the time nor the facilities to carry out the proper preparation of the king's body for burial. It was hastily embalmed, perhaps on the battlefield, without even straightening the limbs from their death-throes. It was then taken back to Thebes for interment in a royal tomb. The king's body was placed in a richly gilded coffin, adorned with his image wearing the royal headdress, the protective cobra at its brow. The inscription named the owner, as he would be revered for generations to come: 'Taa the brave'. Three hundred years after his death, his heroic struggle against the Hyksos was immortalized in literary form, in which it survives to this day: the heroic tale of a young warrior king who gave his life for the liberation of his country.

40 AHMOSE-NEFERTARI
ROYAL DAUGHTER, WIFE AND MOTHER

The three generations spanning the end of the 17th Dynasty and beginning of the 18th Dynasty were a remarkable period in ancient Egyptian history in many ways, not least in the unusual prominence of royal women in affairs of state. Taa II (no. 39) had been supported and encouraged by his powerful mother Tetisheri and his sister-wife Ahhotep. His son, Ahmose, had the support of an equally influential woman in the shape of his own sister and wife, Ahmose-Nefertari (fig. 10), whose influence continued into the reign of her son, Amenhotep I.

Ahmose-Nefertari was born into the Theban royal family during the reign of her father, Taa II. She witnessed his death in battle against the Hyksos, the accession of her brother-husband and his eventual victory against the Asiatic invaders. She played a central role in overseeing Egypt's transition from war to peace, and her own family's elevation from Theban to national dynasty.

In ancient Egypt, religion and politics were inseparable. Ahmose-Nefertari recognized this, and ensured that on the death or retirement from office of her mother, she was appointed by her husband to the highly important role of God's Wife of Amun. Indeed, Ahmose endowed her and her heirs in perpetuity with land and goods, creating an economic base for the position to equal its politico-religious influence. The Amun priesthood was rapidly becoming the most powerful in the land and Ahmose-Nefertari, as God's Wife, was able to play a central role in its affairs. The importance of her new position is reflected in the fact that she often chose to use this title alone, rather than King's Great Wife.

Her role extended into the full range of cultic activities, such as the dedication of ritual offerings, participation in important festivals, and involvement in the construction or restoration of religious buildings. Before Ahmose decided to set up a memorial to his grandmother Tetisheri at Abydos, he sought Ahmose-Nefertari's approval. Her name was recorded in the texts marking the reopening of the limestone quarries at Tura. Her interest and involvement in new foundations culminated in the reign of her son, Amenhotep I, when she acted as joint patron of a new village for the necropolis workmen engaged in building the royal tombs in the Valley of the Kings. For the rest of its existence, the community of the Place of Truth, as it was called, honoured Ahmose-Nefertari side by side with her son as its patron deities.

Ahmose-Nefertari outlived her husband and her son, surviving into the reign of her son-in-law Thutmose I. Her remarkable lifetime thus spanned five, perhaps six reigns. Her death, when it came, was an occasion for national mourning. One private stela described it thus: 'the God's Wife Ahmose-Nefertari, justified before the great god, Lord of the West, flew to heaven.' Gone, but not forgotten. Ahmose-Nefertari was to be the inspiration for a succession of powerful women at key moments in the dynasty of which she was the undoubted founder.

41 AHMOSE SON OF ABANA
WARTIME NAVAL OFFICER

The liberation of Egypt, the expulsion of the Hyksos, and the reforging of a strong and independent nation were the lasting achievements of the early 18th Dynasty kings. The most detailed and vivid account of these momentous events belongs to a naval officer who took a leading part in all the great battles of the age: Ahmose son of Abana.

Ahmose was born and brought up in the thriving city of Elkab (ancient Nekheb), in the far south of Egypt. His father, Baba, served as a soldier in the army of Taa II (no. 39), and the son must have grown up hearing stories of daring military exploits, understanding that they were part of a wider struggle to liberate Egypt from the hated 'rulers of foreign lands'. The young Ahmose followed his father into the military, but chose the navy instead of the army. His first commission was on board the king's ship 'The Offering'. It was a gentle introduction to navy life, but a short one. After marrying and starting a family, Ahmose was transferred to the northern fleet, actively engaged against the Hyksos enemy. Aboard his new ship, 'Shining in Memphis', Ahmose took part in the siege of the Hyksos stronghold of Avaris. The Egyptian fleet engaged the enemy on the city's main canal. Ahmose found himself in the thick of hand-to-hand combat, but distinguished himself by his valour and brought away a rather grisly trophy of his first armed encounter: the hand of a slain enemy fighter. The king rewarded his bravery with the gold of honour, encouraging Ahmose to further acts of courage.

In the midst of the siege of Avaris news reached the king's forces of a rebellion in Upper Egypt, led by a disaffected official. If left to gather momentum, such internal strife might prove disastrous for the wider military campaign. So Ahmose son of Abana was dispatched at once to put down the insurrection. His success was rewarded by a grateful monarch with 'gold in double measure'. Returning to the northern front, Ahmose arrived in time to witness the fall of Avaris to the besieging Egyptian forces. He himself took four prisoners of war, and was allowed to keep them as slaves. The king, determined not merely to drive the Hyksos out of Egypt but to destroy them once and for all, pursued them as far as their Levantine fortress of Sharuhen, to which the Egyptians subsequently laid siege for a gruelling six years. By a combination of resolution and persistence, the Egyptians triumphed. Ahmose's reward was more gold, and more prisoners of war as slaves.

The next major campaign took place, not to the north of Egypt, but to the south, in Nubia. Having re-established national sovereignty throughout the Nile Valley and Delta, King Ahmose now wished to re-build Egypt's empire in the southern lands. His namesake the naval officer, by now a battle-hardened veteran, continued to distinguish himself in combat. However, all was not well at home: political opposition to the new Theban 18th Dynasty was evidently stronger than official records dared admit, and the uprising of a few years before had not, after all, been an isolated phenomenon. For a second, well-organized insurrection broke out, led by 'an enemy from the south'. A detachment loyal to the dynasty, including Ahmose son of Abana, was sent to intercept the rebels; they met at a place called Tynet-ta-amu. The leader of the mutiny was captured together with his followers. Ahmose himself seized two archers aboard one of the enemy ships; he and his fellow sailors were rewarded with slaves and land, to maintain their loyalty. But before the dust had even settled, a third rebellion broke out, led by a man named Tetian. He, too, was eventually defeated, but the atmosphere towards the end of King Ahmose's reign must have been febrile and awash with rumours of internal revolution. By displaying unswerving allegiance to the Theban dynasty, Ahmose son of Abana certainly earned his rewards.

Ahmose I was followed on the throne by his son Amenhotep I, and the efforts 'to extend the borders of Egypt' continued apace. Ahmose son of Abana sailed southwards with the new king to Kush (Nubia south of the Second Cataract), 'fought incredibly', captured the Nubian chief, and conveyed the sovereign back again to Egypt in just two days' sailing. Ahmose was by now speaking patriotically of 'our army', and was rewarded for his efforts with gold, two female slaves and the prisoners of war he had already presented to the king. Moreover, he was appointed a 'Warrior of the Ruler', a mark of great honour.

Once a soldier, always a soldier: even in his mature years, Ahmose's personal involvement in military campaigns did not cease. In the reign of Thutmose I, he conveyed the king to a location in Nubia called Khenthennefer 'in order to cast out violence in the highlands, in order to suppress the raiding of the hill region'. For his bravery and coolness in difficult sailing conditions, he was promoted to 'Chief of the Sailors', at the head of the Egyptian navy. A second Nubian revolt drew a ruthless response from Thutmose I. At the end of a fierce onslaught, the king sailed back to Karnak, under Ahmose's direction, with the dead body of the defeated Nubian chief suspended upside down from the prow of the royal boat – a grim warning to other potential rebels.

Ahmose's long and distinguished military career ended where it had begun, fighting enemies on Egypt's northern border. But this time, the foe was the Kingdom of Mitanni (ancient Naharin), which in seeking to expand its influence throughout the Levant was threatening Egypt's own imperial ambitions in the region. At the head of the Egyptian forces, admiral Ahmose accompanied the king into Syria-Palestine (ancient Retjenu) 'to wash his heart [obtain satisfaction] among the foreign lands'. Fighting on land, Ahmose captured a chariot together with its horses and rider, and presented them to his monarch. He was amply rewarded, with 'gold in double measure'.

In his old age, Ahmose basked in his many honours: 'I was presented with gold seven times in the presence of the whole land; male and female slaves, likewise. I was endowed with very many fields.' He commissioned a rock-cut tomb at his home city of Nekheb with a long text inscribed on the walls to record his achievements for eternity. He had taken part in ten major campaigns under three kings. He had, by his own actions, helped to establish and safeguard the 18th Dynasty on the throne of Egypt. If ever an ancient Egyptian deserved immortality, Ahmose son of Abana certainly did. In his own words: 'The fame of one valiant in his achievements shall not perish in this land forever.'

42 AHMOSE PENNEKHBET
SOLDIER UNDER FOUR SUCCESSIVE MONARCHS

The story of the military exploits of the early 18th Dynasty, recounted in such gripping detail by Ahmose son of Abana (no. 41), is continued in the autobiographical inscription of his near-contemporary, namesake and fellow inhabitant of Elkab, Ahmose, called Pennekhbet. He, too, served a succession of kings, was amply rewarded for valour in battle, and lived to a great age.

Ahmose Pennekhbet was an infantryman, and saw his first action in the twenty-second year of Ahmose I's reign. After the successful siege of Sharuhen, the king pushed on deeper into the Levantine coastal area (ancient Djahi), to mop up any remaining resistance to Egyptian rule. Ahmose Pennekhbet was in the thick of the fighting, as he would be for many years to come: 'I followed Nebpehtyra [Ahmose I], triumphant. I captured for him in Djahi a living prisoner and a hand. I was not separated from the king upon the battlefield from (the time of) Nebpehtyra, triumphant, to Aakheperenra [Thutmose II], triumphant.'

Under Amenhotep I, Ahmose Pennekhbet fought in Nubia and in an unidentified land called Khek. His rewards included two golden bracelets, two necklaces, an armlet, a dagger, a headdress, and a fan. In the campaigns of Thutmose I, he fought in Nubia once again, and against the western Asiatic Kingdom of Mitanni. This loyal service brought even greater acknowledgment, in the form of two golden bracelets, four necklaces, an armlet, two golden axes, six flies and three lions, these last being decorations for valour. Ahmose Pennekhbet's final active service was under Thutmose II against the Shasu (Bedouin) of southern Palestine. The royal rewards on this occasion were the most valuable yet: three golden bracelets, six necklaces, three armlets, and a silver axe – silver was more valuable than gold in the 18th Dynasty. In an apt summary of his army career, Ahmose Pennekhbet stated: 'I followed the Dual Kings, the gods; I was with Their Persons when they went to the south and north, in every place where they went. I have attained a good old age having had a life of royal favour, having had honour under Their Persons and the love of having been in the court.'

His final reward as a loyal servant of the dynasty was to be appointed tutor to princess Neferura, the eldest daughter of 'the Divine Consort, the King's Great Wife, Maatkara [Hatshepsut]', whom he also served as treasurer. Ahmose looked after the little girl in her infancy, 'while she was a child upon the breast'. After a long and highly eventful life, he died in the co-regency of Hatshepsut and the young Thutmose III, oblivious to the former's grander ambitions, unaware that his last royal employer was about to revolutionize the very monarchy that he had served, so faithfully, under four successive kings.

43 HATSHEPSUT
THE FEMALE PHARAOH

In the third reign of the 18th Dynasty, Thutmose I and his principal wife Ahmose were blessed with the birth of a daughter. They named her Hatshepsut, 'foremost of noblewomen'. It was to prove a prophetic choice. For, in a royal house accustomed to king's wives and king's daughters with forceful personalities, the young princess was to outdo all her forebears, winning for herself greater power than all of them.

Little is known of Hatshepsut's early life, during her father's reign. Although she would have grown up among the royal women-folk in one of the 'harem palaces', she must have become aware of her father's growing reputation as a great conqueror; she certainly seems to have inherited his resolution, determination and courage. As a young woman, perhaps still in her teens, she was married, as custom required, to a close royal relative. Her husband was her half-brother (Thutmose I's son by another wife) Thutmose. Together the couple had a daughter, named Neferura. Mother and daughter were to remain close throughout their lives, their fates closely intertwined.

The death of Thutmose I must have come as a crushing blow to Hatshepsut, who already identified herself very much with her father. Moreover, she was now the wife of the new king, Thutmose II – even if she had to share his affections with a secondary consort, Iset, who had already born him a son and heir. None the less, Thutmose II's formal inscriptions gave Hatshepsut prominence, as the King's Daughter, King's Sister, God's Wife and King's Great Wife. One senses a growing awareness in the young woman of her own dynastic importance. Little wonder then, that when her husband died after a brief reign of two years, Hatshepsut seized the moment. An inscription records the new status quo: 'His son (Thutmose III) arose on the throne as king of the Two Lands and ruled on the seat of the one who begot him. His sister, the god's wife Hatshepsut, controlled the affairs of the land.'

It was partly a question of practical politics: since both the designated heir, Thutmose III, and his half-sister, Neferura, were children, a regency was essential. At the start, Hatshepsut continued to refer to herself as King's Great Wife, or as God's Wife, acknowledging that her status as regent derived from her dead husband. But after only a short while, she began to adopt more explicitly kingly titles, such as Lady of the Two Lands, an ingenious female version of one of the traditional monikers of kingship. The calculated use of epithets to enhance her position was accompanied by acts traditionally associated with the royal prerogative, such as the erection of a pair of obelisks at Karnak and temple reliefs showing her making offerings directly to the gods. At some point after seven years as regent, Hatshepsut made her bid for ultimate power, abandoning the pretence of the regency in favour of full kingly status. She adopted the traditional five-fold titulary of an Egyptian monarch and had herself depicted in reliefs wearing the (male) costume of a king (fig. 11).

A woman as regent was one thing: a woman as pharaoh was quite another (there had been only one previous instance in Egypt's long history as a nation-state). Hatshepsut made use of the five-hundred-year-old institution of co-regency to have herself crowned king without needing to oust Thutmose III and risk civil war; as designated heir, he would have had powerful backing, especially among the military. There can be little doubt that she triumphed through the force of her own personality. Yet she cannot have acted alone; she must have been surrounded and supported by officials willing to back her unprecedented bid for power. The most prominent of these was her steward, Senenmut (no. 44); others included the Chancellor

Nehesi, and the administrator of the royal estate, Amenhotep. They all shared one thing in common: as men of humble background, they depended upon Hatshepsut for their continued status. Hence their fate was bound up with hers, and it would have been in their interests to offer her unstinting support.

The office of kingship was inherently male, so Hatshepsut's titles and images had to fudge the issue of her gender, using male as well as female epithets and attributes. She and her advisers embarked on an ever-more-extreme propaganda campaign, rewriting history to legitimize her position. First, she used the same regnal years as Thutmose III, thus effectively dating the beginning of her 'reign' to the death of Thutmose II and the coronation of Thutmose III. Next, she ignored Thutmose II altogether and had herself presented as the anointed heir of her father, Thutmose I: a relief in her mortuary temple at Deir el-Bahri showed her being crowned at court, before Thutmose I, in the presence of the gods, on the auspicious occasion of the New Year's festival. A further step was to invoke the myth of divine birth, promoting the idea that she had been conceived and chosen by the supreme god Amun to be king of Egypt. Perhaps most audacious of all such attempts at myth-making was the inscription she had carved over the lintel at Speos Artemidos, the first rock-cut temple in Egypt, located in an isolated wadi south of Beni Hasan. Although ostensibly dedicated to the cat-goddess Pakhet, the shrine really served to cast Hatshepsut in the role of national liberator, the lintel inscription identifying her as the ruler who drove out the Hyksos (and hence conveniently ignoring the first three kings of the 18th Dynasty).

With her position on the throne secure, Hatshepsut turned her attention to the traditional roles of kingship, not least construction projects. During her decade and a half as king, her architects and artists displayed new heights of creativity, building monuments for their sovereign throughout her realm, from Buhen in Nubia to Serabit el-Khadim in the Sinai. As royal patron, she showered attention on the great temple of Amun-Ra at Karnak, adding two new chambers, an eighth pylon, a processional way and bark-shrines leading from Karnak southwards to Luxor Temple, and an innovative sanctuary of red quartzite (the 'Palace of Maat', also known as the 'Red Chapel'). However, her most ambitious and famous addition to the country's greatest religious complex was a pair of obelisks, erected between the fourth and fifth pylons which her father had built. The inscriptions on the bases of these giant granite needles (the one that remains in situ is the tallest standing obelisk in Egypt) stress Hatshepsut's piety and legitimacy, and give striking insights into her character: 'Let not him who shall hear this say it is a lie which I have said; but say "How like her it is," true in the sight of her father!'

Surpassing even her additions to Karnak, Hatshepsut's best-known building is her mortuary temple at Deir el-Bahri in western Thebes. Named Djeser-djeseru ('holy of holies'), it was modelled on the adjacent temple of King Mentuhotep II (no. 27), but surpassed it in scale and magnificence. It was designed 'as a garden for my father Amun'; its ramps leading from terrace to terrace were lined with trees. Behind the colonnades forming the façade of each level, coloured reliefs depicted the most important events of Hatshepsut's reign: the quarrying, transport and erection of the Karnak obelisks; and the voyage to the distant land of Punt. While Djeser-djeseru was to be the public face of Hatshepsut's mortuary cult, a secret burial was being prepared for her in the traditional resting-place of pharaohs, the Valley of the Kings. She had started her first Theban tomb while still King's Great Wife to Thutmose II. Her kingly tomb was altogether more impressive. It was possibly intended to run right under the mountain, so that the burial chamber would lie under her mortuary temple on the other side of the cliff. However, a seam of poor-quality rock frustrated these ambitious plans. None the less, the tomb remains the longest and deepest in the Valley. Hatshepsut moved her father's sarcophagus into the burial chamber, to lie beside her own: she clearly intended to associate herself with her illustrious parent for the rest of eternity.

Yet Hatshepsut's eventual fate remains a mystery. Her last appearance in the written sources was the twentieth year of her 'reign' (the thirteenth of her co-regency). Most probably, she simply died of natural causes (she would have been in her mid-fifties), for Thutmose III went on to complete, enlarge and decorate many of her temples.

Only late in his reign did he order the persecution of her memory. Her statues were smashed, her images chiselled out, her obelisks at Karnak hidden from view behind screen walls. Yet the destruction was selective: only references to Hatshepsut as king were targeted, while her images and monuments as King's Great Wife were spared. It seems, therefore, that Thutmose III was inspired, not by a personal vendetta against the woman who had kept him from the throne, but by a desire to correct the record and obliterate any sign of a woman having held the sacred office of kingship. The name of Hatshepsut was thus omitted from later king lists, but her monuments and her fame persist to this day: enduring testaments to an extraordinary woman.

44 SENENMUT
FAVOURED COURTIER OF HATSHEPSUT

Hatshepsut's rise from royal widow to king could not have occurred without the backing of a group of powerful officials. Chief among them, and one of the most prominent dignitaries from the entire New Kingdom, was her steward Senenmut. His background was not untypical of Hatshepsut's inner circle, but his destiny was exceptional.

Senenmut came from Armant (ancient Iuny), to the south of Thebes. His parents, although probably members of the small literate class, were untitled. Senenmut grew up with three brothers and two sisters. There are hints of military service during his early adulthood, but his chosen career was in the administration, more particularly the supervision of the huge estates controlled by the temple of Amun at Karnak, which was the largest landowner in the region. It was a steady job, but certainly not the passport to great wealth; when Senenmut's father died, he was afforded only the simplest of burials, without any grave goods. By contrast, when Senenmut's mother died some years later, her own possessions included two silver jugs and a silver bowl, and the equipment provided by her son was of the highest quality, including a gilded mummy mask and a heart scarab of serpentine set in gold. Senenmut was also able to take advantage of his new-found wealth to re-inter his father in more luxurious circumstances.

The explanation for Senenmut's sudden and marked increase in prosperity lies with the regency of Hatshepsut. It was she who appointed him to his most lucrative offices, and he rose to be her most influential courtier. Whether she simply admired him for his administrative abilities, or whether there was some deeper attraction, cannot be determined. There were certainly rumours at court about the nature of the relationship between the monarch and her right-hand man, but these could have been motivated by jealousy at his unrivalled influence. What is clear is that Senenmut enjoyed privileged access to Hatshepsut and to her daughter Neferura, in his capacity as the princess's tutor. Besides Neferura's education, Senenmut's areas of responsibility included the royal treasury, and hence, effectively, the national economy; oversight of the royal audience chamber, giving him control over who Hatshepsut did and did not see; and the stewardship of Hatshepsut's and her daughter's personal property. Senenmut's monuments record over ninety different titles held by him at various stages of his career; in affairs of state, only the vizier was his equal.

He clearly revelled in his new-found affluence: twenty-five statues or statue fragments of Senenmut have survived. No other official of the New Kingdom has left such an array of private sculpture. Many, if not all, were probably gifts from Hatshepsut herself. Several were innovative in form, and marked the first appearance of new types. It is possible that Senenmut devised some of these himself.

His artistic and creative interests were soon recognized by Hatshepsut who promoted him to be Overseer of All the King's Works and Chief Architect. In this capacity, he oversaw the quarrying, transport and erection of her two great obelisks at Karnak. The barges to ferry them from Aswan to Thebes must have been over 90 m (300 ft) long and 30 m (100 ft) wide. He reopened the sandstone quarries at Gebel el-Silsila in preparation for an upsurge in royal construction projects, and personally supervised some of his monarch's highest-profile commissions: 'It was the Chief Steward, Senenmut, who conducted all the works of the king in Karnak, in Armant and Deir el-Bahri;

and of Amun in the temple of Mut, in Ishry and in Luxor Temple...'

The most significant monument by far was Djeser-djeseru, the 'holy of holies', Hatshepsut's mortuary temple in western Thebes. Senenmut's role in its planning and construction is not clear, but he was marked out for special favour in its decorative scheme. Representations of him appear in niches on the temple's upper terrace, and he also appeared in the reliefs of the expedition to Punt. A better insight into his character, however, is provided by a third image, concealed behind the open doors of the small shrine in the upper sanctuary. Here, he had himself depicted kneeling and worshipping. For a commoner to be represented in the most sacred part of the temple, in such close proximity to the god's cult image, was an unthinkable act of *lèse-majesté*; but Senenmut evidently could not resist the chance to buy himself immortality in this way. His unique position in charge of Djeser-djeseru meant that he, and he alone, could get away with such a daring breach of protocol.

Ironically, Hatshepsut's accession as king seems to have brought about something of a decline in Senenmut's standing at court. Perhaps now that she had attained the highest office in the land, she no longer had such a need for him. He was replaced as tutor to Neferura, but continued to enjoy wealth and status as chief steward of Amun, in charge of the extensive estates, granaries, livestock, gardens and craftsmen controlled by the Karnak priesthood. Having devoted many years of his life to Hatshepsut's mortuary temple, he now turned his attention to his own funerary preparations. Like his sovereign, he chose two prime sites. His public tomb-chapel was built in a prominent cemetery at western Thebes. But he also made provision for a more discreet burial-place at Deir el-Bahri. Although the entrance was outside the sacred enclosure, the deep stairway led to a burial chamber right underneath the temple's outer court. He intended to spend eternity in the most auspicious environment possible.

Senenmut's demise is as hazy as his rise to power. He was still active in the sixteenth year of Hatshepsut's reign, but disappeared from the official record soon afterwards. It is not known if he fell permanently out of favour, retired from public life or simply died from natural causes. What is certain is that he was not laid to rest in either of his funerary monuments, and that, at some later date, his memory suffered persecution. Perhaps his enemies – and he must have made many – exacted their retribution when they got the chance. For there were no descendants to look after Senenmut's inheritance: he died without issue and probably never married. That seems to have been the price of winning and retaining the favour of his strong-willed, jealous, female monarch.

45 THUTMOSE III
CREATOR OF AN EGYPTIAN EMPIRE

Like Hatshepsut (no. 43) before him, Thutmose III consciously modelled himself on his illustrious forebear, Thutmose I. For the female king, her father had been a model of royal legitimacy, whose name and reputation she exploited for her own political ends; but for her successor, it was his grandfather's military achievements that provided the greatest inspiration. Thutmose I's conquests in western Asia and Nubia had extended the boundaries of pharaonic rule wider than ever before, effectively creating an Egyptian empire. On achieving sole rule after the demise of Hatshepsut, Thutmose III was determined to equal, even to outdo, these victories. So began the reign of the most successful military leader ever to sit on the throne of Horus.

Thutmose lost little time in pursuing his objectives, launching his first foreign campaign in only the second year of his independent reign. It was to be followed by annual military expeditions for the next eighteen years. The annals describing these epic battles, inscribed on the walls of Karnak temple, constitute the longest historical narrative to have survived from ancient Egypt. They were probably based upon actual campaign journals, such as those kept by the army commander Tjaneny: 'I recorded the victories he [i.e. the king] won in every land, putting them into writing according to the facts.'

The first campaign was carefully planned to achieve maximum strategic impact. Egypt faced three rival centres of power in the

Near East: the Kingdom of Mitanni, with its heartland beyond the river Euphrates; Tunip, in the lower Orontes valley; and an alliance of city states based around the fortress of Kadesh in the middle Orontes valley. A key member of the Kadesh alliance was the town of Megiddo, in the plain of Esdraelon (the Jezreel Valley, northern Israel). Not only was Megiddo a strategically important site in itself, Egyptian intelligence also brought word that it was playing host to a key meeting of the leaders of the Kadesh alliance. As the king himself put it, 'The capture of Megiddo is the capture of a thousand towns.' There was no time to lose.

Thutmose marched his army to Gaza in just ten days, captured the city for future use as a forward base, then pressed on for Megiddo, some 130 km (80 miles) to the north. Halting a little way off, the king consulted his commanders about which of three possible routes to take. Two were straightforward, bringing the army out to the north of the town. The third, southern route passed through a narrow defile and was thus much riskier. In defiance of his officers' advice, Thutmose chose the last and led his army from the front. This was only the first of many instances of strategic brilliance on the king's part. The enemy had assumed that the Egyptian army would take one of the easier routes, and was thus taken completely by surprise when the Egyptian forces appeared. Only the lack of discipline among the Egyptian soldiers – who turned to looting rather than finishing the assault – spared the Kadesh alliance complete annihilation. The princes of the confederation were able to escape back to the fortified town of Megiddo, even if some of them had to be hauled up onto the ramparts by their clothes. But nothing except complete victory would satisfy Thutmose. His forces laid siege to Megiddo for seven months, after which the town capitulated and surrendered to Egyptian might. With such a decisive moral victory, the king's forces swept through the entire region, capturing another 119 towns in swift succession.

Military victories on this scale were rare, and news of the young king's conquests reached as far as Assur, on the banks of the Tigris. The following year, the Assyrian ruler sent tribute to Thutmose III, determined to maintain good relations with the new power in the Levant. Campaign followed campaign in subsequent years, no fewer than fourteen of them directed against a single objective: the city of Kadesh. While it proved stubbornly resistant to Egyptian attack, other towns were less fortunate. The siege and ingenious capture of Joppa (modern Jaffa) passed into folklore, as did Thutmose's achievements in the thirty-third year of his reign. That was the occasion when, aping his great predecessor, he crossed the Euphrates and erected a boundary stela next to Thutmose I's own monument. To achieve this, the Egyptian fleet had to be transported overland by ox-carts from the Mediterranean coast to the Euphrates, a distance of 400 km (250 miles). Not content at such a prodigious undertaking, he also dispatched a trading expedition to distant Punt in the very same year. Never had Egypt's power been felt over so wide an area.

Thutmose's last campaign took place in his forty-second year on the throne, by which time he must have been in his late forties or early fifties. Even so, he led his army from the front. After nearly two decades of warfare, he achieved his ultimate prize: the defeat and capture of Kadesh, combined with the invasion and subjugation of Tunip. All opposition to Egypt in northwestern Syria had been vanquished. Territory was not, however, the only prize: Thutmose also took three women of Syrian extraction (Menwi, Merti and Menhet) as wives, to add to his three Egyptian consorts.

In parallel with these extraordinary victories in the Levant, Thutmose's troops also fought regular campaigns in Nubia, extending Egyptian control as far south as the Fourth Cataract. The booty and tribute which flowed in from such extensive conquests funded an ambitious building programme throughout the empire. Thutmose paid particular attention to restoring the monuments of his illustrious warrior predecessors Senusret I and III, Amenhotep I and Thutmose I. His own greatest projects were at Karnak, the religious epicentre of his new realm. He rebuilt the hypostyle hall of Thutmose I, and covered it with a new ceiling. He dismantled Hatshepsut's Red Chapel, replacing it with a new Sixth Pylon and a red granite bark shrine. He built a hall supported by a pair of unique 'heraldic pillars', and a huge enclosure wall around the central part of Karnak, with rows of chapels and workshops. His most distinctive addition was a mammoth Festival Hall in the eastern part of the temple, begun shortly after the start of his sole reign. Its columns were designed to resemble tent-poles, reminding him of the temporary palaces he used on campaign. The walls of one chamber were covered with a list of sixty-one royal predecessors, reinforcing his own position as the worthy successor of generations of kings; another chamber was decorated with scenes of the exotic flora and fauna 'which His Person found on the hill country of Retjenu [Syria-Palestine]'.

Thutmose's campaigns in the Near East thus dominated his reign and his monuments. By the end of his fifty-three years on the throne, Egypt controlled a vast swathe of territory from the banks of the Euphrates to the distant reaches of the Upper Nile. Never again would the pharaohs rule over such an empire. Moreover, it had been created largely through the energy and determination of one man. Little wonder that the cult of Thutmose III was honoured for another 1,500 years, until the end of the Ptolemaic Period; or that his name, inscribed on scarabs and amulets, was believed to provide magical protection. For he was, without doubt, the greatest of all soldier pharaohs (fig. 12).

46 MENKHEPERRASENEB
HIGH PRIEST OF AMUN

By the middle of the 18th Dynasty, the great temple of Amun-Ra at Karnak had become the most important religious foundation in Egypt. A favoured focus of royal patronage, it was an institution of enormous wealth, with estates throughout the country. The person in overall charge of Karnak, the First Prophet of Amun, was hence one of the most influential individuals in the land. During the reign of Thutmose III, the post was held by Menkheperraseneb, whose lavishly decorated Theban tomb gives an idea of what it meant to be 'superintendent of the priests of Upper and Lower Egypt, administrator of the two thrones of the god, superintendent of advanced offices, superintendent of the double treasuries of gold and silver, superintendent of the temple of Thes-khau-amun, set over the mysteries of the Two Goddesses, first prophet of Amun.'

Menkheperraseneb's very name – 'Menkheperra [Thutmose III] is healthy' – signalled his family's tradition of loyal service to the ruling family. His mother Taiunet had been a royal nurse, while his grandmother had grown up in the palace as a foster-sister of the king (probably the young Thutmose I). The women of Menkheperraseneb's family thus had strong connections with the royal household, and this proximity to the ultimate source of power no doubt played an important part in Menkheperraseneb's promotion. Rising to the office of Second Prophet, Menkheperraseneb began to prepare a tomb, to celebrate his social position. When he landed the top job in the Theban religious hierarchy, he abandoned this monument in favour of an even more lavish burial in a yet more prestigious location.

As head of the Karnak priesthood, the First Prophet of Amun was ultimately responsible for ensuring the smooth running of the temple and the correct performance of its rituals. Especially important were those carried out on auspicious dates in the calendar; and none was more significant than the New Year's festival. For Menkheperraseneb, one of the proudest moments of his life was being presented with a bouquet of flowers by the king, 'after performing rites acceptable to Amun-Ra in his festival of Djeserakhet at his appearances... on his voyage of the beginning of the year'. Naturally, Menkheperraseneb was also concerned with architectural additions to Karnak, and took a keen interest in the king's building projects:

> 'I was witness to how His Person erected many obelisks and
> flagstaffs to his father Amun. I was one who satisfied the
> king by the direction of the work on his monuments. I did
> this without any meanness of spirit and was praised on
> account of it.'

However, it was the economic administration of Karnak that seems to have occupied most of the First Prophet's time. Menkheperraseneb's duties included inspecting the herds and flocks of Amun; presiding over the delivery of agricultural revenues due to the temple from its estates throughout Egypt; receiving tribute from the other subordinate temples under his jurisdiction; and overseeing the restocking of Karnak's granaries at harvest time. He also supervised the receipt of more precious materials, notably 'the gold of the deserts of Coptos, and the gold of vile Kush as the annual tax'. Supplies of precious metals and stones were also offered by the superintendent of the gold(-bearing) deserts of Coptos, who prostrated himself before Menkheperraseneb in an act of obeisance to one of the highest officials in Egypt.

All these precious materials were ultimately destined for the workshops attached to the temple of Amun-Ra. They employed the finest craftsmen in the land, to create rare and beautiful objects for the temple itself and the royal household. As First Prophet, Menkheperraseneb was responsible for inspecting the workshops, overseeing the manufacture of chariots, temple furniture and similar valuable products. To add to such home-produced luxuries, Menkheperraseneb also received tribute from the recently conquered territories of the Egyptian empire in the Near East. One of his most memorable duties was to introduce a large delegation of foreign representatives, bearing rare and exotic goods: Minoans from Crete, in their colourful fringed garments, carrying elaborate *rhyta* (drinking cups) in the form of animal heads; Syrians bringing bears; Hittites from Anatolia, and the chiefs of Tunip and Kadesh bringing weapons and precious metals. Thutmose III's court was colourful and cosmopolitan, and Menkheperraseneb's position gave him a central place in the affairs and pageants of the state.

47 REKHMIRA
PRIME MINISTER OF UPPER EGYPT

Egypt in the New Kingdom was a highly centralized state, and at the nexus of the entire government apparatus was one man, the Vizier. The office of Vizier had come into being in the 3rd Dynasty or earlier, as a response to the need to mobilize the people and resources of the

entire country for large royal construction projects, notably the pyramids. The tripartite title conventionally translated as 'vizier', *taity zab
tjaty*, emphasized the courtly, judicial and administrative roles which
the office combined. However, it would be difficult to reconstruct the
precise nature of the office were it not for a single source from the
mid-18th Dynasty: the Theban tomb of the southern Vizier Rekhmira.
His detailed inscriptions provide the fullest and most important evidence for the vizierate, and indeed the functioning of the Egyptian
government as a whole, at the height of the country's imperial power.

Rekhmira did not achieve the highest office in the land by accident.
He came from a high-ranking family, and succeeded his grandfather
Aametju and his uncle User as southern Vizier. This gave him responsibility for Upper Egypt, stretching from the First Cataract in the south
to Asyut in the north. In this region, his power was absolute: in his
own words, 'I was a noble, second (only) to the king.' His appointment,
like those of all high officials, was confirmed by the king in person at
the royal residence. Thutmose III's speech on the occasion was not,
however, confined to the usual grandiloquent phrases. At its heart
was an exhortation to Rekhmira to act wisely and justly, in accord-
ance with the principles of Maat – Egyptian civilization was founded
upon the concepts of truth, righteousness and correct behaviour, and
the Vizier was their guarantor in practice:

> 'Take heed to thyself, for the hall of the vizier; be watchful over
> all that is done therein…. It is an abomination of the god to
> show partiality. This is the teaching: you shall treat in the same
> fashion him who is known to you and him who is not known
> to you, him who is near and him who is far away.'

At the heart of Rekhmira's duties was his daily audience. It was
a long-standing principle of Egyptian government that any person,
irrespective of social standing, could seek redress or justice from the
Vizier himself. Each day, therefore, petitioners would line up outside
the Vizier's hall, waiting to make their supplications. When their
turn came, they were ushered into Rekhmira's presence. The great
man himself sat with his high officials in front of him, the Master of

the Privy Chamber on his right and the Receiver of Income on his left; scribes were on hand to record the details and outcome of each petition. The precise arrangements for the audience were spelled out in the Vizier's official rubric: 'He shall sit upon a chair, with a rug upon the floor and a dais upon it, a cushion under his back, a cushion under his feet... a baton at his hand; the forty leather-rolls shall be open before him.' These leather rolls were probably legal documents, records of statutes and previous judgments to which the Vizier could refer when making his decisions.

To supplement this daily audience, Rekhmira also made a point of getting out and about among the populace, 'going forth over the land every morning... to hear the matters of the people... not preferring the great above the humble'. He would lean on his staff in the shade of a tree while his scribes went back and forth, receiving and registering petitions. Because the temple of Amun-Ra at Karnak was a major powerhouse of the Upper Egyptian economy, Rekhmira was closely involved with this institution as well. His tours of inspection took in the daily offerings, the monuments themselves, the craftsmen in the temple workshops, and the sculptors and builders at work on new construction projects.

Equally important were his responsibilities as head of government. He was effectively Commissioner of Police, Minister for the Armed Forces, Minister of Agriculture, Interior Minister, First Lord of the Treasury, and Prime Minister, all rolled into one. Each day, Rekhmira received reports from the head of the treasury, from the other major offices of state, and from the garrisons: 'Let every office, from first to last, proceed to the hall of the Vizier, to take counsel with him.' The outgoings and income of the royal residence were reported to him, and dues were brought to him from his local officials. His diverse responsibilities included sealing all property deeds, fixing land and district boundaries (crucial in an agricultural society), staffing the garrison of the residence, levying troops to accompany the king on royal progresses, giving regulations to the Army Council, guaranteeing the water supply, overseeing the work of town councils, procuring supplies of timber, inspecting taxes, and even determining the onset of the annual inundation and the beginning of the calendar year.

Having received information from every department of government, and especially from the Treasury, Rekhmira relayed this to the king at a daily conference. Although the king was head of state, it was the Vizier who translated royal commands into government policy.

The crucial relationship between monarch and vizier lay at the heart of the Egyptian governmental machine. It is easy to imagine, therefore, how nervous Rekhmira must have been when the king who had appointed him, Thutmose III, died and was succeeded by his son Amenhotep II. On hearing the news, Rekhmira set sail immediately downriver to the royal residence town of Hatsekhem in Lower Egypt, to meet the new king and present him, as tradition demanded, with his royal insignia. The audience passed successfully, and Rekhmira returned home to Thebes triumphant, having been confirmed in office.

Despite the detailed narration of his career on the walls of his magnificent funerary monument, the conclusion of Rekhmira's story remains an enigma. His images were systematically mutilated, perhaps suggesting disgrace, his tomb had no burial chamber, and his final resting-place is unknown.

48 DEDI
GOVERNOR OF THE WESTERN DESERT

The deserts to the west of Thebes played a crucial role in the politics and security of Upper Egypt. During the unification of the country in the late predynastic period and the civil war of the First Intermediate Period the desert routes across the Qena bend proved vital for military operations. In the wars against the Hyksos, too, the area had played an important role, allowing the Hyksos and the Kushites to forge an alliance under the noses of the Egyptians. The 18th Dynasty kings had therefore learned from bitter experience that failure to control the deserts could threaten national security. They put in place a system of surveillance and control designed to prevent any further risks.

In the latter part of the reign of Thutmose III and the early years of his successor, Amenhotep II, the governor of the western desert was a man named Dedi. His primary responsibility was the security of 'the back door' to Egypt. He had at his disposal a militia, composed of Nubian recruits and native Egyptians. They maintained a permanent and active presence throughout the western desert, using watchtowers and guard posts to carry out their surveillance operations. More elaborate manoeuvres would also take place from time to time, involving a large detachment of soldiers accompanied by a standard-bearer. The aim seems to have been to mount a deliberate show of force as a warning to any potential trouble-makers.

Dedi's other, related role was as government envoy to the tribes of the western desert. Although the semi-nomadic peoples of the Sahara were most populous and visible further south, in Nubia, their seasonal migrations and trading activities in the oases brought them as far north as Thebes on a periodic basis. It was in Egypt's interests to monitor such movements closely, maintaining peaceful relations while leaving no doubt about Egyptian military dominance. This delicate diplomatic balancing act fell to Dedi. The absence of any significant confrontation during his tenure suggests that he performed his role effectively and diligently.

49 QENAMUN
BOMBASTIC CHIEF STEWARD

The structure of ancient Egyptian society mirrored its most distinctive monuments: at the apex of the pyramid was the semi-divine king, and at the base was the majority of the population; in between were the various ranks of the administration, ranging from the humble functionary to the highest officials of the land. Within this social pyramid, and especially among its intensely hierarchical upper echelons, nuances of status were all important. They were carefully and deliberately expressed by various means, not least an individual's titles and dignities. The royal court of the 18th Dynasty seems to have been particularly obsessed with such advertisements. New epithets were invented purely to denote rank rather than office. Officials collected titles like badges, to display their success and importance to their peers. Qenamun, royal steward during the reign of Amenhotep II, took this practice to its logical, though ridiculous, extreme.

During his career he held over eighty different titles and epithets, although few of them signified real office. Instead, most stressed his virtues and his connections at court: member of the elite and high official, Royal Seal-Bearer, confidential companion, dearly beloved companion, Gentleman of the Bedchamber, Fan-Bearer of the Lord of the Two Lands, Royal Scribe, aide to the king, Attaché of the King in Every Place, Overseer of the Treasure House, Overseer of the Two Gold Houses, *sem*-priest, God's Father, Captain of Bowmen, Head of the Stables, Overseer of the Cattle of Amun, Overseer of Fields, Overseer of the Treasury, Overseer of the Storehouse of Amun, Overseer of the Doorkeepers of the Granaries of Amun... the list is almost endless. One of Qenamun's titles seems to sum up the general principle: Overseer of All Kinds of Work.

That he was obsessed with rank and status is scarcely surprising, given his upbringing. Qenamun's mother, Amenemopet, had been a palace nurse – 'the great nurse who brought up the god' – and he would therefore have been raised in the company of the royal children, as a foster-brother of the future king Amenhotep II. Loyalty to the sovereign would have been inculcated in Qenamun from an early age, and he revelled in being the monarch's most ardent supporter, describing himself as 'doing right by the Lord of the Two Lands', 'being loyal to his benefactor', 'giving satisfaction to the sovereign', 'inspiring the king with perfect confidence', and being 'heartily appreciated by Horus'. More than a streak of vanity, pomposity and self-righteousness shines through these ever-more-elaborate formulations.

Qenamun's actual job was a little more prosaic. He followed in his father's footsteps by becoming steward of an estate, in his case Perunefer, a country residence used for relaxation by senior members of the royal family. The business of running the estate was punctuated by entertainments of various kinds: troupes of dancing girls, musicians, and the presentation of New Year's gifts to the king. This last was one of the highlights of the year, recorded in lavish detail in Qenamun's tomb.

As a childhood companion of the king and now a trusted royal official, Qenamun was ever at his sovereign's side. He claimed to have accompanied Amenhotep II on his journeys 'through vile Syria, without deserting the Lord of the Two Lands in battle, in the hour of repulsing the hordes'. With his position at Perunefer, Qenamun was ideally placed to pick up any gossip at court, and in particular any murmurings against the king. His role as steward thus gave him the perfect cover for his undercover operations as Master of Secrets, the head of the king's internal security apparatus. He boasted of being 'the eyes of the King of Upper Egypt, the ears of the king of Lower Egypt'. It was Qenamun's job to be aware of everything, and to report it to his master: 'when the King is in his palace, he is his eyes.'

This behind-the-scenes power evidently appealed to Qenamun's temperament, and fuelled still further his egotism. Granted permission for a tomb in the Theban necropolis (fig. 13), he employed the best artists of the day and made sure that the tomb-chapel was designed to provide as much wall space as possible. In pictures and words, Qenamun was determined to trumpet his achievements to posterity. His bragging reached new heights, as he lauded himself with ever more grandiloquence: 'chief companion of the courtiers, overseer of overseers, leader of leaders, greatest of the great, regent of the whole land'; and, last but not least, 'one who, if he gives attention to anything in the evening, it is mastered early in the morning at daybreak.' Yet there are signs in the tomb that this rampant self-promotion, coupled with his work in undercover surveillance, made Qenamun more enemies than friends at court. Many of his images and the writings of his name were deliberately effaced after his death. In ancient Egypt, although advancement was the reward of ultra-loyalty, it was not wise to get above one's station.

50 NAKHT
HUMBLE OWNER OF A BEAUTIFUL TOMB

The Tombs of the Nobles at Thebes are one of the great glories of ancient Egypt. The men (women are notable by their absence) for whom they were built represent a 'who's who' of pharaonic society during the New Kingdom. Yet, among the highly decorated sepulchres of viziers, high priests and mayors, there is a small tomb, numbered 52 by modern archaeologists, which was built for a man from the lower ranks of the bureaucracy during the reign of Thutmose IV. Indeed, so lowly was its owner, Nakht, that he had no titles: a striking absence in a society where titles were everything.

It is not even clear why Nakht was able to procure himself a tomb – albeit a modest one – in an area otherwise dominated by impressive funerary monuments. Other than his own burial, he left no trace, made no impact on wider Theban society. In the scanty texts inscribed on its walls, he is referred to simply as a serving-priest of Amun, in other words one of the members of the temple staff at Karnak who, on a rota basis, performed menial, largely non-priestly, tasks. These would have included cleaning the temple precincts and delivering consecrated offerings to their final recipients. Nakht would have worked a fixed period of hours during the day or night, and his temple duties were probably in addition to his (unknown) 'day job'. Like many of his contemporaries, he would probably have considered it an honour to be summoned to perform a period of service in the greatest of Thebes' many temples.

His wife Tawy also had a role in the cult of Amun, as a chantress. Again, this was probably a part-time role performed by local women. Husband and wife would thus have shared, in a modest way, in the great religious rites and festivals that dominated the Theban calendar. One of the most popular of these was the annual Beautiful Festival of the Valley, an occasion for popular participation when Thebans visited the tombs of their deceased relatives for a special meal, often accompanied by music or dancing. Nakht and Tawy hoped that their son, Amenemopet, would do likewise for them after their deaths. In the meantime, they evidently took pleasure in their small household, made complete by a pet cat which from time to time would sit under Tawy's chair eating a fish.

Nakht's chief fame rests, not with his achievements as husband, father or part-time priest, but with his tomb itself. Although small, it is decorated with finely executed and lively paintings which, rarely for an ancient Egyptian monument, can be attributed to a single artist (fig. 14). The master painter, who used an almost impressionistic style in some scenes, remains nameless, but it is likely that he was a friend of Nakht's. His work has endured over thirty centuries, bringing unexpected fame to an otherwise faceless functionary, one of the multitude of lowly workers whose unsung dedication built and sustained ancient Egyptian civilization.

51 SENNEFER
MAYOR OF THEBES

The idealizing image preserved in ancient Egyptian art is almost certainly as false as it is alluring. It is only through the less formal written record of private correspondence that we can catch glimpses of the unvarnished reality. A case in point is Sennefer, Mayor of Thebes in the reign of Amenhotep II.

He had all the attributes of a successful bureaucrat. First, he was fortunate in his relatives. His father had been steward to the God's Wife of Amun, and his brother had risen even further, becoming Vizier. With such useful connections, it was only to be expected that Sennefer, too, would achieve high office. He served as Overseer of Priests of the God's Wife, steward of the temple of Amenhotep I and Festival Leader of Thutmose I, before being promoted to the mayoralty. This gave him civic responsibility for one of the great cities of Egypt and oversight of the Amun cult's cattle, double-granary and timber plantation.

Second, Sennefer was surrounded by a loyal and loving family. He was married twice, to a royal wet-nurse named Senay and a chantress of Amun named Merit. Third, he enjoyed royal favour as 'one who satisfies the heart of the king', and could boast that he had 'reached old age in the praise of the Lord of the Two Lands'. This patronage manifested itself in concrete terms. Sennefer was granted the privilege of a Theban tomb, famous for the ceiling of its burial chamber, which is covered with a representation of a vine, laden with pendant bunches of black grapes. He may have been responsible for the vineyards of Amun, or perhaps he was just a wine connoisseur and bon viveur, 'the mayor who spends his time in happiness'. The pillars of the tomb, a feature found in royal sepulchres of the same period, also suggest an owner who aspired to the very best. Indeed, Sennefer may even have usurped a tomb in the Valley of the Kings, originally intended for Hatshepsut, for himself and his family.

Another impressive mark of the king's esteem was being granted permission to have a granite pair-statue of himself and his wife Senay placed in Karnak temple, where it might receive offerings from worshippers. The statue showed the couple at the height of their prosperity: Senay wearing a formal dress and a huge wig, Sennefer adorned with the gold of honour, the rolls of fat around his torso demonstrating his wealth. He also sported his most treasured possession, an amulet in the shape of two hearts conjoined, inscribed with the throne-name of Amenhotep II.

The pair-statue was evidently well used by visitors to Karnak, and the lap was worn away by the repeated presentation of offerings. Unusually, the piece was signed by the sculptors who made it, Amenmes and Djedkhonsu, 'outline draughtsmen of the temple of Amun'. In this small detail, the two worlds of a high official are revealed: the public reputation and the private relationships. Sennefer seems to have used his contacts within Karnak temple to procure the services of skilled craftsmen for his own personal project. Such arrangements must have happened all the time, but are rarely attested in the written record.

The final piece of evidence for Sennefer's life and character is an even more remarkable survival: a sealed and unopened letter addressed to a tenant-farmer named Baki who worked in the town of

Hu (ancient Hut-sekhem). In the correspondence, Sennefer announced that he was due to arrive in Hu in three days' time, and ordered Baki to have supplies ready. The tone of the letter is both imperious and hectoring. Sennefer warned Baki: 'Do not let me find fault with you concerning your post', and admonished him again a few sentences later: 'Now mind, you shall not slack, for I know that you are sluggish and fond of eating lying down.' Baki may, of course, have been particularly lazy or inept, but it is equally possible – and perhaps more likely – that this was the way Sennefer addressed all his subordinates. Egyptian officials were not always as perfect as their tomb reliefs and statues tried to suggest.

52 AMENHOTEP III
RULER OF A GOLDEN AGE

The conquests of the early 18th Dynasty created an Egyptian empire in the Near East and Nubia, stretching 'from Karoy [el-Kurru, near the Fourth Cataract] in the south to Naharin [the Kingdom of Mitanni, beyond the Euphrates] in the north'. Egypt prospered from this huge hinterland as exotic and valuable goods flowed into the treasury and royal workshops. Control of the Nubian deserts gave the pharaohs access to unparalleled quantities of gold, promoting trade and increasing national prosperity still further. The late 18th Dynasty was, therefore, quite literally a 'golden age' of power and prestige. Its zenith coincided with the reign of a king who consciously surrounded himself with gleaming objects as a metaphor for the brilliance of the sun: Amenhotep III.

He was born around 1403 BC, late in the reign of his grandfather Amenhotep II, after whom he was named. The boy was given the additional epithet *mer-khepesh*, 'he who loves strength'; however, the strength of his reign was to be economic rather than military. When Amenhotep was only about two years old, his father acceded to the throne as Thutmose IV. The young prince probably grew up in the royal nursery within the harem palace at Gurob, on the edge of the Fayum. Here, he would have come to appreciate the lavish decoration and furnishings that were to be an abiding passion for the rest of his life.

When he was still a boy, Amenhotep suffered the loss of his older brother, Amenemhat. Not only must this have been a devastating personal bereavement, it also changed Amenhotep's life forever, since he was now his father's eldest surviving son and heir. By way of an induction into his new office, the Crown Prince was taken by his father on campaign in Nubia, to experience the military role of kingship at first hand. Amenhotep seems not to have taken to army life: with a single exception (a minor skirmish in Nubia), his reign of thirty-seven years would be devoid of campaigns, in stark contrast to the frequent battles waged by his predecessors.

His preparation for the throne was all too brief. At the tender age of about twelve, he became king in succession to his father. The mix of emotions must have been compounded by the untimely death, in the same year, of his sister Tentamun. The young Amenhotep had to perform the burial rites for both a father and a sister; this was followed soon afterwards by his coronation at Memphis (ancient Ineb-hedj). To complete a momentous year, Amenhotep issued a commemorative scarab announcing his marriage to the lady Tiye (no. 53), the woman who was to be his constant companion throughout his reign.

At first, affairs of state were handled by Amenhotep's mother, Mutemwia, in her capacity as regent. Amenhotep himself set about demonstrating his virility, in preparation for assuming the reins of power as soon as he reached adolescence. To this end, in the second year of his reign, he took part in a staged bull-hunt in the Wadi Natrun. In a single day's hunting, he claimed to have killed fifty-six bulls out of a total of 170 slaughtered by the royal party. After resting his horses for four days, he rode out again and killed another forty, commemorating the whole event on another set of specially issued scarabs. Kingship required not just brute strength and mastery of the untamed forces of nature, but also concrete expressions to impress the people and propitiate the gods: temples. So Amenhotep set his architects and builders to work on a series of projects, from a small temple to the vulture-goddess Nekhbet at Elkab (ancient Nekheb) to a limestone shrine at Heliopolis (ancient Iunu). Work was begun on a tenth pylon in the temple of Amun-Ra at Karnak, and on Amenhotep's royal tomb in the isolated western branch of the Valley of the Kings.

The pace of building increased with the appointment of Amenhotep son of Hapu (no. 55) to the ministry of works, and the king also took steps to tighten his grip on the powerful priesthoods, appointing his brother-in-law Anen as Second Prophet of Amun in Thebes and Chief of Seers (High Priest of Ra) at Heliopolis. With the wealth of the great temples at his disposal, Amenhotep could lavish ever greater resources on his building projects, magnificent statuary, and the dedication of new cult images.

In the tenth year of his reign he issued a further commemorative scarab to record the number of lions (102) he had killed during his first decade on the throne, and, in the same breath, to note his diplomatic marriage to princess Gilukhepa, daughter of Shuttarna II, king of Mitanni. The lady arrived in Egypt with a retinue of 317 women. She was not Amenhotep's only foreign wife. He also married two unnamed Babylonian princesses; the daughter of the king of Arzawa; and princess Tadukhepa, the daughter of Tushratta, Shuttarna II's successor as king of Mitanni.

Despite such a collection of consorts, it was Amenhotep III's first wife, Tiye, who remained undisputed favourite, and the most influential woman at his court. Her position is reflected in the fifth and final commemorative scarab issued by the king, to mark the excavation of a ceremonial lake for Tiye in her town of Djarukha (perhaps her birth-place, Akhmim). It measured 3,700 by 700 cubits (1,938 by 367 m, 6,358 by 1,204 ft), and the lavish opening ceremony involved the king and queen being rowed on it in the royal barge 'The Aten [sun disc] Gleams'. This name reflected the increasing focus on solar worship under Amenhotep III: his palace at Thebes was called 'Splendour of the Aten', while one of his favourite epithets which he applied to himself was Aten-tjehen, 'dazzling Aten'. This fixation on the visible disc of the daytime sun as a metaphor for kingship was to be the defining characteristic of his son's reign.

After more than two decades on the throne, Amenhotep's thoughts turned to the royal succession, and he appointed his eldest son, Crown Prince Thutmose, to the High Priesthood of Ptah in the capital city of Memphis. Father and son officiated together at the funeral and burial of the Apis bull. Back in Thebes, the king inaugurated work on one of his most significant projects to date, a temple at southern Ipet (modern Luxor). This bold new edifice, aligned towards Karnak rather than the river, was designed to serve as the backdrop for the annual Opet Festival at which the king communed in secret with the supreme god Amun-Ra, being rejuvenated by the experience and emerging to popular acclaim as 'Foremost of all the living *kas*'. The implicit deification of the living king was made rather more explicit in the decoration of one of the inner chambers, which described Amenhotep's birth as having arisen from a union of his mother and the god Amun. Shortly after work began at Luxor, tragedy struck when Crown Prince Thutmose died; his place as heir was taken by his younger brother (no. 56), who was to carry Amenhotep's glorification of the monarchy to its extreme.

The king's thirtieth anniversary jubilee was an occasion for national rejoicing. The festivities were overseen by the trusted official Amenhotep son of Hapu, and took place at Thebes, which from now on was the court's permanent home. At the climax of the celebrations, the king, his mother Mutemwia, his consort Tiye and his daughter Sitamun, newly elevated to the rank of 'King's Great Wife', sailed together across an artificial harbour in a dazzling golden bark. The solar imagery could not have been more explicit, with the three generations of royal women symbolizing the goddess Hathor's roles as mother, wife and daughter of Ra. Two further jubilee festivals followed, in the king's thirty-fourth and thirty-sixth years on the throne; at the latter celebrations, Amenhotep appeared covered from head to toe in gold jewelry. But no amount of formal association with the sun god could change his inescapable mortality. After a reign of thirty-seven years, Amenhotep III died, aged about fifty. Egypt's dazzling sun had finally set.

53 TIYE
QUEEN WITH AN INTEREST IN POWER-POLITICS

In the official record, the reigns of Egyptian monarchs often look like one-man shows, dominated by the person of the king, with other members of the royal circle afforded only minor bit-parts. By contrast, Amenhotep III's glittering reign was very much a double-act. From his first year on the throne to the end of his life, his wife Tiye was his constant companion and support. In state texts, her name was closely associated with her husband's. She was the recipient of the king's favour to an extraordinary degree, the monuments dedicated to her ranging from a boating lake in Middle Egypt to a temple in Nubia. In common with earlier generations of 18th Dynasty royal women, Tiye exercised considerable influence at court and took an active and public role in government. She thus, unwittingly, set the scene for the extraordinary rise to power of her daughter-in-law, Nefertiti (no. 57).

Tiye was the daughter of middle-ranking provincial officials from Akhmim in Middle Egypt. Her father, Yuya, was a priest in the local temple of Min and overseer of its herds of cattle. Tiye's mother, Tuyu, was a songstress in the cults of Amun and Hathor, and a leading temple musician 'Chief of Entertainers' in the cults of Amun and Min. Both parents were therefore closely involved in their local communities, but did not hold high office in regional or national government. When the newly crowned Amenhotep III chose Tiye as his wife, in the first year of his reign, he was therefore breaking with recent royal tradition by marrying a commoner from such an obscure background. But the bond between the couple, neither of them much older than twelve, was clearly strong from the start. Amenhotep promoted his parents-in-law, appointing Yuya as Master of the Horse and lieutenant-commander of the king's chariotry, while bestowing on Tuyu the dignity of King's Mother of the King's Great Wife. Tiye's brother, Anen, likewise received promotion. The king was keen to admit his wife's family into the inner royal circle.

Tiye clearly took to royal life, enjoying the luxury and sophistication of Amenhotep III's court. New fashions of clothing were sweeping Egypt, under the influence of its extensive foreign contacts, and Tiye enjoyed her fair share of elaborate garments. One of her most exotic creations was a feather dress with two vulture-wings that wrapped around the hips and thighs, tightly belted at the waist and held in place by wide shoulder straps. But Tiye was no mere dilettante. With her husband's encouragement, she began to involve herself in affairs of state. She sent letters on her own behalf to foreign rulers, and received their replies, contributing to the upsurge in diplomatic correspondence characteristic of Amenhotep III's reign.

On the domestic stage, she fulfilled the female roles necessary to complement her husband's preferred model of divine kingship. Hence, she was Mut to his Amun; she adopted the horns and disc of the goddess Hathor to his Horus; she associated herself with Nekhbet to draw an explicit parallel between the vulture goddess who helped the sun god in his journey across the heavens and a royal consort supporting her husband through his earthly reign. The royal iconographers also cast Tiye in a more fearsome role, as defender of the king: in one relief, she is shown as a sphinx, trampling the enemies of pharaoh in a scene adapted straight from the imagery of kingship. It is highly probable that Tiye was closely involved in this carefully worked-out propaganda: the pouting lips and downturned mouth seen on her statues suggest a steely resolve behind the façade of queenly beauty. Indeed, Tiye employed her own sculptor, a man named Iuty, to create her likenesses; he was but one member of her extended household, led by her steward Kheruef.

From shortly after her husband's coronation until his third jubilee festival, Tiye was ever at Amenhotep's side. In the last year of his reign, a statue of Ishtar, Mesopotamian goddess of love and fertility, was sent to Egypt by Tushratta, king of Mitanni. It might have been intended as a symbol of the royal couple's enduring affection, but with Amenhotep III's death just a year later, Tiye found herself suddenly alone. She moved her household to the palace at Gurob to live out her widowhood surrounded by her faithful female staff: the head of the household, Teye; the singer, Mi; the maids, Nebetya and Tama. To placate her son, the new king Amenhotep IV (later Akhenaten), Tiye (no. 56) also maintained a residence at his new city of Akhetaten (Amarna); here her household was supervised by the steward Huya.

Tiye seems to have been a formidable presence in the early years of her son's reign. Having embarked on a revolution in government, he could not afford to do without her experience and counsel. On one occasion, Tushratta wrote to Amenhotep IV (as he then was), urging him to consult his mother on matters of state, since she was the only one who understood Amenhotep III's policies in detail. That a foreign ruler held Tiye in such high regard is testimony to her profound influence and political nous.

Having survived her husband by almost a decade, Tiye died in her early sixties; she is generally thought to have been buried by her son in the royal tomb at Amarna. However, the discovery of two *shabti*-figurines, referring to her as the King's Mother, in Amenhotep III's tomb at Thebes, suggests that she may in fact have been laid to rest next to her husband – as she would certainly have wished. Her influence as the matriarch of the family continued for another generation: her grandson Tutankhamun was buried with objects bearing her name, including a lock of her hair. Devoted wife, wise mother, beloved grandmother; diplomatic correspondent, official consort, patron of the arts: Tiye was all of these and more, a larger-than-life figure who continues to fascinate, thirty-three centuries after her death.

54 USERHAT
LOWLY SCRIBE, ARTISTIC PATRON

To be able to read and write was a rare and valuable skill in ancient Egypt. Membership of the country's tiny literate class opened doors to a career in the administration, to the corridors of power. Hence, to be a 'scribe' was something to boast about. A good example was Userhat, who lived and worked in Thebes in the reign of Amenhotep III. Userhat's motley collection of titles included scribe of the census of bread of Upper and Lower Egypt, Overseer of the Cattle of Amun, and deputy herald; but, more often than not, he referred to himself simply as 'scribe'. His entry into the lower echelons of government had been helped, no doubt, by his distant royal connections: he had been brought up as a 'child of the royal nursery'.

He remained, however, a lowly official, a small cog in the huge wheel of Theban bureaucracy. What has guaranteed Userhat's lasting fame is not his career but his choice of artist to decorate his Theban tomb. By chance, he clearly knew one of the best artists of the day, someone able to bring new verve and vigour to the traditional stable of motifs. As a result, the scenes in Userhat's tomb are some of the most famous in the whole canon of New Kingdom private funerary art. In the hands of the anonymous artist, a standard scene of hunting in the desert was transformed into a dynamic composition of colour, movement and pathos: desert hares and antelope flee in panic before a hail of arrows; a wounded fox, caught in a thorn bush, slowly bleeds to death. Such emotion and sense of action are rare indeed in tomb art; the artist of Userhat's tomb was clearly a master.

Other details in the tomb reflected Userhat's life and interests, such as his supervision of the annual cattle count and his presentation of flowers to the king, enthroned beneath a brightly coloured pavilion. A small, naturalistic detail was included in a formal banquet scene in the form of a pet monkey, squatting beneath his wife Mutnofret's chair, eating fruit from a basket. In the depiction of Userhat's funeral procession, the tomb owner's chariot and favourite pair of horses featured prominently, suggesting that chariot-riding as a leisure activity was not confined to the highest echelons of society, but enjoyed by a wider section of the population. A genre scene, included to add colour but probably not directly related to Userhat's own experiences, was the recruitment of young conscripts into the army. As soon as they were enlisted, they waited in line to have their hair cut short by the army barber: an induction common to new recruits throughout history. It was through such acutely observed details that the artist raised the decoration of Userhat's tomb above the commonplace, offering instead lively snapshots of life among the lower ranks of the administration in 18th Dynasty Thebes.

55 AMENHOTEP SON OF HAPU
THE KING'S RIGHT-HAND MAN

Although it was a society in which inherited office was the ideal, ancient Egypt none the less prided itself on giving men of talent the opportunity to rise to the very top through their own abilities. Indeed, there are examples throughout pharaonic history of individuals of humble birth achieving high office. One man, however, outdid them all: Amenhotep son of Hapu rose, not from rags to riches, but from drudgery to divinity.

Amenhotep was born around 1435 BC, during the reign of Thutmose III (no. 45), a son to Itu and his wife Hapu. He grew up in the small provincial town of Athribis (ancient Hut-hery-ib), capital of the tenth nome (province) of Lower Egypt. As a boy, his intellectual abilities must already have been recognized, as he was sent to attend the House of Life attached to the local temple. This institution housed both the sacred library and the scriptorium where priests composed new religious texts. The young Amenhotep would have received a thorough induction in Egyptian reading and writing, an education shared with very few of his contemporaries: 'I was inducted into the gods' books and beheld the words of Thoth [hieroglyphs]. I penetrated their secrets and learned all their mysteries, and I was consulted on their every aspect.'

Having learned to read and write, he no doubt entered the lower ranks of the local administration, and seemed destined for a comfortable, though unspectacular career. All that changed at the accession of Amenhotep III (no. 52), by which time Amenhotep son of Hapu was already in his mid-forties. The new reign brought with it new opportunities for men of learning, and Amenhotep became a royal scribe and chief priest of his local temple of Horus-Khentikheti. Still, his world did not extend beyond the confines of his home town in the central Delta. At some point during the next decade, however, word must have reached the king about the abilities of this local administrator. For, in his fifties, Amenhotep was summoned south to Thebes – more than 650 km (400 miles) away – to take up the position of scribe of recruits, responsible for levying and deploying manpower throughout Egypt for royal construction projects. So successful was Amenhotep in this important role, that he was subsequently promoted to Overseer of All the King's Works; he now had direct managerial responsibility for Amenhotep III's lavish projects, ranging from the temple of Soleb in Nubia to the king's mortuary temple and colossi on the West Bank of Thebes. These last were among the largest royal statues ever commissioned, and Amenhotep was understandably proud of his part in their creation:

> *'I directed the king's likeness in every hard stone like heaven, directing the work of his statues, great of breadth. I did not imitate what had been done before... and there has never been anyone who has done the same since the founding of the Two Lands.'*

As a reward for his excellent work, Amenhotep received a signal honour: the king ordered statues of his favourite high official to be placed along the main processional route in the great temple of Amun-Ra at Karnak. This unusual mark of royal esteem conferred on Amenhotep the role of intermediary in other people's prayers. In his own words, 'I am the spokesman appointed by the king to hear your words of supplication.'

Although by now in his seventies, Amenhotep was still the ablest of the king's ministers, and was therefore given a challenge of special significance: coordinating the lavish jubilee celebrations to mark Amenhotep III's thirty years on the throne. The festivities took place at Thebes, and involved the construction of a jubilee palace, and the staging of elaborate water-borne processions and other visual spectacles. As Festival Leader and 'member of the elite in the offices of the *sed*-festival', Amenhotep son of Hapu had to make sure that everything went according to plan; there was no room for mistakes in such a symbolically charged event. The jubilee passed off in exemplary fashion, and Amenhotep was showered with honours by a grateful monarch. Among his rewards was a decorated, commemorative headband (the ancient Egyptian equivalent of a jubilee medal), which he proudly wore in later years.

Amenhotep never held one of the great offices of state – vizier, chancellor, High Priest of Amun, army commander – yet enjoyed an exceptional degree of royal favour because of his personal and intellectual qualities. In recognition of these, he was brought into the royal household as steward to the king's eldest daughter, Sitamun. Amenhotep was now firmly established as the grand old man of the court, feted for his achievements, beloved of the people. Already in his eighties, he must have seemed immortal, even to himself: 'I have reached the age of eighty years. I am greatly praised by the king, and I will complete 110 years.' But that was a little too ambitious, even for Amenhotep. At around the time of the king's second jubilee festival, the old man died, his final wish being 'to go out into the sky and be united with the stars, acclaimed in the boat of the sun god'. He was interred in a tomb in the hills of western Thebes, and was given the unique honour of his own mortuary temple – unprecedented for a private individual. Here, his cult was still maintained three centuries after his death.

The posthumous reputation of Amenhotep son of Hapu gained a popular following, especially in the Theban region where so many of his great projects had been carried out. A 22nd Dynasty inscription at Karnak addressed him as a great sage: 'O Amenhotep, in your great name you know the secret power in the words of the past, that date back to the time of the ancestors.' By the reign of Ptolemy II (180–164 BC), Amenhotep son of Hapu had been formally deified, worshipped at two sites on the West Bank of Thebes (Deir el-Medina and Deir el-Bahri) as a god of learning and healing. From there, the cult of Amenhotep spread throughout the Nile Valley and continued to be observed until the period of Roman rule: a remarkable legacy for a man of humble origins.

PART 5

The Great Heresy
AMARNA PERIOD

The reign of Akhenaten and its immediate aftermath have prompted more interest and more controversy than any other phase of ancient Egyptian history. The Amarna Period, as it is known, lasted barely two decades, yet transformed every aspect of pharaonic civilization, from art and religion to politics and government. There is no doubt that the instigator of these revolutionary changes was Akhenaten himself (no. 56), aided and abetted by his wife Nefertiti (no. 57). But no revolution can succeed without its loyal adherents, and the main protagonists of the Amarna Period emerge as complex and fascinating individuals in their own right: from the High Priest Meryra (no. 58), in charge of promoting Akhenaten's new religious doctrine, to the sculptor Bak (no. 59), instructed by the king himself in the bold, new artistic style of the age, to Mahu (no. 60), the Chief of Police responsible for maintaining tight security in the new capital city of Amarna (ancient Akhetaten). It is perhaps because of such colourful characters that the reign of Akhenaten seems more vivid, more accessible than other eras of the pharaonic past.

While the revolution was most vigorously promoted in Amarna itself, its effects were felt throughout the country. Temples were closed, priesthoods disbanded; monuments to gods other than Aten, the sun disc, were systematically defaced; new shrines to Aten were built in the major centres of the old religion, including Thebes and Memphis. There is evidence that Akhenaten's new doctrine failed to find favour among the general population, and there must have been a widespread sense of unease at the fundamental changes being wrought in every area of public life. Only perhaps beyond Egypt's borders, in its foreign territories, did life continue much as before: the scenes from the tomb of Huy, Viceroy of Nubia (no. 61), suggest a seamless continuation of the traditional Egyptian policy of political control and economic exploitation.

As much as the personalities, the archaeology of the Amarna Period has contributed to its fame and popularity. The fact that Akhenaten's new capital city was abandoned almost as swiftly as it was founded, and has been rediscovered through decades of careful survey and excavation, means that we can reconstruct life in Amarna to a degree impossible for any another ancient Egyptian city. We can reconstruct its palaces and temples, its workshops and houses; we can imagine the king's progress along the ceremonial road, and the appearance of the royal couple on the balcony of the King's House; we can, in our mind's eye, wander the streets of Akhetaten in a way that is impossible for Thebes or Memphis. Furthermore, the art of the Amarna period is undeniably engaging, if somewhat surreal. The colossal statues of Akhenaten and the painted bust of Nefertiti (fig. 15) have a power and immediacy unmatched by other ancient Egyptian sculpture.

But perhaps the most important reason for the endless fascination with the Amarna Period is the mysterious manner of its passing. So many questions remain unresolved about the events surrounding and following the end of Akhenaten's reign. Who was Smenkhkara? Did Nefertiti succeed her husband as 'king' in her own right? Where was Akhenaten buried and where is his body now? Which widowed queen wrote a desperate letter to the Hittite king begging for a husband to rule Egypt alongside her? Add to these intriguing puzzles the life, death and burial of Akhenaten's sole surviving child, the boy-king Tutankhamun (no. 62), and it is little wonder that the Amarna Period continues to inspire so much study and speculation. The tomb of Tutankhamun remains the single most spectacular archaeological discovery ever made in Egypt. Yet despite its fabulous treasures, it has yielded surprisingly little information about the king himself, his queen (no. 63) or his successor (no. 65). Much more informative are the Memphite tombs of Tutankhamun's high officials, such as his treasurer Maya (no. 64), recently excavated from the sands of Saqqara. They promise new insights into events at the end of the

18th Dynasty. But the allure of the Amarna Period is likely to remain. For, as Lady Burghclere famously remarked about the discovery of Tutankhamun's tomb, 'A story that opens like Aladdin's Cave and ends like a Greek myth of Nemesis cannot fail to capture the imagination of all men and women.'

56 AKHENATEN
THE HERETIC PHARAOH

Religious visionary or fanatical zealot? Enlightened ruler or tyrannical despot? Inspirational hero or destructive heretic? No other individual from ancient Egypt, and few others from world history, inspires such passionate and contradictory reactions as Akhenaten. He has been called 'the first individual in history' and he certainly imposed his own personal beliefs on his country to an unprecedented extent. His break with the past – in art, religion, even the location of the capital city – changed Egypt utterly, but the revolution lasted a mere decade. It caused such revulsion that the whole episode, and the king who directed it, were excised from the official history by those who came afterwards. Akhenaten is an endlessly fascinating figure, made and re-made by each new generation in its own image. It is sometimes difficult to disentangle truth from fiction, but the historical facts of his life bear repeating, since they help us enter into the mind of Egypt's most radical pharaoh.

Virtually nothing is known about the young prince Amenhotep who was destined to rule as Akhenaten. His elder brother, Thutmose, was the heir apparent; so, for the early years of his life, Amenhotep could have had no expectation of succeeding to the throne. Thutmose's premature death changed all that. Not only was Amenhotep the new Crown Prince, he was subsequently crowned at Karnak as his father's co-regent, Amenhotep IV, to smooth the succession when the old king died. The younger Amenhotep would have witnessed, perhaps even taken a formal part in, his father's dazzling jubilee celebrations at Thebes, involving boats covered in gold and electrum sailing in a specially constructed artificial harbour. The effect must have been mesmerizing, and when Amenhotep IV became sole ruler, he seems to have resolved to outshine even his father.

From the beginning of his sole reign, Amenhotep IV inaugurated a radically new style of representation, characterized above all by the physical exaggeration of the human figure: elongated and attenuated limbs, distended belly and broad hips, ovoid head. So different was this new canon of proportions that it must have been ordered by the king himself. By making such a decisive break with the past, Amenhotep IV had announced to the world that his reign marked a new beginning. It was both a promise and an omen.

The first large-scale project to bear the hallmarks of the new style was a shrine to the Aten, called Gempaaten, to the east of the main temple of Amun-Ra at Karnak. The sun-disc or Aten presented an appropriate metaphor for the dazzling pharaoh bringing light and life to his subjects. Amenhotep IV, however, did not just regard Aten as a metaphor, but as his personal god. It was to become his overriding obsession.

The Aten temple at east Karnak evidently struck Amenhotep as unsatisfactory: his god deserved a much grander edifice on a virgin site, not a subsidiary shrine tacked on to the cult centre of another deity. After a short time, therefore, all building work at Karnak was halted. Amenhotep ('Amun is content') changed his name to Akhenaten ('effective for Aten') to signal his devotion to the sun-disc above all other deities; and he resolved to find a site at which Aten could be properly worshipped. He alighted upon a natural embayment in the cliffs on the east bank of the Nile in Middle Egypt.

In late spring in the fifth year of his reign, Akhenaten made a formal visit to his chosen site. He appeared on his electrum-plated chariot, dazzling like Aten itself. In front of his assembled courtiers, he gave a decree establishing his new capital city, Akhetaten ('horizon of Aten', modern Amarna). He supervised a spectacular offering to Aten in front of the cliffs, and worshipped the sun-disc as it hovered over the scene. Next, the entire court was summoned and officials prostrated themselves at Akhenaten's feet. He told them that Aten himself had instructed him to found the city at Amarna, since it 'did not belong to a god nor a goddess', and that it would belong to Aten forever as his monument 'with an eternal and everlasting name'. The courtiers replied enthusiastically: they had little choice.

Just in case there were any doubters, the king made abundantly clear his resolution and single-mindedness to see his project through to completion. Not even his wife, Nefertiti, would be able to divert him from his chosen path: 'Nor shall the King's Great Wife say to me "Look, there is a nice place for Akhetaten somewhere else", nor shall I listen to her.' The king decreed that the city would contain a suite of principal buildings. Moreover, Amarna was not just to be the new royal residence, but the eternal resting-place for the king and his immediate family: 'If I should die in any town of the north, the south, the west or the east in these millions of years, let me be brought back so that I may be buried in Akhetaten.'

The whole ceremony was recorded on two boundary stelae, cut into the cliffs at the northern and southern limits of Amarna. Exactly one year later, Akhenaten paid another visit to his city to inspect progress. He issued a second decree, defining the boundaries more precisely. Copies of this proclamation were similarly memorialized on boundary stelae around the perimeter of the site. By the eighth year of Akhenaten's reign, the sacred precinct of Amarna was demarcated by fifteen such markers. The city itself grew as a linear development along the east bank of the Nile. The major ceremonial buildings specified by Akhenaten were linked by the Royal Road. This formed the processional avenue along which the king rode in his chariot each day from his residence to the seat of government. The royal progress mirrored the path of the sun-disc across the heavens, and formed the central daily ritual for the city and its inhabitants.

Indeed, Akhenaten's new world order put himself and the royal family at the centre of public and religious life. The king's affection for his wife and daughters was celebrated as a sign of Aten's beneficence. However, the image of a strong and loving royal family masked a more complex reality. Akhenaten displayed a suffocating closeness to the female members of his family. When his mother Tiye died in the twelfth year of his reign, he had her buried in the royal tomb at Amarna, against her late husband's (and probably her own) wishes. Nefertiti's prominence in the official ideology was unprecedented, yet, for at least the first decade of his reign, Akhenaten also had a secondary wife, Kiya, who probably bore him at least one son (Tutankhuaten, later Tutankhamun, no. 62). Her eventual fall from grace and the systematic usurpation of her monuments may mirror Nefertiti's remorseless rise to power.

The latter years of Akhenaten's reign were marked by growing religious fanaticism. After eleven years on the throne, he decided to 'purify' the names of Aten – written in two cartouches to symbolize the joint rule of king and god – in order to eradicate all traces of the old religion. Throughout the country, on the king's orders, the names of other deities, especially Amun, were systematically erased from monuments. Masons scaled obelisks and clambered up temple walls to obliterate all references to gods and goddesses other than Aten. There could be no other deity in Akhenaten's universe. Everyone in Egypt was expected to follow the king's 'Teaching', but only the upper echelons of society, dependent upon royal favour for their position, seem to have embraced the new religion, and probably with little real enthusiasm. Monotheism or simple egoism, it was radically different from orthodox Egyptian beliefs, and there is no doubt that it flowed from Akhenaten's own mind.

Its ultimate expression was the *Great Hymn to the Aten*. The work's authorship is not certain, but it was very probably written by the king himself, as the central element of his Teaching. Its message was clear and uncompromising: 'There is none who knows thee except thy son Akhenaten. Thou hast made him wise in thy plans and thy power.'

Akhenaten died after seventeen years on the throne. He was buried in the royal tomb at Amarna. Despite his vehement antipathy towards traditional Egyptian religion, his sarcophagus of pink granite was nevertheless accompanied by all the usual funerary equipment: a canopic chest, magic bricks, even *shabti*-figurines to serve him in the next world. Before the heretic king was even cold in his grave, it seems, orthodox beliefs were reasserting themselves. Like all revolutions, Akhenaten's was swift, dramatic and ruthless. Like so many, it died with its instigator.

57 NEFERTITI
THE POWER BEHIND THE THRONE

Nefertiti has become synonymous with the extravagant, exotic court created at Akhetaten. She has inspired almost as many theories as her husband, yet comparatively little is known about her background and her ultimate fate remains shrouded in mystery. None the less, the evidence for her meteoric rise to power and her unrivalled place in her husband's radical plans paints a portrait of an intelligent, ambitious and ruthless woman.

The name Nefertiti means 'the beautiful one is come', an appropriate moniker for a king's wife whose exquisite painted bust – excavated in the workshop of the sculptor Thutmose and now one of the treasures of Berlin's Egyptian Museum – is revered as an icon of ancient beauty (fig. 15). Just where Nefertiti came from, however, was never stated; it probably served her interests to keep it deliberately obscure. It was perhaps not seemly for the quasi-divine king's wife to admit to an earthly, even a humble, origin. Although a foreign ancestry has been suggested – equating Nefertiti with the Mitannian princess Tadukhepa, known to have been sent to Egypt in the reign of Amenhotep III (no. 52) – it is more likely that she came from the same powerful provincial family that had already married into the royal family in the person of Tiye (no. 53). Indeed, Nefertiti may have been Tiye's niece, and hence Akhenaten's first cousin. She was certainly brought up as a baby in the household of Ay (no. 65), probably at Akhmim in Middle Egypt, with Ay's wife Tey acting as her wet-nurse. Nefertiti's only known relative was a sister, Mutbenret, with whom she probably shared her childhood.

Nefertiti married her husband when he was still a prince, or else very early in his reign when he was still known by his birth-name Amenhotep. When he changed his name to Akhenaten, signalling the start of his revolution, she responded in kind, adding the epithet Neferneferuaten, 'beautiful are the beauties of Aten', to her name, to proclaim her devotion to the new god. From now on, husband and wife acted together, co-instigators of the changes that swept aside hallowed customs, co-beneficiaries of the new order which put the royal couple at the centre of popular worship. In the new religion,

Aten was the creator while Akhenaten and Nefertiti were his children. Together they formed a divine triad – ironically, the unit at the heart of the traditional Egyptian pantheon – but theirs was an exclusive claim to divinity. To emphasize their roles, Akhenaten associated himself with Shu, son of the creator and god of light and air, while Nefertiti took the part of Tefnut, Shu's sister-wife. She adopted Tefnut's flat-topped headdress, and made it the very symbol of her authority, wearing little other headgear in public after her husband's fourth year on the throne.

On the rock-cut stelae marking the boundaries of the new capital city, Akhenaten lauded Nefertiti as 'great in the palace, fair of face, beautiful in the double plumes, the mistress of joy, at the hearing of whose voice one rejoices, possessor of graciousness, great of love, whose arrangements please the Lord of the Two Lands'. Indeed, the intimacy of their relationship was made a central element of the new religion and was publicized for all to see. Reliefs from the city showed the King's Great Wife ever present at her husband's side. In one, Nefertiti was shown exchanging looks with Akhenaten as she sat on his lap and fastened a bead collar around his neck. On another, she was depicted glancing fondly towards him while the couple's three eldest daughters played on their parents' laps. There had never been a royal partnership quite like it.

In offering scenes, Nefertiti was shown equal in size to her husband. Indeed, in the Aten temple at Karnak, she had her own shrine, and reliefs depicted her offering directly to the Aten without the king's presence. This represented a marked departure from previous usage. On a private stela from Akhetaten, both husband and wife were shown wearing crowns. Another block went one stage further, depicting Nefertiti in the act of smiting a (female) captive, echoing the quintessential pose of kingship. It was unprecedented for anyone other than the king himself to be shown performing this highly symbolic action, and it proclaimed Nefertiti's exceptional role beside her husband.

More was to follow. In reliefs in the tomb of Meryra (no. 58), carved late in Akhenaten's reign, the overlapping figures of Akhenaten and Nefertiti were almost joined into a single outline, suggesting the divine unity of the royal couple. Nefertiti added further epithets to her name, including 'beloved of Aten' and even 'ruler', hinting at a steady elevation of her status to that of co-regent with her husband. Then, at the zenith of her powers, she disappeared from view, following the burial of her second daughter Meketaten. Had she died or fallen from grace, or had she rather undergone an even more profound transformation? It is tempting to speculate that Nefertiti followed the logic of her own life, adopting a fully kingly titulary to match the iconography, and shedding her previous persona in the process.

However, when Akhenaten died a few years later, the next king to emerge, after a brief hiatus, was one Smenkhkara. Had Nefertiti finally been eclipsed, or had she perhaps undergone yet another change of image and name to suit her sole reign? If she did rule independently, it was only for a very short time. The throne soon passed to a royal relative who was probably related only by marriage to Nefertiti, the boy-king Tutankhuaten (who later adopted the name Tutankhamun). In the power-struggle surrounding the end of the Amarna Period, Nefertiti's faction was the loser. What ultimately became of her is not known. Perhaps she was laid to rest in the royal tomb at Amarna, beside her husband: that would certainly have been his dying wish. For, in the ultimate gesture of affection, Akhenaten's own sarcophagus was decorated at its four corners not with images of the traditional protector goddesses, but with figures of Nefertiti. It was perhaps an acknowledgment that his revolution would never have happened but for the extraordinary woman at his side and behind his throne.

58 MERYRA
ZEALOT OF A NEW RELIGION

At the heart of Akhenaten's 'heresy' was, of course, his religious doctrine. At the core of this was the Aten. And at the centre of Aten-worship was the Great Aten Temple at Amarna. The High Priest of the Aten was thus at the very nexus of the Amarna revolution, and for most of Akhenaten's reign the office was held by a man called Meryra.

Besides the usual indicators of rank, Meryra's principal title, in its full form, was Greatest of Seers of the Aten in the Temple of Aten in Akhetaten. Greatest of Seers was traditionally the designation for the High Priest of Ra at Heliopolis (ancient Iunu). Now that Ra had been supplanted by Aten as the sun god, the title was transferred to the head of the Aten priesthood. It was a particularly appropriate designation, since the Aten was explicitly the visible sun: Aten temples were dominated by great open courts, where the solar disc could be observed and worshipped in all its glory, unhindered and unmediated.

There was a further element in Atenism which differentiated it from the traditional cults of Egypt. According to the purest form of Akhenaten's doctrine – 'the Teaching' – the king was the only one who knew the Aten, the only channel of communication between god and people. Official texts made it quite clear that Akhenaten and the Aten were co-regents, the sun-disc ruling in the heavens while the king ruled on earth. Moreover, Atenism was essentially a cult of the royal family, whereby ordinary people, if they wished to worship the Aten, were encouraged to do so via images of Akhenaten, Nefertiti and their daughters. This made a priesthood somewhat redundant, yet Akhenaten retained one. Perhaps the pattern was simply too ingrained in the Egyptian consciousness, or perhaps it was a matter of practicality, since the king could not be expected to officiate at every daily ceremony in the Great Aten Temple at Amarna, let alone at cult centres in other cities. So, there remained a need for a High Priest, even if his secondary titles, 'fan-bearer on the king's right hand' and 'greatly praised of the good ruler', made it clear that his position was subordinate to the king himself.

Around Akhenaten's ninth year on the throne, Meryra was promoted to the position of High Priest of the Aten, an office he was to hold for the next seven years. He carefully ensured that his previous career and background remained hidden; but, like many of Akhenaten's inner circle, he probably came from nowhere and owed everything to the king's favour. The investiture took place at the royal palace in the centre of Amarna. The king and queen, accompanied by their eldest daughter Meritaten, appeared at the balcony, leaning on a sumptuously embroidered cushion. Meryra, wearing a long white gown and a decorative sash, and attended by members of his household, entered into the royal presence and knelt before the king. Scribes were on hand to make an official record of the proceedings. Four sunshade-bearers were in attendance to provide relief from the heat of the day. And, in the background, four policemen carrying batons stood ready in case of any sign of trouble. It was, after all, an autocratic regime, and the royal family never went anywhere without a security presence.

Akhenaten spoke to Meryra, confirming his appointment with a formal speech. The crowd of onlookers, including a troupe of female dancers with tambourines, shouted their acclamation and, when the clamour had died down, Meryra replied. As was appropriate to the occasion, his words were brief and to the point: 'Abundant are the rewards which Aten knows to give, pleasing his heart.' His friends then raised him up on their hands, and he left the palace as one of the king's inner circle.

A second milestone in Meryra's career came some time later when he was rewarded for his ultra-loyalty to the king with the conferment of the 'gold of honour'. This was the highest mark of esteem that could be bestowed on a commoner, and it consisted of heavy collars of gold beads that were placed around the recipient's neck during the investiture. The ceremony took place between the storehouses, where much of the wealth of the Great Aten Temple was stockpiled, and the riverbank of Amarna. Meryra was decked out in all his finery, wearing earrings and a festal costume. His attendants included the usual fan-bearers, sunshade-bearers and scribes, as well as three members of his temple staff. He was received in the outer court of the granary by Akhenaten and Nefertiti, accompanied by two of their daughters and a large retinue. As soon as he beheld the pharaoh, Meryra raised his arms in salutation and worship. The king advanced, hung the gold collars around his neck, and addressed the assembled company. The speech was verbose, stilted, rather legalistic and anything but brief, like so many dictators' speeches throughout history. Meryra seems not to have made a reply: perhaps he was simply overwhelmed by the occasion.

The whole episode was recorded in detail in Meryra's tomb. Hewn into the northern cliffs of Amarna, it was the finest sepulchre in the whole necropolis, with an impressive façade nearly 30 m (100 ft) wide. It reflected his high status at court. His wife, Tenra, was depicted in the tomb reliefs, but there was no mention anywhere of the couple's children. Indeed, scenes of the king, the royal family and their retinue dominated the monument. Each of the door jambs was carved with salutations to the Aten, Akhenaten and Nefertiti. The majority of the decoration was concerned with the activities of the king and queen. The tomb owner himself was relegated to an almost secondary position. There could be no stronger indication of the essence of Atenism – the centrality of the king in the lives (and deaths) of all his people.

Curiously, Meryra was never laid to rest in his splendid tomb; its burial chamber was never finished. His end remains a mystery. For the High Priest of Akhenaten's new religion, in which there was no afterlife, only earthly existence under the beneficent rays of the sun-disc, this seems entirely appropriate.

59 BAK
SCULPTOR WHO LED AN ARTISTIC REVOLUTION

Since the very beginnings of pharaonic civilization, Egypt's rulers appreciated the power of art to express, reinforce and immortalize royal authority. The formal art of the Egyptian court symbolized the ordered universe over which the gods and their earthly representative, the Egyptian king, presided. This world-view found expression in two-dimensional reliefs and three-dimensional sculpture. Artists working in the official tradition – and there was little scope for anything else – were thus very much servants of the state. The close relationship between the king as head of state and the artists who glorified him is exemplified in the career of Bak, chief sculptor during the early years of Akhenaten's reign.

Bak grew up in an artistic family. His father, Men, was chief sculptor in the reign of Amenhotep III, and had married a woman from Heliopolis named Ry. Bak, in turn, entered the family profession, rising to the position of 'chief sculptor in the great and mighty monuments of the king in the house of the Aten at Akhetaten (Amarna)'. Father and son had themselves depicted in an inscription in the granite quarries at Aswan ('the Red Mountain'), source of some of the best sculptural stone. Men is shown in front of a colossal statue of his royal master, perhaps one of the Colossi of Memnon that stood before Amenhotep III's mortuary temple at western Thebes. Bak, in turn, is shown worshipping a statue of *his* sovereign, Akhenaten. Particularly striking is the difference in style between the two scenes. While Men and Amenhotep III are depicted according to the traditional, hallowed canon of Egyptian court art, Bak and Akhenaten are shown in the revolutionary style introduced by the king as part of his decisive break with the past. Father and son must therefore have been well aware of the differences.

The art of the Amarna Period, especially that from the early part of Akhenaten's reign, is utterly distinctive. The elongation of the head, the distortion of the body's proportions, the androgyny in royal representations – these were bold departures from the accepted norms, and must have been sanctioned at the highest levels. In an inscription next to the scene in the Aswan quarries, Bak confirms the source of the new art style, describing himself as 'a disciple whom His Person himself instructed'. We must therefore imagine Akhenaten, at the beginning of his reign, laying down the guidelines for his artistic revolution to his leading painters and sculptors. Since the king's word was the law, there would be no reversion to the traditional canon without express direction from the palace.

Bak clearly took the king at his word and embraced the royal directive with enthusiasm. Like all converts to Akhenaten's 'Teaching' who relied on royal patronage for their continued status, Bak was a passionate advocate of the new way of doing things. He expressed his public devotion to the king in his Aswan inscription, which is labelled 'Giving adoration to the Lord of the Two Lands and kissing the ground to Waenra [Akhenaten]'.

As chief sculptor, Bak supervised a team of craftsmen, and was responsible for training them in the new style. One of the finest products of his workshop was his own commemorative stela, sculpted from reddish-brown quartzite (fig. 16). It depicts Bak next to his wife Taheri; she has one arm around her husband's shoulder in a gesture of affection. She wears a simple sheath dress, while he is clothed in a more elaborate, pleated garment, in tune with the fashion of the reign. He is also shown as rather corpulent, emphasizing his wealth and status. Unusually, the two figures – and especially that of Bak – protrude from the background of the stela so as to be rendered in three dimensions. We can see here the hand of the master sculptor, unable to leave his preferred medium behind even when commissioning a two-dimensional piece. Indeed, it is tempting to speculate that Bak carved the stela himself. He would, after all, have been the most accomplished sculptor of his day. Could the work of an inferior talent possibly have satisfied him for his own memorial? If this is correct, Bak's stela is the oldest self-portrait in history.

60 MAHU
AKHENATEN'S CHIEF OF POLICE

Fundamentalist and despotic regimes have always governed with an iron fist. They brook no opposition, but at the same time they are in constant fear of plots and coups. So they surround themselves with security, and often adopt an overtly militaristic or paramilitary style of rule. There can be little doubt that ancient Egypt, too, was a dictatorship at many, if not most, periods of its history. The king's word was the ultimate authority and must have been backed up by force, or at least the threat of coercion. The police and army units which formed the internal security forces left little trace in the official record, probably because their very existence was at odds with the

Utopian image the elite wished to promulgate; but exist they did, and one individual from the Amarna Period provides us with an insight into this largely hidden aspect of ancient Egyptian society.

Mahu was the Chief of Police of Amarna (ancient Akhetaten). Like most security chiefs serving authoritarian rulers, he was an ultra-loyalist. He probably came from a modest background, and was one of Akhenaten's personal appointments. As such, Mahu would have owed everything – his position, status and wealth – to the king's continued patronage. There is an inkling of this in Mahu's tomb in the northern cliffs at Amarna. The texts inscribed on the walls include no fewer than four copies of the Hymn to the Aten, the official creed of Akhenaten's new religion. Including it once would have served as an explicit statement of loyalty to the regime. Repeating it four times left no room for doubt.

The accompanying scenes in Mahu's tomb provide fascinating snapshots of his official duties. The prosecution of criminals was straightforward enough, but there were other, more unsettling, aspects to Mahu's role. Akhenaten's radical policies must have aroused deep unpopularity among certain sections of the population, and the fear of insurgency must have haunted his regime. Mahu was all too aware of 'the people who would join those of the desert hills' in waging sporadic attacks on government forces. Amarna was thus a city crawling with security personnel. As well as the police force under Mahu's direct command, there were the soldiers and 'leaders of the army who stand in the presence of His Person'. Every time the king or other members of the royal family left their fortified palace compound by the riverside, they were accompanied by a large security presence. On occasions, Mahu himself may have joined the squads of police running in front of and beside the royal chariot. More usually, he would have ridden in his own chariot, at the head of his forces.

Public expressions of loyalty were evidently *de rigueur* in Akhetaten, and Mahu knew what was expected of him. His speech before the king was a model of sycophancy:

> 'O Waenra [Akhenaten], you are forever, O builder of
> Akhetaten, whom Ra himself made!'

However, in such an atmosphere of paranoia, even an arch-loyalist Chief of Police was not given unfettered control of royal security. There is evidence that the king's elite bodyguard comprised foreign soldiers who were thought less likely than native Egyptians to harbour a grudge against the revolutionary pharaoh.

The frequent formal processions and appearances by Akhenaten and Nefertiti that framed life in Amarna must have preoccupied Mahu for most of his career, yet he also found time – whether through personal piety or duty – to visit the temples of Aten at the religious heart of the city. Kneeling in front of the temple, he made the most of this public display of loyalty by leading his fellow policemen in singing Akhenaten's praises:

> 'May the pharaoh – life, prosperity and health – be healthy!
> O Aten, make him continual, this Waenra.'

Such regular and repeated demonstrations of faithful devotion were eventually rewarded, and Mahu was summoned to the palace to be thanked for his loyal service. Filled with pride, he emerged from his royal audience with his arms raised in ecstatic triumph. Perhaps on this occasion, his words were more heartfelt than usual, as he declaimed 'May you raise up generations to generations, O Ruler!'

For Mahu himself, however, a single lifespan was his allotted frame. He died before the withdrawal of the court from Amarna, and thus never lived to see the downfall of the regime of which he had been the staunchest supporter.

61 HUY
VICEROY OF KUSH

'Gold – everywhere the glint of gold': the fabulous treasure of Tutankhamun (no. 62) caused a sensation at its discovery in 1922 and has come to symbolize the opulence of the pharaohs. Egypt's wealth in the New Kingdom was recognized and envied throughout the Near East, and was largely based upon its abundant resources of one commodity, gold. In a letter to the court of Amenhotep III, the king of Mitanni, Tushratta, wrote: 'In the land of my brother is not gold as the dust upon the ground?'

In fact, by the 18th Dynasty, the gold of the pharaohs came not from Egypt itself, but from its conquered and annexed territories in Nubia. The gold-bearing rocks and alluvial deposits of Wawat (Lower Nubia) and Kush (Upper Nubia) supplied the Egyptian treasury with its main currency for foreign trade, and the craftsmen in the royal workshops with the material for fashioning dazzling objects for the king's palace and tomb. Access to gold was the main reason for Egypt's interest in Nubia. Ensuring regularity of supply fell upon the shoulders of the Egyptian administrator, the King's Son (Viceroy) of Kush.

Huy, Viceroy of Kush during the reign of Tutankhamun, was thus the man ultimately responsible for the manufacture of the king's golden treasure. Amenhotep-Huy (to give him his full name) secured a closer connection to the royal court through his marriage to the lady Taemwadjsi, since she was an acquaintance of Amenhotep III's parents-in-law, Yuya and Tuyu. During the troubled reign of Akhenaten and its immediate aftermath, Huy's fortunes are not known. Perhaps he simply kept his head down, waiting and hoping for better times. These came with the accession of Tutankhamun, when Taemwadjsi was appointed head of the new king's harem palace while her husband Huy landed the plum job of Viceroy of Kush.

His formal appointment took place at the royal palace, in the presence of the boy king himself. After courtiers had paid homage to Tutankhamun on the steps of the throne dais, Huy's appointment was read out, not by the king – on account of his youth – but by the Overseer of the Treasury. The proclamation was brief and to the point,

'Thus speaks Pharaoh: there is handed over to you from Nekhen to Nesut-tawy', confirming Huy's jurisdiction over a vast expanse of territory stretching from Hierakonpolis in Upper Egypt to Napata in Upper Nubia. Huy replied, in turn, 'May Amun Lord of Nesut-tawy, do according to all that you have commanded, O sovereign, my lord.' He then received the badges of his new office, a rolled-up scarf and a gold signet-ring. As he left the palace, a bouquet of flowers in each hand, Huy was welcomed by the officials of his new department. In front of him marched the Viceroy's sailors, preceded by their chief standard-bearer. The whole joyous procession was accompanied by a lutenist and other musicians, while Huy's servants and onlookers shouted blessings.

Huy's first act as Viceroy was to give thanks for his appointment in the temple of Amun, where he made libations of myrrh. Only after carrying out this solemn act did he don his ceremonial robes, gold armlets and gold collar, signifying his new status as 'the prince, the great courtier, important in his high office, great in his dignity, the true scribe of the king, his beloved, Amenhotep'. His whole family was there to witness the moment, including his four sons, his mother Wenher, his sister Gu and other female relatives, joined for the occasion by members of Huy's household, friends and neighbours.

The celebrations over, it was time for Huy to begin his official duties. He journeyed from the royal residence to Nubia by river, aboard the splendid viceregal boat. His beloved horses had their own stall, while Huy had the benefit of a cabin shaded by a large awning. When the boat arrived at Faras (ancient Sehetepnetjeru), the Egyptian seat of government in Nubia, Huy was greeted by local dignitaries bearing symbolic offerings of food and bags of gold dust. But the Viceroy's chief interest would have been his first meeting with his full team of officials: the Deputies of Wawat and Kush; the Mayor of Soleb (ancient Khemmaat); the Overseer of Cattle; the Lieutenant of the Fortress of Faras; the Mayor of Faras; and the High Priest, Second Prophet and *wab*-priests of the local cult of the deified Tutankhamun.

Of course, Huy's principal job was to oversee Egypt's exploitation of Nubia's economic resources: cattle and gold. The importance of the latter was reflected in his titles Overseer of the Gold-Countries of Amun and Overseer of the Gold-Countries of the Lord of the Two Lands. On regular occasions, Huy inspected the revenue destined for the royal treasury. Sitting on a simple stool, carrying his sceptre of office, he watched while gold rings and bags of gold dust were brought in, weighed and counted. Regular shipments of gold, minerals, livestock and exotica were dispatched from Faras, and Huy was responsible for inspecting the transport boats to ensure they were in good condition for the long journey by river. He could certainly not afford for a precious cargo to founder en route. He also had to ensure that the fortress of Faras itself, Egypt's power-base in annexed Nubia, was re-supplied on a regular basis with all necessary produce, including oxen, horses, donkeys, goats and geese.

The culmination of his official duties was the formal presentation of Nubian produce to the king. The extensive scenes in Huy's Theban tomb which record the event, be they first-hand or imagined, certainly present a magnificent spectacle. Huy appeared in all his finery, holding the sceptre of viceregal authority and waving an ostrich-feather fan to signify his courtly status as 'fan-bearer on the king's right hand'. Offering-bearers paraded before the enthroned monarch with red and green minerals, ivory tusks, ebony logs, shields, furniture, and the most important commodity of all in the form of a model golden chariot, gold rings, bags of gold dust, and elaborate gold table decorations. At the end of the ceremony, Huy emerged from the palace having received his highly appropriate reward: 'gold on his neck and arms, time after time, exceedingly many times.'

62 TUTANKHAMUN
THE BOY KING

He came to the throne as a child, died on the threshold of adulthood, and never really exercised control over his kingdom; yet his lavish burial has become synonymous with the power of the pharaohs. His monuments were systematically usurped by his successors, he was airbrushed out of history by later chroniclers, and little is known about his reign; yet today he is undoubtedly the most famous of ancient Egypt's kings. His background and personality remain obscure, yet his face is an icon, known to millions the world over. These are just some of the paradoxes surrounding the boy-king Tutankhamun: as Howard Carter noted, 'the mystery of his life still eludes us'. The discovery of his tomb in 1922 caused a sensation and ignited a popular fascination for ancient Egypt that has never abated. The 'wonderful things' with which Tutankhamun was buried continue to awe and enthral. But what of the king himself, the boy behind the golden mask?

His parentage is nowhere made explicit. The best clue is an inscription on a block from Amarna, found reused at Hermopolis. It carries the words 'the king's son of his body, his beloved, Tutankhuaten'. This strongly suggests that Tutankhuaten was Akhenaten's son, probably by a secondary wife called Kiya. Certainly the baby's given name, 'living image of Aten', is as devout as one would expect from the founder of the Aten cult. As the king's son, Tutankhuaten would have been brought up at Amarna, probably in the North Palace which seems to have served as the household of the royal women and children. Curiously, there are no surviving images of the boy from Amarna; this invisibility from the official record, together with Kiya's sudden fall from grace and similar 'disappearance', may perhaps be attributed to Nefertiti. As mother of the king's daughters and an ambitious woman in her own right, she would scarcely have welcomed the birth of a son and heir by another wife.

In due course, the two competing lines were united when Akhenaten's son by Kiya married his daughter by Nefertiti. Tutankhuaten's union with Ankhesenpaaten (no. 63) must have greatly strengthened his claim to the throne, not least because his wife had effectively become heir apparent following the promotion of one older sister and the premature death of the other. However, the succession, when it arose on Akhenaten's death, was far from straightforward. Only after one or two other claimants had come and gone could Tutankhuaten claim his inheritance. He was a boy of about nine years old.

The court continued to be based at Amarna, but the sands were shifting rapidly and the Aten cult was about to be swept away. Those behind Tutankhuaten's elevation to the kingship were older, experienced men: the God's Father Ay (no. 65) and the military commander Horemheb (no. 66). They realized that the restoration of the old cults and certainties was the only option: Akhenaten's reforms were simply too unpopular in the country at large to be sustained after his death. The reversal of policy came swiftly. In his second year as king, Tutankhuaten changed his name to Tutankhamun, signalling the reinstatement of Amun as chief state god and the demotion of Aten. At the same time, the royal residence was moved back to Thebes, and Amarna was abandoned. To mark this decisive break with the Atenist heresy, Tutankhamun issued a formal decree from the capital at Memphis. It recorded the restoration of the old deities, the reopening and rebuilding of their temples, the reinstatement of local priesthoods, and the dedication of new cult statues. Tutankhamun praised himself as the one who 'performs benefactions for his father and all the gods... having repaired what was ruined... and having repelled disorder throughout the Two Lands'. Moreover, the king adopted a new title, 'Repeater of Births', making it quite explicit that he was the initiator of a new age.

Rebuilding and beautification of the major state temples began apace. At Karnak, the Aten temples were dismantled and the damage inflicted by Akhenaten's henchmen was repaired. A figure of Tutankhamun was added to the decoration of the Third Pylon to record his decisive role for eternity. At Memphis, the king dedicated a new temple ('the House of Nebkheperura'), and marked the restoration of traditional practices with the ceremonial burial of the Apis bull. In distant Nubia, temples were built at Kawa (ancient Gempaaten) and Faras, and restoration work carried out at Amenhotep III's temple at Soleb. Indeed, Tutankhamun – or, rather, his backers – was particularly keen to associate himself with the golden age of his grandfather, who was now seen as the last legitimate king before the heresy. Thus, at one of Amenhotep III's grandest monuments, Luxor Temple, a new processional colonnade was added in front of the peristyle forecourt; its walls were decorated with scenes of the Opet Festival, one of the holiest events of the Theban religious calendar.

With the restoration of the old religion came the reinstatement of long-standing beliefs about the afterlife. These required Tutankhamun to make proper provision for his burial and mortuary cult. He seems to have begun a mortuary temple in western Thebes, not far from his grandfather's, and a royal tomb in the western branch of the Valley of the Kings, similarly close to Amenhotep III's burial. But dramatic events intervened to thwart these plans.

Just as he reached maturity, around the age of nineteen or twenty, Tutankhamun died – whether from natural causes or from foul play remains a cause of much speculation. It is tempting to suggest that the prospect of the king governing for himself, perhaps reversing the policies put in place by his puppet-masters, or at the very least dispensing with their services, was too unwelcome a prospect for powers behind the throne; certainly the main beneficiary from Tutankhamun's untimely death was Ay. Whatever the circumstances, the funeral arrangements were unusually hurried. A small, non-royal tomb on the floor of the main Valley of the Kings was pressed into service as the royal resting-place. Several grave goods were reused or adapted for Tutankhamun's burial. Even the king's sarcophagus was second-hand, and had probably been made originally for one of the royal burials at Amarna; a new lid was found to fit the box, and even though it was made from a different stone, granite instead of quartzite, it had to suffice.

Tutankhamun was laid to rest in early spring. His tomb was broken into by robbers not long afterwards, but it was re-sealed with most of the contents intact. Later covered by spoil from another royal tomb, it was lost and forgotten for over 3,000 years. Tutankhamun himself was consigned to oblivion: despite his restoration of the old ways, he was too closely associated with 'the enemy of Akhetaten' to be counted as a legitimate pharaoh, so his name was deliberately excluded from the king lists.

But, against all the odds, the vulnerable and manipulated boy king was redeemed; the discovery of his tomb and its marvellous contents brought him back to life and made his name live again, to be celebrated beyond all other pharaohs.

63 ANKHESENAMUN
TUTANKHAMUN'S CHILD BRIDE

Akhenaten's religion was essentially a cult of the royal family, in which the king, his wife and their three eldest daughters played leading roles. Although the king and Nefertiti were pre-eminent, forming a triad with the heavenly Aten, the daughters were none the less essential to the image of a 'holy family' that the king wished to project. Hence, from the moment of her birth, Ankhesenpaaten, the third daughter of Akhenaten and Nefertiti, was a public commodity, used by the royal court for its own ends. Her particular fate was to remain the plaything of more powerful individuals for the rest of her life.

Ankhesenpaaten ('she lives for the Aten') was born in or around her father's ninth year on the throne. If the official propaganda is to be believed, father, mother and daughters enjoyed a close and loving relationship. A stela used for private worship shows the king and queen sitting facing each other, with their three eldest daughters playing around them. Ankhesenpaaten stands on her mother's shoulder and plays with one of the uraeus-ornaments hanging down from her crown, as any small child would. But this was no ordinary family.

When she was just eight years old, Ankhesenpaaten's father died, and her life was thrown into turmoil. Since her eldest sister, Meritaten, had been elevated to the role of King's Great Wife, and her other sister, Meketaten, had died in childbirth some years earlier, Ankhesenpaaten found herself in the position of heir apparent. After a few years of uncertainty as to which party would prevail, the throne passed, not to Ankhesenpaaten herself, but to her husband and half-brother, Tutankhuaten. He was no more than nine or ten, and unable to dictate policy. The young couple found themselves mere ciphers in the hands of older, more experienced operators. The adherents of the old religion saw in Tutankhuaten and his young bride the perfect cover for a swift abandonment of Atenism. To mark this decisive break with the Aten 'heresy', Tutankhuaten and his wife changed their names: the Aten element was dropped, to be replaced by the old state god, Amun. Hence Tutankhuaten became Tutankhamun (no. 62), while Ankhesenpaaten became Ankhesenamun.

Despite the circumstances of their union, they seem to have felt real affection for each other. However, their married life would be struck by tragedy. Their attempts to start a family came to nothing when two successive daughters died in the womb or were stillborn. One was seven months old, the other eight or nine months. Despite these sadnesses in their family life, Ankhesenamun and her husband enjoyed some relatively untroubled times together. A series of eighteen scenes on the little golden shrine from Tutankhamun's tomb show the couple at intimate moments. When Tutankhamun was hunting, Ankhesenamun would pass him arrows. At other times she might fasten a collar around his neck, support his arm, or play a sistrum for him. He reciprocated this affection, pouring liquid into his wife's cupped hands, or greeting her fondly when she came to him in his open-air pavilion.

But such companionship was not to last. Tutankhamun died tragically young, just as he and his wife reached adulthood. Ankhesenamun was left a widow before her twentieth birthday. She may have been desperate enough to write to the Hittite king Shuppiluliuma, begging him to send her one of his sons to marry. It seems she knew only too well the alternative: a ring-bezel with the paired names of Ankhesenamun and the God's Father Ay seems to indicate that the latter bolstered his claim to the throne by taking his predecessor's widow as his own consort. The fact that Ay may have been Ankhesenpaaten's grandfather, and was certainly many decades older than her, was not going to stand in the way of his ambition. For Ankhesenamun, this turn of events must have compounded her grief at the loss of her young husband. What became of her, however, is not known. The ring marking her union with Ay is the last record of Ankhesenamun. Thereafter, she disappears from history: an ignominious end to a life that was never her own.

64 MAYA
ROYAL TREASURER

'My God, it's Maya!' These immortal words, beamed around the world, were uttered by a Dutch archaeologist on 8 February 1986 when he stumbled into the underground chamber of a tomb at Saqqara and caught sight of an inscription naming its owner. They convey the excitement generated by the rediscovery of the lost burial-place of Maya, one of the most important officials of the late 18th Dynasty. Not only was Maya a key player in the reign of Tutankhamun, his career spanned the entire Amarna Period and its immediate aftermath. His story demonstrates how some of those most closely associated with the heretic regime of Akhenaten changed sides with unseemly haste to save their own careers.

Maya did not come from a particularly high-ranking family. His father, Iuy, was a mere 'official', while his mother, Weret, was a song-stress and musician in the cults of Amun and Hathor – common part-time roles for the wives of New Kingdom bureaucrats. Weret seems to have died when Maya was still young; the maternal role in the family was taken by Iuy's second wife, Henutiunu. She evi-dently forged a strong bond with her stepson, since he gave her a prominent place in the decorative scheme of his tomb. Three further boys, Nahuher, Nakht and Parennefer, completed the family. Some or all may have been Iuy's sons by his new wife, and hence Maya's half-brothers.

Whether by talent or good fortune, Maya grew up in close prox-imity to the court of Amenhotep III (no. 52). He boasted later in life of 'the presence of the King having been granted to me since I was a child'. Under Amenhotep's successor, Akhenaten, Maya received promotion to his first significant office of state. Indeed, his rise seems to have been swift. By the middle part of Akhenaten's reign, he had already garnered a host of important dignities and roles: true and beloved scribe of the king, Fan-Bearer on the King's Right-Hand and Overseer of All the Works of the King. His principal office, however, was a military one, Overseer of the Army of the Lord of the Two Lands. This must have brought him into close contact with another aspiring army officer, Horemheb (no. 66). The two men's careers were to remain intertwined. Like other senior courtiers, Maya began a tomb for himself, cut into the hillside at Amarna. He would have been as shocked as the rest of the government when Akhenaten died after seventeen years on the throne, and his entire revolution faltered.

Maya decided to back a return to orthodoxy. He had by now married a woman named Meryt ('beloved'), and was undoubtedly assured of continued wealth and status if he supported the counter-revolution, led by his old colleagues Ay (no. 65) and Horemheb. The latter had moved swiftly to take control of the army after Akhenaten's demise, so, wisely, Maya concentrated on civilian affairs; perhaps the two men simply divided the reins of power between them. Maya retained his former role as Overseer of Works, taking responsibility for Tutankhamun's royal building projects in the Valley of the Kings, which may have included the reburial of Akhenaten and members of his family in a Theban tomb. At Karnak, Maya supervised work on the avenue of sphinxes leading to the Mut complex, in the hypostyle hall, and on the Second, Ninth and Tenth Pylons. To speed up the work, he ordered the dismantling of Akhenaten's Aten Temple at Karnak and reused the blocks as filling for Tutankhamun's own constructions – a complete refutation of the old regime and everything it represented. At the same time, he may have ordered the scenes and texts in his unfinished tomb at Akhetaten to be carefully erased and covered with plaster, to expunge any record of his involvement in the government of Akhenaten.

Maya's enthusiasm for the restoration of the old order extended also to economic matters. As Overseer of the Treasury under Tutankhamun, he led a royal mission to levy taxes and restore cults – the first may have been a necessary prerequisite for the second – throughout the entire length of Egypt, from the First Cataract to the Delta. He was rewarded for his loyal service with the 'gold of honour' and prisoners of war brought back from military campaigns in Asia. He enjoyed direct access to the palace and glorified in epithets normally reserved for the king: 'who appeases the Two Lands', 'who unites the Land with (his) plans'. Indeed, the decoration of Maya's

Memphite tomb, begun at the height of his powers, recalls a royal sepulchre, with reliefs in monochrome golden-yellow, the colour of resurrection. With Ay and Horemheb, Maya was one of the triumvirate of powerful men behind the throne of the boy king.

When Tutankhamun died prematurely, Maya was responsible for the hurried preparation of the royal tomb and its contents. To ensure his own immortality, he had his name and titles inscribed on two objects destined for the king's grave goods. Later, he would re-seal Tutankhamun's tomb, after robbers had entered it, and supervise the beginning of work on a royal tomb for his long-standing colleague, Horemheb. The two men evidently continued to get along well, since Maya retained his high-ranking posts even after Horemheb had assumed the kingship. One of Maya's final acts as Overseer of Works was to carry out the reburial of king Thutmose IV; an inscription in the tomb recording the operation may even be in Maya's own handwriting.

Just a year later, he died, aged probably in his late fifties. His young daughters, given the touching names Maya-menti ('Maya remains') and Tjau-en-Maya ('breath of Maya'), were adopted by another Memphite couple, Djehuty and Tuy. Despite Maya's happy marriage, he and Meryt had no surviving sons. So it fell to Maya's younger half-brother, Nahuher, to act as heir and supervise the couple's burial in their lavish tomb on the Saqqara plateau – to await the excitement of rediscovery 3,300 years later.

65 AY
THE GREAT SURVIVOR

Ay was born into a powerful provincial family in the region of Akhmim in Middle Egypt. It seems likely that he was a son of Yuya and Tuyu. If this was the case, the marriage of his sister Tiye to Amenhotep III propelled Ay into the inner circle at court, and gave him special access to the ultimate source of authority, the king. Whether by accident or design, Ay also had the good fortune to have in his household, as nursling and ward of his wife Tey, a baby girl who was destined for unparalleled power: Nefertiti. By the time she had grown up and married, and her husband had succeeded to the throne as Amenhotep IV/Akhenaten, Ay thus found himself with unrivalled connections. He was both foster-father to the King's Great Wife and, probably, uncle to the king. He exploited his position to the full, rising swiftly to a position of prominence at the heart of Akhenaten's regime. Ay's military offices included Overseer of All His Majesty's Horses and Commander of Chariotry, while his courtly status was expressed in his titles Fan-Bearer on the King's Right Hand and royal scribe (private secretary to the king). Tey, for her part, was lauded as 'greatly favoured of Waenra [Akhenaten], whom the King's Great Wife favoured'.

Success and status under Akhenaten depended, more crudely than ever before, on the king's personal favour. Absolute loyalty to the royal couple was a prerequisite; public devotion to the king's new religion was also expected from high officials, and Ay knew very well what he had to do to retain his position at court. In his tomb, the largest private sepulchre at Amarna, granted by the king himself, Ay proclaimed his zeal for the new religious order by covering its walls with the most complete version of the *Great Hymn to the Aten*, the definitive expression of Akhenaten's doctrine. Moreover, Ay consciously referred to himself as 'one who listens to the king and follows his Teachings'. His reward was commensurate with such a lavish display of allegiance: the gold of honour, bestowed by the king, and a shower of other accolades including a pair of red leather riding gloves – the perfect gift for a keen horseman.

Ay must have expected to finish his career and end his days at Amarna, comfortable in his position at the king's right hand. But the untimely death of Akhenaten changed everything. The king's mysterious and ephemeral successor, Smenkhkara, had none of Akhenaten's personal authority, nor perhaps the same extreme enthusiasm for his religious reforms. The once-powerful Amun priesthood who had been unceremoniously evicted from their temples by Akhenaten's henchmen were determined to seize the opportunity to reassert themselves and return Egypt to orthodoxy. The general population, too, may have grown weary of Akhenaten's excesses, while the army was pragmatic enough to see that the tide was turning. In a blatant but brilliant volte-face, Ay turned his back on Akhenaten's regime and presented himself instead as a counter-revolutionary who could and would restore the old order. He was clever enough to realize his usefulness to Akhenaten's opponents: a public repudiation of the king and all his works by the man who had been their greatest champion would deal a fatal blow to Akhenaten's entire project.

As the new cheer-leader for the traditionalists, Ay used his military connections to ensure that the throne passed swiftly to the young prince Tutankhuaten, too young to rule in his own right and utterly dependent upon his advisers. Having manoeuvred himself into position as fan-bearer to Tutankhamun and 'the confidant of the king throughout the entire land', Ay may have been instrumental in the abandonment of Akhetaten, the relocation of the court to Thebes, and the restoration of the old religion, proclaimed by royal decree. But Ay had unwittingly unleashed forces that threatened his own position. There were now other, equally ambitious, men surrounding the new king, individuals for whom Ay's tainted background was anathema. More dangerous still, they had a figurehead in the person of Horemheb, an army commander who quickly established himself as a major power in the land, combining the highest military, diplomatic and administrative titles.

Tutankhamun's brief, nine-year reign must have been both exhilarating and anxious for Ay, as he ruled through the young king while constantly watching his back for rivals. When Tutankhamun died unexpectedly early, Ay had, once again, to move swiftly to secure his position, and he did so in the most audacious manner. According to Egyptian custom, the individual who carried out the burial of the deceased became the legitimate heir, whether or not there was any blood relationship. At Tutankhamun's death, there were no surviving descendants and the main royal line had become extinct. This left two possible successors, Ay and Horemheb. The latter probably enjoyed the backing of the army, but may well have been away on campaign. By contrast, Ay was in the right place at the right time to make his move. A speedy burial for Tutankhamun was essential if

Ay was to stage-manage the occasion and thereby take the throne for himself. The tomb intended for the boy king was not yet finished, so a small, non-royal tomb on the floor of the Valley of the Kings was hurriedly pressed into service. Funerary objects were requisitioned and Tutankhamun was hastily buried. Moreover, to emphasize his legitimacy, Ay had himself depicted on the walls of Tutankhamun's burial chamber in the act of 'opening the mouth' of the dead king's mummified body. Such a scene was unparalleled in the decoration of a royal tomb, but Ay's purpose was clear, and he had already proved himself a master of propaganda. Just as he had used the walls of his own tomb at Akhetaten to proclaim his loyalty to Akhenaten and the Atenist religion, so he was now using the walls of Tutankhamun's tomb to support his own accession to the throne.

Through a combination of political skill and crude ambition, Ay had reached the very pinnacle of Egyptian society. But his triumph was short-lived. He had waited a lifetime for the ultimate prize, and reigned for just three years. His hope of founding his own dynasty was also dashed when his son and Crown Prince, Nakhtmin, was shunted aside by Horemheb. This time around, nothing and nobody was going to keep the army commander from the throne. It was Horemheb who would be regarded by later generations as the first legitimate king since Amenhotep III; Ay would be expunged from history.

Ay's entire life had straddled the fault-line between heresy and orthodoxy. He had turned both to his advantage, but in the end faced an insuperable dilemma: his close association with Akhenaten and the royal family had brought him power, even the kingship, but damned him forever in the eyes of posterity. His restoration of the old religion saved his career but sealed his fate.

PART 6

Imperial Egypt
RAMESSIDE PERIOD

The fabric of national life in Egypt had been left in shreds by Akhenaten's ill-fated revolution. After the end of the Amarna Period, it fell to an army general, Horemheb (no. 66), to re-establish order. With military precision, he restored the orthodox religion, re-staffed the demoralized priesthoods with tried and trusted army colleagues, and reformed the law by means of a careful and thorough edict. Without any heirs of his own, he chose another army officer as his successor. The latter ascended the throne as Ramesses I, and kings of the Ramesside dynasty – most of whom also bore the name Ramesses – ruled Egypt for the next 200 years.

True to their origins, the Ramessides were soldier pharaohs. Egypt's foreign possessions had been rather neglected during the Amarna Period, and now there were new threats to contend with, notably the Hittite empire. So the first kings of the 19th Dynasty embarked on a series of military campaigns to re-establish Egyptian control in the Near East. They were assisted by mercenaries and by other soldiers of foreign origin who had settled in Egypt and adopted Egyptian customs – men such as the general Urhiya (no. 68) and his son Yupa (no. 69). Indeed, Ramesside Egypt was a decidedly cosmopolitan society, with people from Syria-Palestine, the Mediterranean, Libya and Nubia living happily side by side with native Egyptians. Though the memory of their foreign ancestry might endure for generations, like the draughtsman Didia (no. 74) they were only too happy to enjoy the benefits of living and working as loyal subjects of the pharaoh.

Despite concerted military campaigns by Ramesses II (no. 70) and his successor Merenptah (no. 75), it proved impossible to impose

Egyptian supremacy throughout the Near East. Indeed, the Battle of Kadesh, which Ramesses II presented as a famous victory, was notably inconclusive and led to the establishment of peaceful relations between Egypt and the Hittite kingdom as a more productive long-term solution than permanent conflict. But other, third-party powers were now in the ascendant throughout the eastern Mediterranean, and they proved a persistent irritant to Egypt. The most serious threat came in the reign of Ramesses III (no. 78), when a combined land-force and naval armada of Sea Peoples nearly overwhelmed Egypt's defences. Decisive leadership and forceful military action won the day for Egypt, but national security of the kind understood in previous eras could not be re-established.

Aside from the complications of foreign relations, Ramesside Egypt was a dynamic and prosperous place. The ancient cities of Thebes and Memphis had been joined by a third capital city, the Ramessides' dynastic stronghold of Per-Ramesses (modern Qantir) in the northeastern Delta. Each of these three great centres of court culture had its distinctive attributes. Per-Ramesses was the centre of royal ceremonial, where Ramesses II received dignitaries and celebrated many of his jubilee festivals. Memphis remained the seat of government where officials great and small, like Raia (no. 71) and Mes (no. 73), served out their careers and built their tombs for the afterlife. The more ancient funerary monuments of the Memphite necropolis, notably the pyramids of the Old Kingdom, attracted the attentions of the first recorded Egyptologist, Ramesses II's son Prince Khaemwaset (no. 72). His restorations and small-scale excavations at Saqqara and Giza marked an upsurge of interest in Egypt's own past, a development that also led to the compilation of the most comprehensive of all king lists, the Turin Canon.

It is not Per-Ramesses or Memphis, however, that dominates the archaeological record of the Ramesside Period, but Thebes. Both Ramesses II and his father Seti I commissioned spectacular additions to the great temple of Amun-Ra at Karnak, while the 19th and 20th Dynasty royal mortuary temples on the West Bank were even more impressive than their 18th Dynasty precursors. Members of the Theban religious and administrative hierarchies continued to be buried in lavish tombs, adorned with images and texts relating to their official duties. A few individuals, such as the scribes Thutmose (no. 81) and Butehamun, left copious personal correspondence. An extraordinary survival from the same period is the will of an ordinary Theban woman named Naunakht (no. 80), which sheds light on the ancient Egyptian law of inheritance as well as on her own personal circumstances. An even more important source of evidence for daily life in New Kingdom Thebes is the community of necropolis workmen at Deir el-Medina. Here, 'Servants in the Place of Truth' like Sennedjem (no. 67) lived with their extended families. They were prone to the same joys and the same irritations as every community, with the serial criminal Paneb (no. 76) proving a particular thorn in the village's side.

The royal court itself was not immune to serious criminal activity, as the plot to assassinate Ramesses III demonstrates. This was, however, merely the latest episode in a long-running series of dynastic intrigues which had plagued the Ramesside ruling family since the end of the 19th Dynasty. The role played by senior courtiers like Bay (no. 77) remains murky, but it seems that, beneath the veneer of dignified order, the royal succession was riven by disputes. Egypt had experienced on previous occasions the destabilizing influence of a weakened kingship, but it failed to learn from its own history. A succession of feeble and ephemeral kings in the middle of the 20th Dynasty, balanced by powerful dynasties of officials (for example Ramessesnakht, no. 79), set the stage for the civil disturbances and power politics of Ramesses XI's reign. Under the competing egos of strongmen like Panehsy (no. 82) and Herihor (no. 83), the government was torn asunder. Egypt once again split along regional lines, never again to regain its national vigour. The era of the last great pharaohs had passed.

66 HOREMHEB
FOUNDER OF A NEW AGE

The rise of a permanent, professional army is a distinctive feature of the New Kingdom. The wars of liberation against the Hyksos and the consequent involvement of Egypt in the wider Near East created the need for a well-organized military class. Warrior pharaohs such as Thutmose I and III defined their reigns by their foreign conquests, extending the borders of Egypt to encompass most of Syria-Palestine and much of Nubia. At first, the army had little apparent influence in domestic politics, but in the wake of the Amarna period, that changed fundamentally.

Akhenaten's revolution closed most of the major temples, scattering and neutralizing the previously powerful priesthoods. Most of his own appointees to high office were parvenus, men who depended for their position on the king's personal favour. Hence, when Akhenaten died, the country was left with no obvious organ of government to pick up the pieces: none, that is, apart from the military. The man who stepped forward to restore order and dignity to a profoundly disturbed nation, to 'calm the Palace when it had fallen into a rage', was a career army officer. He would be revered by later generations as the first legitimate pharaoh since Amenhotep III and the founder of a new dynasty. His name was Horemheb.

His background is virtually unknown, other than that he came from the town of Herakleopolis (ancient Hnes) in Middle Egypt and was apparently of fairly humble parentage (although he later hinted at a descent from the great pharaoh Thutmose III). Like many of his generation, he achieved success by his own merits, and chose the army as the best route to promotion. Born in the reign of Amenhotep III, he would already have been rising through the ranks by the time Amenhotep IV/Akhenaten came to the throne. Given Horemheb's later repudiation of the heretic king, it is scarcely surprising that he kept quiet about what he was doing during Akhenaten's reign. Perhaps, as a senior army officer, he was able to spend most of his time outside Egypt, keeping his head down.

Horemheb rose rapidly to prominence after the accession of Tutankhamun. Indeed, the range and seniority of Horemheb's titles at this time demonstrate the extraordinary scope of his powers: King's Two Eyes Throughout the Two Banks (Egypt), King's Deputy in Every Place, Foremost of the King's Courtiers, Overseer of Generals of the Lord of the Two Lands, Overseer of Every Office of the King, Overseer of Overseers of the Two Banks, Overseer of All Divine Offices, Hereditary Prince of Upper and Lower Egypt. The last title designated Horemheb as heir apparent. He certainly seems to have been closely involved in every department of government, and it may be suspected that he was the effective power in the land, the *de facto* ruler in a country where the king was still a minor.

Despite such a raft of responsibilities, Horemheb did not turn his back on his main profession and power-base, the army. His private tomb at Saqqara, built during the reign of Tutankhamun, was decorated with scenes from his career, and military episodes featured prominently. As Commander-in-Chief, Horemheb led at least two campaigns, one to Syria and one to Nubia. In his own words, 'He was sent as the king's messenger to the very limits of Aten's rising, returning when he had triumphed.' He was shown observing the scribes as they registered prisoners of war from the latter campaign, and being rewarded by the king with the gold of honour. Horemheb's Memphite tomb served as the burial-place for his first wife, Amenia, but not for Horemheb himself, for he proceeded to take a step that would relegate his life as a private citizen to history.

Although he was the heir apparent, Horemheb did not succeed to the throne after Tutankhamun's untimely death. Whether he missed his chance, being away on campaign, or simply came to an arrangement with Ay (no. 65), it was his rival, the great survivor of Akhenaten's reign, who became the next king. Horemheb must have known that the old man would not last long; indeed, within three years, Ay too was dead. With the powerful backing of the military, Horemheb seized his chance and the throne. He immediately signalled his policy direction by dating his reign from the death of Amenhotep III: under Horemheb, the Amarna Period – 'the time of the enemy belonging to Akhetaten [Amarna]', as he called it – would be erased from the national consciousness.

Official inscriptions might be able to rewrite history, announcing that Horemheb had been singled out for kingship while still a child; but, for pragmatic reasons, it was none the less important to establish his legitimacy, after a sequence of four tainted rulers. His bold and calculated move was to timetable his coronation to coincide with the annual Opet Festival at Thebes. What more powerful sanction for his accession could there be than the patronage of Amun-Ra himself? After communing with the image of the god in the sanctuary of Luxor Temple, Horemheb emerged, wearing the blue crown, to popular acclaim. As a further sign of the return to orthodoxy, he made his first priority the restoration of the temples closed by Akhenaten:

> 'From the Delta marshes to Ta-Sety [Nubia] he renewed the gods'
> mansions and fashioned all their images... they having been
> found wrecked from an earlier time.'

He reinstated the daily rites and re-staffed the depleted and demoralized priesthoods with new appointees 'from the pick of the home troops': Horemheb the army officer was relying on his tried and trusted colleagues to help restore stability to the country. He carried out reforms of the army itself, separating it for operational purposes into northern and southern divisions, each with its own commander.

As king, it was Horemheb's duty to enhance and embellish the great temples of Egypt, but he showed little appetite for grand construction projects. Even his new, royal tomb in the Valley of the Kings (fig. 17) remained unfinished. Of far greater interest to a career tactician was the thorough-going reform of government. To this end, Horemheb issued an edict which remains one of the most extensive examples of pharaonic legislation. In its prologue, he set out his purpose: 'His Person took counsel in his heart... to crush evil and destroy iniquity.' Moreover, he described himself as 'a ruler zealous and watchful against greedy men': those opposed to his reforms had been warned. The decree contained nine principal measures. All were concerned in some way with rooting out corruption, in economic or judicial practice.

There were new laws to prohibit the requisitioning of slaves and of boats required for state purposes, and to guard against the seizure of hides during the annual cattle count; new penalties for fraud in the assessment of taxes, combined with the abolition of the state tax on animal fodder; reform of the system for provisioning the court during the regular royal progresses; new regulations for local law courts, including the introduction of the death penalty for judges found guilty of corruption; general guidelines for the application of justice, warning against bribery and partiality; and, last but not least, new regulations to ensure that the royal bodyguards were well and regularly rewarded – Horemheb had seen enough of palace intrigue to take a keen interest in his personal security. The end result of this raft of new legislation was that 'Maat returned and reoccupied her place... and the people rejoiced.'

As he neared the end of his reign, Horemheb's final task to embed stability and security was to pave the way for a smooth succession. His second wife, Mutnojdmet, had died in childbirth, and the king thus had no heirs of his own. Ever the military man, he turned to his fellow army officers for the solution, and in particular to his close colleague Paramessu (Ramesses I), who was duly proclaimed heir apparent. It was an inspired choice: Paramessu already had a son and grandson, and the Ramessides would provide stability to the monarchy for generations to come. As for the great legislator himself, the epilogue to his edict turned out to be a fitting epitaph for his impact on Egypt:

'I shall be renewed unceasingly, like the moon... one whose limbs shed light on the ends of the earth like the disc of the sun god.'

67 SENNEDJEM
WORKMAN IN THE VALLEY OF THE KINGS

The most important construction project of any reign was the royal tomb, designed not only to afford eternal protection to the king's body, but also to provide him with the wherewithal, practical and magical, to be reborn into the afterlife. The very public royal tombs of the Old and Middle Kingdoms – the pyramids – had invited robbery, and the rulers of the New Kingdom were determined to provide themselves with greater security. So they chose an isolated valley in the Theban hills as the location for their tombs, which were to be hewn into the cliff, thus remaining out of sight. The work of cutting, dressing and decorating the tombs in the Valley of the Kings was highly sensitive, and steps were taken to prevent details of the work becoming generally known.

Most significant in this respect was the foundation, in the early 18th Dynasty, of Deir el-Medina, a special walled community isolated from the rest of the Theban population, to house the necropolis workmen and their families. It remains a time-capsule of daily life in the New Kingdom. It has yielded a wealth of evidence relating to local economic activity, social relations, judicial proceedings, religious beliefs, and so on. Many of its inhabitants are known to us by name and one of them, Sennedjem, left behind a particu-larly rich store of information. His life provides an insight into the goings-on in the workmen's village in its heyday at the beginning of the Ramesside period.

Sennedjem was a simple necropolis workman, a Servant in the Place of Truth. Like most of his fellow workers, he had a large family. He and his wife Iyneferti shared their compact house with their ten children: four sons, Khabekhenet, Bunakhtef, Rahotep and Khonsu; and six daughters, Irunefer, Taash-sen, Hetepu, Ramessu, Anhotep and Ranehu. The house itself was divided into two parts. Fronting onto the narrow street was the public room, in which guests were received and entertained. Behind it, at the back of the house, were the family's domestic quarters, including a kitchen area. A staircase led to the roof, which provided additional sleeping space. It was crowded

10 Painting from the tomb of Kynebu at Thebes, 20th Dynasty, showing Ahmose-Nefertari (no. 40) with black skin. The early 18th Dynasty queen was revered by subsequent generations and her cult became the focus of popular worship among workers in the Theban necropolis. Her black skin and the lotus bloom both symbolize regeneration.

11 Brown granite bust of Hatshepsut (no. 43), 18th Dynasty. Representations of Hatshepsut are numerous, especially from Thebes where she commissioned major projects on the east and west banks. Some statues emphasize her traditional, kingly attributes while others, such as this bust, display softer, more feminine features. The tension between her gender and her office was a defining feature of Hatshepsut's reign.

12 Standing siltstone statue of Thutmose III (no. 45) from Karnak temple, 18th Dynasty. The symmetry, balance and beautifully rendered details of the king's wig, beard and kilt make this one of the finest surviving examples of royal sculpture from ancient Egypt.

13 *Shabti*-figure of Qenamun (no. 49) from his tomb in western Thebes, 18th Dynasty. Shabti figures were designed to answer the call-up in the afterlife, performing menial tasks on behalf of their owners. As a high official, Qenamun would have been spared such duties during his lifetime, but did not want to take any chances in the hereafter.

14 Painted relief from the tomb of Nakht (no. 50) at Thebes, 18th Dynasty, showing him hunting in the marshes, accompanied by his wife. Standing on a papyrus skiff (reed boat), he uses a throwstick to bring down waterfowl.

15 Painted bust of Nefertiti (no. 57), from the workshop of the sculptor Thutmose at Amarna, late 18th Dynasty. Ever since its discovery in 1912, this sculptor's model, a remarkable survival of ancient art, has been regarded as an icon of female beauty.

16 Quartzite stela of Bak (no. 59) and his wife Taheri, late 18th Dynasty. Bak's exaggerated corpulence indicates his worldly success. In the surrounding text, Bak claims to have been instructed in the new and radical art style of the Amarna period by the king himself.

17 Painted relief from the royal tomb of Horemheb (no. 66) in the Valley of the Kings, late 18th Dynasty. When he became king, Horemheb abandoned his earlier tomb at Saqqara and began work on a new, royal monument at Thebes. Here he is shown offering to the goddess Isis.

and noisy, fairly typical of an Egyptian dwelling. During the day, the children played in the streets with their friends and neighbours, while Iyneferti carried out the essential economic transactions of the household, often meeting the other womenfolk of the Place of Truth by the village well. She was as fashion-conscious as the next woman, and enjoyed wearing her long wig.

For Sennedjem, the rhythm of life followed a weekly routine. At the start of each working week, he and the other necropolis workmen left their houses, to walk up the hill behind the village and along the edge of the cliffs until they reached the col overlooking the Valley of the Kings. Here there was an encampment of small, stone-built huts, where the workmen slept at the end of each day's work. After leaving some of their personal belongings at the camp, the men continued down the hillside to the tomb construction site itself. Sennedjem himself worked on the tomb of Seti I – at that point the most magnificent in the valley – and perhaps on the tomb of his son, Ramesses II. Using copper tools and wicker baskets to collect the chippings, the stone-cutters slowly chiselled their way into the bedrock, following the guidance of the architects and foremen, to create the long descending corridor of the tomb. Behind them came plasterers and painters to finish and decorate the walls. It was long, hot and tiring labour, but work in which the men could take pride.

The necropolis workmen were well paid, but not wealthy. They lived in comfort, not opulence. Leisure pursuits were simple, such as playing the board-game *senet*. They did, however, have the advantage of access to some of the best craftsmen available: their own colleagues. The objects in Sennedjem's tomb attest to the skills of his neighbours. They included a bed, a chair inscribed with the name of his eldest son, and six walking sticks. There were also some of Sennedjem's own tools, such as a cubit measure. Iyneferti's treasured possessions included a wooden box decorated with the figure of a leaping gazelle, a toilet box and a vase.

The tomb is justly famous for its decoration; again, it seems likely that this was carried out by one of Sennedjem's workmates. Reflecting his personal priorities, prominence was given to depictions of Sennedjem's extended family. The most striking scenes in

Sennedjem's tomb, however, are those which envisage life beyond the grave. He is shown adoring the open Gates of the West, the entrance to the next world; and an entire wall is devoted to a detailed portrayal of the Fields of Iaru, the agricultural idyll in which Sennedjem and his family hoped to spend eternity. A blessed afterlife was not just the reward of the pharaohs buried in the Valley of the Kings: it was equally within reach of the men who built the royal tombs with the sweat of their brows.

68 URHIYA
FOREIGNER WHO BECAME AN ARMY GENERAL

In pharaonic times, to be considered an Egyptian it was merely necessary to adopt Egyptian customs and an Egyptian way of life. Ethnicity and background were irrelevant so long as an individual lived according to Egyptian norms. At all periods, Egyptian society welcomed and incorporated people of foreign origin, from the lands bordering the Nile Valley and from further afield. At certain times, increased immigration or forcible re-settlement of prisoners of war boosted the number of 'foreigners' within Egyptian society. The Ramesside Period, when the pharaoh ruled an empire extending from Upper Nubia in the south to Syria in the north, was one such time. Egypt in the 19th Dynasty was especially cosmopolitan. The army that defended Egypt's empire drew upon large numbers of foreign mercenaries. Ethnicity was no bar to success, and at all levels of society, people of foreign origin achieved positions of importance.

The influence of foreigners at the Ramesside court is epitomized by the life and career of a man called Urhiya. His name is Hurrian (the main language spoken in eastern Anatolia and northern Mesopotamia from around 2500 to 1000 BC) and means 'true'. It is striking that Urhiya kept his own foreign name rather than adopting an Egyptian one in order to assimilate more readily into Egyptian society. He was clearly confident of his own abilities and felt no need to hide his ancestry. This self-confidence and resilience found their perfect outlet in the Egyptian army. Urhiya had been born in the reign of Horemheb, the general who became pharaoh, and therefore grew up in a society where the military played a central role. The army offered the best chance of advancement to an ambitious young man. Joining up when he reached adulthood, just as Seti I came to the throne, Urhiya rose prominently through the ranks. He was promoted to troop-commander, in charge of a section of several hundred men, and ultimately to the rank of general.

After three decades of active service, Urhiya made the move into civilian life when Seti I was succeeded by his son, Ramesses II. The loyal military man was given a key position at court, that of High Steward to the new king. This meant that Urhiya had overall responsibility for administering the pharaoh's personal estates and income. This was a highly responsible job, entrusted only to the king's most loyal officials. Urhiya clearly discharged his duties in an exemplary manner, for he was further promoted, in Ramesses II's tenth year, to Steward of the Ramesseum. For a decade Urhiya was ultimately responsible, in a practical sense, for the king's immortality: the Ramesseum was Ramesses' cult temple for eternity; the proper maintenance of the royal mortuary cult depended upon a steady flow of income; that income was derived from the Ramesseum's own estates; and those estates were administered by Urhiya.

For a man of foreign extraction to have ended his career in charge of the king's mortuary provision is a powerful demonstration that Egyptian society rewarded ability and loyalty above narrow ethnic considerations. Urhiya not only integrated himself into pharaonic culture, he also achieved the same for his family. His wife Tuy became a lay servant of two of Egypt's major cults, as chantress of Amun and songstress of Hathor. His brother Tey went one step further, entering the priesthood. And, as we shall see, in the next generation, one of Urhiya's three sons, Yupa (no. 69), rose to even greater prominence than his extraordinary father.

69 YUPA
SUCCESSFUL SECOND-GENERATION IMMIGRANT

Yupa was born under Seti I, but his career was contained within the long reign of Ramesses II. Like his father Urhiya (no. 68) before him, Yupa decided to join the army as the best path to prominence. As a second-generation immigrant, he had the considerable advantage that his family was already fully integrated into Egyptian society, and reasonably affluent. His father's influence no doubt helped his career progression, but he still had to start at the bottom and work his way up. Hence, at the time of the Battle of Kadesh, in Ramesses II's fifth year, the teenaged Yupa was a trainee stable-master in the King's Great Stable, one of forty young recruits charged with various lowly jobs. His particular task was the production of a fixed quota of 2,000 bricks. It was hardly exciting or challenging work, but a necessary training for the rigours and discipline of army life that lay ahead. And it had its compensations: the camaraderie among the recruits led to the formation of life-long friendships, especially for a popular figure like Yupa. Decades later, he would be mentioned on the stelae of totally unrelated contemporaries, perhaps friends from his army days.

He served in the army for twenty-five years before following in his father's footsteps and entering civilian service, first as High Steward of the king and then as Steward of the Ramesseum. However, in Yupa's case, this was not the pinnacle of his achievements. In his mid-sixties, he was given the honorific but highly prestigious role of royal jubilee-herald. In this capacity, he was responsible for organizing the formal proclamation throughout Egypt of the king's ninth to fourteenth jubilee festivals. The fact that the previous holders of the post had been the king's favourite son, Khaemwaset (no. 72), and the Vizier Khay shows the esteem in which Yupa was held at court.

He was able to commission a kneeling statue of himself and a fine sarcophagus, and even had himself immortalized in an inscription inside the temple of Montu at Armant. Like all good Egyptians, he left behind descendants to honour his memory. But none was to equal his own success. Despite his foreign name and background, Yupa's career was characterized by ambition, hard work, family influence and royal patronage: a quintessentially Egyptian combination.

70 RAMESSES II
THE GREATEST OF ALL PHARAOHS

'My name is Ozymandias, king of kings:
Look on my works, ye Mighty, and despair!'

The fallen colossus which inspired Shelley's famous poem stands to this day in the Ramesseum, the Theban mortuary temple of Ramesses II (Ozymandias is a Greek corruption of his Egyptian throne-name, Usermaatra). The mighty who ruled Egypt in subsequent generations might well have despaired, for Ramesses built more temples and erected more colossal statues of himself than any other pharaoh, before or after. He seemingly left his mark at every major site the length and breadth of Egypt and Nubia. Determined to ensure that his name could not be removed or his monuments usurped by his successors, he had his cartouches carved unusually deeply into the stone. Ramesses II – 'the Great' as he is often called – is thus the most ubiquitous and the most recognizable royal builder on the modern tourist itinerary.

In keeping with his unparalleled architectural legacy, Ramesses bestrode his own age like a colossus. He fathered more children than any of his royal predecessors or successors: as many as fifty sons and fifty-three daughters. It is therefore a fair bet that most of the native-born pharaohs who ruled Egypt after Ramesses were his descendants, by one route or another. For his sons, he built the largest tomb in the Valley of the Kings, possibly the largest in the whole of Egypt; it is still under excavation, and the number of its chambers has already surpassed 150. Ramesses commissioned temples on an equally lavish scale. In Nubia alone, he built at Beit el-Wali, Gerf Hussein, Wadi es-Sebua, Derr and Napata. In Egypt, his construction projects were concentrated in the three great cities of the age: the dynastic capital of Per-Ramesses (modern Qantir), the traditional capital of Memphis and the religious capital, Thebes. The Theban monuments have survived the best, and none is more impressive than the Ramesseum. Inscriptions in the sandstone quarries at Gebel el-Silsila record that 3,000 quarrymen were employed in supplying stone for this project alone. It was designed to perpetuate the name and cult of Ramesses for eternity, as expressed in its official name, The Mansion of Millions of Years of Ramesses in the Domain of Amun United-with-Thebes. The Ramesseum was an ingenious blend of traditional and innovative features, a masterpiece of logistics and ambition. As such, it was the perfect embodiment of its creator.

Ramesses was born during the reign of Horemheb, before his grandfather Paramessu (Ramesses I) had been designated as heir. The family's swift rise from provincial obscurity to the throne of Egypt had a profound effect on the young Ramesses' upbringing. At the age of thirteen or fourteen, he accompanied his father Seti I on campaign for the first time. Ramesses had already been granted the titular rank of Commander-in-Chief, and he seems to have relished army life. He rode out again at his father's side a year or two later, to confront Egypt's most feared enemy, the Hittites. It was the beginning of an involvement that would characterize Ramesses' entire reign.

When he reached adulthood, at the age of sixteen, he was granted his own household, complete with concubines, to join his two existing wives, Nefertari and Isetnofret. As time went by, Ramesses was entrusted with more and more of the affairs of state such as supervising quarrying work at Aswan, and overseeing the construction of the grand hypostyle hall at Karnak. Aged twenty-two, Ramesses led his first military campaign, putting down a minor rebellion in Nubia. Following in the family tradition, he took along with him two of his own young sons, Amenhirwenemef and Khaemwaset (no. 72). Then, in his mid-twenties, Ramesses became sole monarch on the death of his father. One of the longest and most magnificent reigns of Egyptian history had started in earnest.

To confirm his accession, Ramesses participated in the Opet Festival in the first year of his reign, rejuvenating himself through close association with the god Amun. True to his instincts as a prodigious builder, Ramesses ordered that construction should start on a grand addition to Luxor Temple (the setting for the Opet Festival), and that work on his father's temple at Abydos should begin again after years of neglect. To tighten his grip on the influential Theban priesthood, Ramesses appointed a new High Priest of Amun, Nebwenenef. Within a year, he had signalled that he was indisputably in charge.

Foreign affairs then took centre stage, as Ramesses launched a campaign to restore Egyptian control over the province of Amurru. This was a mere prelude, however. In the fifth year of his reign, he decided to win back all the conquests his father had made, even if it meant confrontation with the powerful Hittite army. Ramesses led from the front, riding in his chariot at the head of his four divisions as they left Per-Ramesses, bound for the fortified city of Kadesh. A gifted tactician, he took the precaution of sending a support force up the Mediterranean coast to rendezvous with the main army at Kadesh. Within a month of leaving Egypt, 2,000 men were making camp on a ridge to the south of the city. They faced a Hittite force nearly twice as numerous. Without warning, the Hittite chariotry attacked one of the Egyptian divisions as it made for camp, scattering the infantry. Ramesses found himself isolated except for his personal bodyguard and shield-bearer, surrounded on all sides by the enemy, with the Egyptians in panic. In an impressive display of decisive action under fire, he rallied his troops to defend themselves, just long enough to allow the support force – which had arrived from the coast in the nick of time – to engage the Hittites and save the Egyptians from utter annihilation.

Through his own leadership, Ramesses had prevented a crushing defeat. Although the Battle of Kadesh was, in reality, a stalemate, the king presented it as a famous victory, not least because of the part he had played in the turn of events. He had scenes and accounts of the battle included in the decoration of all his major building projects. Further Syrian campaigns would follow, three and five years later, but none would equal the Battle of Kadesh for sheer drama.

The long-term consequence of Kadesh was a remarkable peace treaty with the Hittites. It was an inspired piece of diplomatic compromise. It secured continued Egyptian access to eastern Mediterranean ports, and free passage as far north as Ugarit (modern Ras Shamra), in exchange for Egypt ceding control of the province of Amurru to the Hittites. Both sides signed up to a mutual non-aggression pact and defensive alliance, recognizing each other's laws of legitimate succession, and entering into an unprecedented extradition agreement. To seal the agreement, senior members of the Egyptian and Hittite royal families exchanged letters of friendship.

On the domestic stage, Ramesses vigorously promoted a personality cult, through which he took the deification of kingship to new heights. This trend reached its apogee in the temples at Abu Simbel, inaugurated by the king and his chief wife, Nefertari, in the twenty-fourth year of his reign. The main temple was precisely oriented so that, at sunrise on 22 February and 22 October (one of which is assumed to have been Ramesses' birthday), the sun entered the sanctuary and illuminated the figures of three of the four gods worshipped there: Amun, Ra and Ramesses himself (Ptah, as a god of the underworld, remained in the shadows). The king evidently felt he could get away with more in Nubia than he could in Egypt proper; his temple at Aksha was explicitly dedicated to 'Ramesses, the Great God, Lord of Nubia'.

But Ramesses' thoughts were not fixed entirely on himself. His beloved wife, Nefertari ('the beautiful companion'), 'for whose sake the very sun does shine', had been his constant companion since before his sole reign. Even for a man with as many wives as Ramesses, he must have been grief-stricken when Nefertari died, shortly after the official opening of Abu Simbel. The funeral ceremonies over, Isetnofret was promoted to the position of King's Great Wife, the second of eight women to hold this rank during Ramesses' sixty-seven-year reign. Marriage was, of course, a useful tool in the diplomatic armoury, and Ramesses carried out protracted negotiations to secure himself a Hittite bride. After a year of discussions, a Hittite princess set out from the citadel of Hattusas (modern Boghazköy) and arrived at Per-Ramesses to be received by the king in his palace and given an Egyptian name, Maathorneferura. Her dowry included gold, silver, bronze, slaves, horses, cattle, goats and rams. She joined a cosmopolitan harem which included Babylonian and Syrian women, reflecting the multi-ethnic and multicultural nature of Ramesses' court. Some time later, Ramesses welcomed an even more distinguished visitor from Hatti, in the person of the Hittite Crown Prince, Hishmi-Sharruna. Ramesses' suggestion of a visit from the Hittite king met with a cool response, but it is possible that a high-level summit between the two greatest leaders of the Near East did in fact take place on neutral territory. It would have been an extraordinary encounter.

The second half of Ramesses' reign seems to have been dominated, above all else, by frequent jubilees. The first took place in his thirtieth year, in the Festival Hall at Per-Ramesses. This was followed by further celebrations at periodic intervals of every two or three years, until the thirteenth jubilee (there may have been a fourteenth). If the country was exhausted by so much festivity in honour of the king, Ramesses himself revelled in it. When he died at the age of ninety-two, the expression on his face was one of pride, dignity and contentment. He must have been confident that his magnificent reign would never be eclipsed. He was truly a 'king of kings'.

71 RAIA
A MUSICIAN FROM MEMPHIS

The music of ancient Egypt is lost forever. Without musical notation (at least until the Ptolemaic period), the songs and tunes that played such a large part in Egyptian life, in private and public spheres, in secular and religious celebrations, can never be recovered. Some of the instruments survive but we can only guess at the melodies and harmonies they produced. However, there is no doubting the centrality of music and musicians in pharaonic culture. In his life and death, Raia offers us a glimpse of that vanished world of sound.

Raia was Chief of Singers in the temple of Ptah at Memphis in the reign of Ramesses II. Although his title referred only to singing, he was an all-round musician and his official duties included playing the harp before statues of Ptah and Hathor Lady of the Sycamore. Raia directed the temple's all-male choir; several of its members, such as Ray, Neferptah and Ptahhotep, were probably close friends.

Raia's wife Mutemwia shared his musical interests. She was a Chantress of Amun, a role which involved singing and probably playing a musical instrument in the daily service of the god. At their home in Memphis, Raia and Mutemwia and their daughter enjoyed a life of simple domesticity. They shared their house with Mutemwia's unmarried sisters Iuy and Kuyu, while a pet monkey completed the household. Raia and his wife got on well with their neighbours, Paser the builder and his brother Tjuneroy, the overseer of works. Indeed, it was probably through these friends' influence at court that Raia was able to build for himself a tomb-chapel in the prestigious necropolis of Saqqara.

Lacking great means, Raia's funerary monument was a tiny affair. It was marked above ground by a small brick pyramid, resting on a slab of limestone which formed the roof of the tomb-chapel. This room was so small that a visitor could only just stand up in it. Raia made all the necessary provisions for his afterlife, appointing a lector-priest called Shedamun to look after his mortuary cult, but there was hardly any space for the priest to perform his duties!

Despite the modesty of his tomb, Raia's popularity among his family, friends and colleagues was amply demonstrated at his funeral. His mummy was borne to the tomb on a catafalque drawn by oxen. It was received at the tomb entrance by a priest wearing a mask of the god Anubis, before being lowered into the burial chamber. (Later, Mutemwia would be interred beside her husband, so that they might spend eternity together.) His widow threw dust over her head in the traditional sign of grief, accompanied by other female mourners, some of them perhaps hired for the occasion. Most fitting of all, the surviving members of Raia's temple choir gave their much-loved director a musical send-off, singing him to the grave.

72 KHAEMWASET
THE FIRST EGYPTOLOGIST

The pyramids of the Memphite necropolis were already over a thousand years old at the height of the New Kingdom. How did the Egyptians of that 'golden age' regard their own past and its striking architectural remains? An answer is to be found in the life of Khaemwaset, the fourth son of Ramesses II.

Born early in his father's co-regency with Seti I, Khaemwaset was groomed from an early age for his royal destiny and received the full training appropriate for a king's son. At the age of just five, he had his first taste of military action when he accompanied his father and elder brother Amenhirwenem on a campaign to crush a minor rebellion in Lower Nubia. Both boys rode in their own war chariots, albeit driven by experienced officers. In his early twenties, Khaemwaset was given religious responsibility as *sem*-priest of Ptah, deputy and assistant to the High Priest in the national capital's main temple. For Khaemwaset, this appointment may have felt like a homecoming. His mother, the King's Great Wife Isetnofret, had spent time in the region of Memphis, and the prince himself may have been born there. Certainly, the capital and its ancient necropolis were to occupy and fascinate Khaemwaset for the rest of his life.

One of his first official duties was to participate in the burial of the Apis bull in the sixteenth year of his father's reign. Khaemwaset contributed objects for the tomb and must have been deeply affected by the ceremony with its combination of powerful symbolism and great antiquity. When he found himself directing the funeral rites for the next Apis fourteen years later, having succeeded as High Priest of Ptah, Khaemwaset decided to make the occasion grander still and leave his mark for posterity at the same time. To replace the earlier, single interments, he therefore inaugurated a vast underground gallery at Saqqara; opening off the gallery, a new burial chamber would be carved for each successive Apis burial. On the surface, the cult of the Apis was honoured in a new temple, which also served as the final resting-place for each bull's mummified body on the day before its burial. In the temple's dedicatory inscription, Khaemwaset made his bid for immortality, addressing future generations thus:

'It will indeed (seem) to you a benefaction, when you behold (in contrast) what the ancestors have done, in poor and ignorant works. Remember my name.'

His wish was to be answered: the underground gallery, or Serapeum as it later came to be known, remained in use, just as Khaemwaset had intended, for the next thirteen centuries.

His interest in the past went beyond reverence for the cult of the Apis. Khaemwaset was clearly impressed and enchanted by the Old Kingdom monuments that still dominated the skyline of the Memphite necropolis. In his own words, he 'loved the noble ones who dwelt in antiquity before him, and the excellence of everything they made, in very truth, a million times.' Crucially, he also had the resources to indulge his passion. In his late thirties, he therefore he set about visiting, inspecting and restoring the pyramids and sun-temples of the 3rd, 4th and 5th Dynasty kings. On each monument he investigated he had a standard inscription carved to record his work. The inscription on the Great Pyramid ran:

'It is the High Priest, the sem-priest, the King's Son Khaemwaset who has perpetuated the name of King Khufu.'

While conducting his tour of inspection at Giza, Khaemwaset even undertook a small-scale excavation, anticipating the work of archaeologists by more than three thousand years. He was rewarded with a remarkable discovery:

'It was the High Priest and King's Son Khaemwaset who delighted in this statue of the King's Son Kawab, which he discovered in the fill of a shaft in the area of the well of his father Khufu.'

The statue was subsequently erected in the temple of Ptah at Memphis, so that its discoverer could admire it on a daily basis.

Beyond his religious duties, Khaemwaset was responsible for the administration of the Memphite area. He also acted as royal herald, making the official proclamation of his father's first five jubilees. By the time he had reached his late fifties, Khaemwaset's three older brothers had predeceased him, making him Crown Prince and heir apparent. But Khaemwaset's time on earth, too, was fast running out, and he died in his father's fifty-fifth regnal year, having given forty years of devoted service to Memphis, its cults and its monuments.

A great builder and restorer, a model priest and prince, Khaemwaset was remembered for centuries after his death, featuring as the hero of a popular cycle of stories over a millennium later. In his beloved Memphite necropolis, his memory was honoured in a hilltop sanctuary at Abusir with a view of all the pyramids: the perfect monument for the first Egyptologist.

73 MES
VICTOR IN A LONG-RUNNING COURT CASE

There is a tendency to view ancient Egyptian civilization through rose-tinted spectacles. The Egyptians themselves desired and strove to portray themselves and their culture in ideal terms, since the very act of recording a person or event conferred immortality; and there was an overriding and understandable wish to perpetuate the best, not the worst, aspects of their lives. This idealizing view of the pharaonic world is beguiling to the modern, jaundiced eye, yet it is as false as it is alluring. For example, when it comes to the ancient Egyptian family, it is tempting to focus on the exemplary model portrayed on stelae and in tomb paintings: parents, children and relatives living in harmony and mutual support. This may have been the case for a few lucky individuals, but experience – especially in societies where large extended families live in close proximity – suggests that disagreements, jealousies, strife and even open hostility were probably closer to the norm.

A unique inscription from the early 19th Dynasty proves that the ancient Egyptians, too, were prone to complex and often stormy family relationships. The author of the account was a man named Mes. He lived during the reign of Ramesses II and, like his father before him, rose to the modest office of Treasury Scribe in the temple of Ptah at Memphis. But his claim to fame, the proudest moment of his life, was nothing to do with his career. Rather, it concerned his victory in a court case, an internecine legal battle between relatives, that by its close had dragged on for a full century.

The background to the case went back to the very beginning of the New Kingdom and the reign of Ahmose. Mes's distant ancestor, Neshi, had been superintendent of the seal and admiral under Ahmose, and had fought valiantly in the wars of liberation against the Hyksos. Like other loyal officers, Neshi was granted an estate near the capital city of Memphis as a reward for his military service; it came to be known as 'the settlement of Neshi'. The estate passed down through the generations, eventually being inherited by Mes's great-grandmother, the lady Shentra. Shentra had several children and this is where the trouble first arose. For when Shentra died, in the reign of Horemheb, one of her daughters, Wernuro (probably the eldest), evidently believed she should inherit everything; her siblings thought otherwise. Wernuro therefore went to court to uphold the legal unity of the estate and confirm her position as sole heir. She was only partly successful, winning the right to act as administrator of the estate while having to accept that the law recognized the shares of her co-heirs.

This decision was evidently too much for one member of the family, Wernuro's sister Takhuru. She now filed a second lawsuit to gain formal control of her portion of the inheritance. When this was granted, Wernuro and her son Huy (Mes's father) counter-sued to win back their administrative rights over the whole estate. The dispute had now split the family asunder. The level of ill-feeling was acute, and was to be passed on to the next generation. Hence, when Huy died, perhaps some forty or more years later, his relatives decided to settle the matter once and for all. They hired a dubious character called Khay to expel Huy's widow Nubnofret and her baby son Mes from their land.

Facing destitution and permanent exclusion from her family estate, Nubnofret filed a fourth lawsuit. Her aim was to regain control of the estate, but she was thwarted by Khay's machinations on behalf of her relatives. He conspired with a court official to falsify the tax records held at the Delta city of Per-Ramesses. These would have shown that Huy had indeed farmed the land, upholding Nubnofret's claim. But when the documents were brought before the High Court of the Vizier in Heliopolis (ancient Iunu) no mention of Huy was to be found in them. Khay's assertions were vindicated, and it looked as though Mes and his mother had lost everything.

However, the gloating family had not reckoned on the young boy's determination to right the wrongs done to his mother. When he came of age, he filed a fifth lawsuit in the Great Lawcourt at Memphis. His case against Khay comprised two charges. The first was to re-establish his right to the ancestral land-holding as a direct descendant of Neshi. The second was an accusation against Khay and an accomplice of falsifying the tax records. On the first charge, Mes was cleverer than his opponent. Realizing that the documentary record had been tampered with and would not substantiate his claim, Mes appealed directly to the local inhabitants in the vicinity of 'the settlement of Neshi'. They were able to testify to his descent and therefore his right to the land. Living witnesses were more powerful evidence than mere documents, and even Khay had to admit Mes's legitimate descent before the court. His inheritance established, Mes brought in other documents to support the accusation against Khay.

With bated breath, plaintiff and defendant awaited the final verdict. It was announced by a scribe in front of the bench of judges. Like all ancient Egyptian legal decisions it took the form 'A is right, B is wrong'. The court found in Mes's favour, and he lifted his hand to greet the verdict. Khay, by contrast, bowed his head under the stick wielded by the court officer. Mes was triumphant and left the court with his arms held high; his opponent left in disgrace. To celebrate his historic victory and ensure that his claim was upheld in perpetuity, Mes had the full details of the case inscribed on the walls of his tomb-chapel at Saqqara.

Mes the litigant, unafraid to go to law to gain justice, is a curiously familiar figure in the modern, western world. He is also a stark reminder that family feuds are a universal human experience.

74 DIDIA
CHIEF DRAUGHTSMAN OF FOREIGN ANCESTRY

One of the chief wishes of an ancient Egyptian was to bequeath his office to his children. A draughtsman named Didia, who lived in Thebes in the reign of Ramesses II, exemplifies the realization of this wish. For Didia was the seventh generation of his family to hold the office of Chief Draughtsman of Amun. His distant ancestor, named Pada-Baal ('Baal redeems'), had come to Egypt from Syria-Palestine, perhaps as a prisoner of war, in the mid-18th Dynasty. Evidently keen to assimilate into Egyptian society, he gave his children Egyptian names. Yet, the family retained a sense of its origins, most of the male members marrying women who were themselves foreigners or of foreign ancestry. Didia was proud of his genealogy, inscribing it on a stela.

As Chief Draughtsman of Amun, Didia's skill was in drawing, painting and designing. His work was not, however, confined to mere sketching. He served the Vizier Paser in the construction and decoration of the great hypostyle hall at Karnak, begun under Seti I and finished under Ramesses II. Next, as Didia himself recorded, 'I was charged by His Person to do work for Amun, to restore monuments in Karnak and on the Great West (Bank) of Thebes.' His commission was to restore the temples of the 18th Dynasty and earlier periods that had fallen into disrepair, namely the Festival Hall of Thutmose III at Karnak; the joint funerary temple of Amenhotep I and Ahmose-Nefertari, and the mortuary temple of Thutmose III in western Thebes; and the temple of Mentuhotep II, the Amun temple of Thutmose III, and the mortuary temple of Hatshepsut at Deir el-Bahri.

Didia was also able to produce, or commission from colleagues, his own finely executed stelae and a black granite statue. His inscriptions invoked a plethora of gods and goddesses: Amun of Karnak and Mut, naturally, but also the Heliopolitan deities Ra, Atum, Shu, Tefnut, Geb and Nut; the Elephantine triad of Khnum, Satet and Anket; Horus of Behdet; Nekhbet; Hathor of Gebelein; Sobek-Ra Lord of Sumenu; and Montu the Theban. After seven generations of living and working in Thebes, a family of Syro-Palestinian origin had become more Egyptian than the Egyptians.

75 MERENPTAH
THE PHARAOH WHO SUBDUED ISRAEL

During his extraordinarily long reign, Ramesses II had deliberately blurred the distinction between the divinity of his office and his own human frailty. Moreover, he must have seemed practically immortal to the thousands of his subjects whose entire lives were contained within his sixty-seven years on the throne. His heirs, too, must have wondered if the old king would ever die, and a succession of crown princes had their expectations thwarted as they predeceased their father. When Ramesses finally departed his earthly life, in his nineties, the next in line to the throne was not his first, second or even third son, but his thirteenth, a prince named Merenptah.

He was himself an elderly man, probably in his sixties at the time of his accession. Married with three or four children, the prince Merenptah must have spent the majority of his adult life completely unaware of his eventual destiny; but as one older brother after another died, he rose inexorably in the line of succession. When the moment came for him to assume the kingship, the unexpected heir must have realized that his reign would be a short one. Work began straight away on his tomb in the Valley of the Kings, and his mortuary temple was built in record time by reusing blocks from the nearby monument of Amenhotep III. It was a race against time and not even respect for his royal ancestors could be allowed to stand in the way.

Merenptah's instinct to emulate the glory of his father Ramesses II was at odds with the pressing urgency to complete his own architectural legacy. The new king's mortuary temple exemplified this tension: its entrance pylon was nearly as large as the Ramesseum's, proclaiming the grandeur of its royal builder; but the temple behind the façade was only half the size of his father's colossal edifice.

Ever conscious of the need to fulfil the traditional role of pharaoh, one of Merenptah's first acts as king was to order a thorough inspection and refurbishment of temples throughout Egypt. For good measure, he had his own name added to many of them; in this, he certainly took after his father. In international relations, too, Merenptah honoured his predecessor's accomplishments. Under the terms of the peace treaty with the Hittites, which had followed the inconclusive Battle of Kadesh, Merenptah shipped grain to the Hittite kingdom to relieve a famine. However, it was not all peace and friendship in the Levant.

The early years of a new reign were always a vulnerable time. The death of a king and the inauguration of an untested monarch presented the perfect opportunity for foreign adversaries and rebellious provinces to launch an offensive. When the death in question was that of the great pharaoh and military commander Ramesses II, and the new king was a sexagenarian, the temptation was irresistible. In Merenptah's first year on the throne, the cities of Ashkelon, Gezer and Yanoam in Syria-Palestine revolted against Egyptian domination. Merenptah had to act decisively to prevent the break-up of the empire his father and grandfather had so determinedly created. So he sent his Crown Prince, Seti-Merenptah, to crush the rebels and restore control. A fortified well was subsequently established at a strategic location in the hills outside Jerusalem, to provide drinking water for Egyptian trading, diplomatic and military expeditions in the Levant. The 'Well of Merenptah' served its purpose, and normal communications across Syria-Palestine were resumed within a year of the unsuccessful rebellion.

But a far greater threat to Egypt was still to come. In Merenptah's fifth year on the throne, Nubians in the south of the Nile Valley launched their own revolt. This was no ordinary insurgency: it seems to have been a deliberate diversionary tactic, designed to lure the Egyptian forces away from the real attack. For, along the western edge of the Delta, a full-scale invasion was under way, led by the Libyans in alliance with the mysterious and much-feared Sea Peoples. The latter included the Ekwesh (probably Achaeans from mainland Greece), together with Sherden – some of whose compatriots had served in Ramesses II's army – and Shekelesh, Teresh and Lukka. Together, these peoples from the eastern Mediterranean made up perhaps a third of the total invasion force. It was the deciding moment of Merenptah's reign. He had to act quickly and decisively if Egypt was not to labour again under a foreign yoke.

The king mobilized his forces quickly. He ordered the Viceroy of Kush into action against the Nubians, who were crushed with relative ease. The main Egyptian army marched at once for the western Delta, engaging the invaders near the twin cities of Pe and Dep (Greek Buto, modern Tell el-Fara'in). After a ferocious six-hour battle, the Egyptians claimed victory. The invasion had been stopped in its tracks. No doubt mightily relieved, and buoyed up by this stunning military success, Merenptah followed his father's example and had an account of his triumph inscribed for eternity. In fact, not one account but two: just as Ramesses II had commissioned both a poetic and a prose record of the Battle of Kadesh, so his son composed two versions of his own victory. The poem was a masterpiece of hyperbole. It included a graphic account of the rout of the Libyan troops; the flight of their chief Merey, referred to as 'the abomination of Memphis'; and the desolation of their homeland in the wake of defeat. Moreover, the king was extolled as victor over all Egypt's enemies: Tjehenu (Libya), Canaan, Ashkelon, Gezer, Yanoam, Khor and – most famously of all – Israel. This reference to the people of the Old Testament is the only known occurrence of the name Israel in a hieroglyphic text. It is a supreme irony that, despite his genuine military successes and efforts to defend his father's glorious achievements, Merenptah's place in history was ultimately secured by this one, brief, and perhaps fictional reference.

76 PANEB
NOTORIOUS CRIMINAL

Ancient Egyptian art presents a perfectly ordered view of the world
in which people go about their daily lives in peace and contentment,
families are loving and close-knit, and the social hierarchy is universally
respected. Of course, no society in history has been such a Utopia,
and ancient Egypt certainly had its fair share of disease, delinquency
and strife. But we must look to other sources of evidence other than
art for insights into the grittier realities of life. Administrative and
legal texts, in particular, were created to record factual occurrences
rather than to immortalize an idealized picture of society. They can
therefore provide fleeting glimpses of the social ills that lurked beneath
the outward semblance of order and harmony. One such collection of
documents from the end of the 19th Dynasty highlights the crimes
and misdemeanours of a notorious Theban criminal.

The miscreant in question was a man called Paneb. He lived in
Deir el-Medina, the village of the necropolis workmen tucked away
in a secluded valley of western Thebes. Paneb's father and grandfather had both been workmen employed in the construction of the
royal tombs. Nefersenet, Paneb's father, had worked on the tombs of
Ramesses II and his sons, and was evidently well known in the local
area, being mentioned in several graffiti. His son was to become even
more of a household name, but for rather different reasons.

Paneb had a typically large family. He shared his small house
with his wife Wabet, their three or four sons, and five daughters;
but it was not a picture of unalloyed domestic bliss. In the cramped
conditions of the village, living cheek-by-jowl with other households,
the opportunity for extra-marital affairs was ever-present, and Paneb
seems to have found the temptation irresistible. He had sexual relations with at least three married women, one called Tuy and two
by the name of Hunro, transgressions which must have made him
unpopular, especially with his own family.   ·

In his work, too, Paneb was deceitful and unscrupulous. On
reaching adulthood, at the end of the long reign of Ramesses II,
he had joined the team of necropolis workmen, following in his

father's footsteps. As a 'man of the crew', Paneb laboured through the decade-long reign of Merenptah and into that of Seti II. Five years into the new king's reign, an opportunity suddenly presented itself for promotion when the chief workman, Neferhotep, died or retired. In ancient Egypt, important offices were usually passed down through a family, and Neferhotep's younger brother, Amennakht, expected to succeed as chief workman. However, he had reckoned without Paneb who was quite prepared to do whatever it took to advance his own career, even at others' expense. Paneb simply bribed the Vizier to appoint him chief workman, passing over Amennakht. Subsequently, to cover his tracks, Paneb made a complaint against the Vizier which led to his dismissal from office.

As one of two chief workmen, responsible for the 'right side' of the crew, while his colleague Hay led the 'left side', Paneb now had ample opportunity to feather his own nest. He had already begun work on his own tomb when he was a humble stone-cutter; but he now had at his disposal the entire workforce of his team. He lost no time in using them for his own projects, taking them away from their contracted work in the Valley of the Kings. For example, one of Paneb's subordinates, Nebnefer son of Wadjmose, failed to turn up for work because he was feeding Paneb's ox. Such behaviour was probably quite widespread among those in minor positions of authority, and would not have been considered a serious transgression. However, Paneb's criminal activity went further. He stole tools from his place of work, taking away pick-axes and a hoe belonging to the state for the construction of his own tomb. He also used his influence and access to commit much graver crimes. Seti II had now died and had been laid to rest in the Valley of the Kings. If Paneb's later accusers are to be believed, he plundered the royal tomb on which he had himself worked and robbed it of a chariot cover, incense, oil, wines and a statue. He compounded his offence by sitting on the dead king's sarcophagus, an act of appalling desecration.

Theft, tomb-robbery, blasphemy against the gods: Paneb had descended from petty wrongdoer to major criminal, and his enemies seized their chance to bring him to justice. Amennakht, who harboured a lasting grudge against Paneb for dishonestly depriving him of the office of chief workman, dictated a series of charges to a scribe, then laid them in writing before the Vizier Hori. In his submission, he even accused Paneb of murder. The defendant's own son, Aapehty, himself a necropolis workman, weighed in with accusations against his father of adultery and fornication. Condemned on all sides, by colleagues and family members, Paneb's criminal career had run its course. But had it? Frustratingly, we know nothing of his ultimate fate, whether he was convicted or managed to escape justice by some clever ruse. Whatever the court's decision, Paneb had ensured his immortality, not by good deeds but by infamy.

77 BAY
KING-MAKER

The sixty-seven-year reign of Ramesses II dominated the 19th Dynasty. While it had been a source of great stability at the time, its effect on later generations was seriously destabilizing, as a succession of either aged or immature kings followed. In such a situation, there was abundant scope for dynastic intrigue, for plots and counter-plots. The record of such events is, naturally, rather opaque, but it is clear that one man in particular took advantage of the circumstances to promote his own interests; his name was Bay.

During the reign of Seti II, Merenptah's short-lived successor, Bay held the office of chancellor. His background is obscure, but he was possibly of Near Eastern origin. He was clearly an accomplished politician. He needed to be, since Seti II's reign was far from trouble-free. In his second year on the throne, a usurper called Amenmesse was proclaimed king in the Nile Valley south of the Fayum, leaving Seti with effective authority over just the Delta and Memphite area. Amenmesse may have been Seti's son who, frustrated at being passed over as heir apparent, decided to launch his own bid for power and oust his father in the process. He held out as king for nearly four years, before

Seti II managed to restore royal authority throughout Egypt and its conquered territories. It is not clear what part, if any, Bay played in these events; even if he was not involved in Amenmesse's coup, he evidently saw the damage that had been done to the authority of the monarchy and decided to exploit it for his own purposes.

Seti II's restoration to full power was short-lived, as he died a year or so after ousting Amenmesse. The Crown Prince and legitimate heir had been Seti's son Seti-Merenptah, but he was either dead already or unable to assert his rights to the succession in the face of powerful opponents. Leading the opposition camp was Bay. His preferred choice as the next king was a young prince called Siptah, very probably the son of Amenmesse; in texts at Aswan and Gebel el-Silsila, Bay boasted that he had 'established the king in the seat of his father'. Bay's candidate had good connections in Nubia, giving him access to its mineral wealth. Better still, as a mere child, he was ripe for manipulation by older, more experienced courtiers, and Bay fully intended to exert his own authority by ruling through the young king.

Siptah was duly proclaimed king, but power was exercised through a regency headed by Seti II's widow, Tawosret. At least, this was the official version of events, but in reality Bay was the power behind the throne. He used his new-found power to the full, commissioning a tomb of regal proportions for himself in the Valley of the Kings. However, his influence at the heart of government did not last long. In the fifth year of Tawosret's regency, she made her bid for full power, a decision which precipitated Bay's downfall. He was executed on Tawosret's orders and his name was systematically erased from the record, with the exception of an oblique reference to 'the great enemy'. His tomb was never used.

A year or less later, Siptah himself, still only in his teens, was dead. The counter-revolution was complete. The young king's name was removed from his own unfinished tomb, and from Tawosret's nearby sepulchre in the Valley of the Kings. She continued to rule as sole king, but the country was split asunder. Civil war ensued and order was only restored by the advent of a new strong-man, Sethnakht, the founder of the 20th Dynasty. He and his descendants wrote both Siptah and Tawosret out of history, regarding Seti II as the last legitimate king of the 19th Dynasty royal line. As for the king-maker Bay, history was even more damning: a 20th Dynasty source called him simply 'the Syrian upstart'.

78 RAMESSES III
THE LAST GREAT KING OF EGYPT

Ramesses III has been called the last great pharaoh. Certainly, his thirty-one years on the throne of Egypt were not short of glories: temple-building on a grand scale, epic military victories, expeditions to bring back exotic materials from distant lands. But the manner in which his reign came to an end – a court conspiracy, attempted assassination and untimely death – was less glorious, presaging the breakdown in central authority that was to characterize the Third Intermediate Period.

Ramesses was born in the dying days of the 19th Dynasty. His father, Sethnakht, was probably an army general, in charge of the troops garrisoned in the eastern Delta. In the aftermath of the troubled reigns of Siptah and Tawosret, the military class turned to Sethnakht as the man best able to restore stability. But he was already elderly. Effective power during his brief, two-year reign was therefore exercised by his son Ramesses, who, like his father, had probably started his career in the army.

When Ramesses himself acceded to the throne, he brought with him the promise a better future. Here was a vigorous and healthy king, to restore stability and glory to the Egyptian throne after a succession of weak and ineffectual rulers. He consciously modelled himself on Egypt's last great king, Ramesses II, choosing a throne-name (Usermaatra-mery-amun) which deliberately recalled that of his illustrious predecessor (Usermaatra-setepenra). Ramesses III may perhaps have been the great-grandson of Ramesses II: he was certainly a ruler in the same mould. He named two of his sons after Ramesses II's sons, even appointing them to the same offices as their forebears.

Just as Ramesses II had built a magnificent mortuary temple (the Ramesseum) on the West Bank at Thebes, so Ramesses III set about doing the same. Proclaimed as 'The Mansion of Millions of Years of King Ramesses, United With Eternity in the Estate of Amun', the temple at Medinet Habu was to be the last great architectural achievement of the New Kingdom. Its massive pylons, two columned forecourts, hypostyle hall, and adjoining palace were all contained within a fortified enclosure wall. The gateway to the entire sacred space was modelled on a Syrian fortress (*migdol*), and the king reserved its upper chambers for his private use, decorating them with intimate scenes of himself and his wives.

The fact that Ramesses' mortuary temple employed Syrian-inspired architectural motifs illustrates the cosmopolitan nature of his reign. Even his favourite wife Iset may have been of foreign origin. But Egypt's foreign relations were not confined to cultural influences and diplomatic marriages. Peoples to the north, east and west were undergoing internal convulsions; restless foreign rulers and displaced people alike viewed Egypt's legendary wealth with greedy eyes. Would the young king Ramesses III live up to the bravery and resolve of his famous forebear? His first five years on the throne passed in peace, but this was the calm before the storm. From the king's fifth to eleventh years, Egypt suffered no fewer than three attempted invasions, testing its defences, and the king's military leadership, to the limit.

The first attack was led by the Libu people of Cyrenaica (coastal Libya). It was swiftly countered but much worse was to come. In the king's eighth year, Egypt faced one of the most dangerous situations it had ever known. Political and military unrest in the far-off Mycenaean world may have been the trigger: according to the Egyptian account, 'the foreign countries plotted in their islands, and the people were dislodged and scattered by battle all at one time and no land could stand before their arms.' The displacement of large numbers of people from the Aegean and Anatolia caused a massive population movement. The migrants, known collectively as the Sea Peoples, comprised at least nine distinct ethnic groups: Denyen (perhaps the Danaoi from mainland Greece), Ekwesh (Achaeans?), Lukka (Lycians),

Peleset (Philistines), Sherden, Shekelesh, Teresh, Tjeker (Teucrians?) and Weshesh. Together, they moved out from their homelands, through the eastern Mediterranean, ravaging coastal towns and cities, attacking Cilicia, Cyprus and Syria, and even destabilizing the once-mighty Hittite empire.

They pressed on towards Egypt; a land invasion, including women and children in carts, headed for Egypt's northeastern frontier while a sea-borne force made for the Delta. On learning of the two-pronged invasion, Ramesses immediately sent orders to the frontier fortresses to stand firm and hold the enemy at bay until the main Egyptian army arrived. When the two forces met at the border, there was a mighty battle with massive loss of life; but the Egyptians prevailed. Attention now turned to the Delta coast. The enemy fleet made for the mouth of one of the Nile branches, no doubt intending to sail upstream to Memphis; but the Egyptians engaged them in the open sea, assisted by archers firing from the shoreline. At the end of the epic encounter, Egypt was victorious and Ramesses recorded the whole conflict in texts and images on the outer wall of his mortuary temple. The description of the battles is the longest surviving hieroglyphic inscription. Although Egypt secured its continued liberty and independence, routing the invaders, the effort placed great strains on the country and must have severely dented its confidence. Moreover, some of the Sea Peoples settled on the coastal plain of the Levant, uncomfortably close to Egypt, while others, notably Sherden, made their homes in the Nile valley itself. The geo-politics of the Near East were changing, and nothing could stop the process.

Ramesses was eventually able to turn his attention to more peaceful activities, such as sending expeditions to distant lands to bring back precious materials for the royal treasury: myrrh and incense from Punt, copper from Timna, and turquoise from Sinai. The wealth generated by these missions was put to work in a new round of temple-building, including at Karnak.

As he neared his thirtieth year on the throne, and the occasion of his jubilee festival, Ramesses III had proved himself a worthy successor of his hero Ramesses II, leading his people bravely and wisely in war and peace. But all was not well in the corridors of power. Just months before the jubilee, the necropolis workmen went on strike four times to demand their monthly wages in grain. The government, it seems, was too preoccupied with preparations for the forthcoming celebrations to meet its more mundane responsibilities. The jubilee itself passed off smoothly, but disguised the simmering resentment building at court. The cause of conflict was the ambition of one of Ramesses III's wives, Tiye, to place her son, prince Pentaweret, on the throne in place of his father. The plot to assassinate the king was hatched in the harem palace. Those involved included members of the king's inner circle – such as the Chief of the Chamber, butlers, an Overseer of the Treasury and a Commander of the army – as well as officials and others directly connected with the harem.

The coup plot was foiled, and Ramesses set up a high-level commission of enquiry to try the accused and carry out the sentences. The intention may have been to insulate the king from any further direct involvement. But it was to be Ramesses III's last act, the exhortation 'May all that they have done fall upon their heads' his final royal command. The king died shortly afterwards, perhaps as a result of injuries sustained in the assassination attempt. With his death, the self-confident and secure model of kingship passed away too. Egypt would never fully regain its former glory.

79 RAMESSESNAKHT
HIGH PRIEST UNDER THE LATE RAMESSIDES

The remaining years of the 20th Dynasty following the death of Ramesses III were characterized by a swift succession of kings, as one heir after another succumbed after only a few years on the throne. Yet alongside and in contrast to this unsettling transience in the office of kingship, Egypt witnessed some remarkably lengthy and stable careers among the upper echelons of the administration. It was as if the mantle of national continuity had passed from the pharaoh to his high officials. One such man was the High Priest of Amun, Ramessesnakht.

Unusually for someone who was to become head of the all-powerful Amun priesthood, Ramessesnakht was not a Theban by birth. His family came from Hermopolis (ancient Khemnu) in Middle Egypt, where his father, Meribast, held a raft of important local offices. Ramessesnakht married a woman named Adjitsherit and started a family, before finally attaining high office in his thirties or forties, when he was promoted by Ramesses IV to the office of High Priest of Amun. The new king thereby signalled his independence, presumably passing over other, Theban candidates (who might have expected promotion) in favour of a talented outsider. Ramessesnakht swiftly assumed responsibility for matters far beyond his primary religious duties. In the third year of Ramesses IV's reign, he was put in charge of an expedition to the siltstone-quarries of the Wadi Hammamat. With 9,000 men, it was the biggest such expedition since the reign of Senusret I in the early 12th Dynasty.

Just a few years later Ramesses IV was dead. For the next two decades, kings came and went; but Ramessesnakht continued in post. In a term of office lasting at least twenty-seven years, he served under six monarchs, from Ramesses IV to Ramesses IX. He also succeeded in making his family's control of the High Priesthood unassailable: first one son (Nesamun) then another (Amenhotep) succeeded him in that office, while his daughter Aatnmeret married another senior cleric. When Ramessesnakht died, in his late sixties or seventies, he had achieved everything dreamt of by an ancient Egyptian official:

a lifetime of service to the king (or, in his case, six); a goodly burial in the west (in his case, a fine tomb in the Theban necropolis); and, best of all, the inauguration of his own, family dynasty.

80 NAUNAKHT
WOMAN WHO DISINHERITED HER UNGRATEFUL CHILDREN

Despite the relatively low profile of women in the official record of ancient Egypt, they enjoyed far greater equality in social and legal matters than their counterparts in other civilizations of the ancient world. Indeed, the position of women in many modern states has not yet reached the same level of equality as in ancient Egypt. The legal status of women was on an equal footing with that of men – if they wished, wives could testify against their husbands – and they maintained control of their own property, even after marrying. Women were also free to dispose of their wealth as they wished. The best and most famous example of an ancient Egyptian woman doing exactly this is contained in the last will and testament of Naunakht, an inhabitant of Thebes in the late Ramesside Period.

Naunakht was a woman of modest means. She held no particular rank, describing herself simply as 'a free woman', although she may occasionally have served as a songstress of Amun in the temple of Karnak. Her first husband was a scribe named Qenhirkhepeshef. He had been involved in work on the royal tombs, and was probably therefore a man of means. It may thus have been a marriage motivated by financial considerations rather than a love-match. Certainly, it seems to have produced no offspring. Naunakht's second marriage, to a servant in the Place of Truth named Khaemnun, was altogether more fruitful. They had eight children, four boys and four girls.

To be blessed with many children was the ancient Egyptian ideal, for in a society without social security, the next generation offered the only means of being looked after in old age. But some of Naunakht's offspring did not exactly live up to their mother's, or society's, expectations. The unvarnished details are all contained in Naunakht's will, declared before a court and recorded in writing on the fifth day of the fourth month of the season of inundation in the third year of the reign of Ramesses V – around November 1147 BC. The court comprised fourteen individuals, varying in rank from humble workmen to district officers. Naunakht was about to disinherit three of her children, and she did not mince her words:

'I brought up these eight servants of yours… But see, I am grown old, and see, they are not looking after me in my turn.'

The trade-off was simple:

'Whoever of them has aided me, to him I will give of my property; he who has not given to me, to him I will not give of my property.'

The losers were Naunakht's two daughters, Wosnakht and Manenakht. While they could not be prevented from inheriting the two-thirds of the matrimonial property that under law belonged to the husband (Khaemnun), they could, and would, be excluded from any part of Naunakht's share:

'They shall not participate in the division of my one-third.'

In a similar vein, one of Naunakht's sons, Neferhotep, was cut out of the will because he had already received more than his fair share in the form of copper vessels, which he had squandered. By contrast, his brother Qenhirkhepeshef was singled out for special favour 'over and above his fellows', receiving not only his one-fifth share of Naunakht's estate but also her single most valuable asset, a bronze washing-bowl.

A year or two after the testament was made verbally and in writing, the whole family – Khaemnun and the eight children – had to suffer the indignity of appearing before a second legal hearing to confirm that they were content with, and would respect, the terms of the will. Even though none of Naunakht's possessions was worth very much, being mostly pieces of furniture and kitchen utensils, the rebuke to her wayward daughters must have been keenly felt. They had learned the hard way what could be expected by the ungrateful children of a woman who knew her own mind.

81 THUTMOSE
CORRESPONDENT IN A TIME OF TROUBLE

Literacy was restricted to a tiny minority in ancient Egypt. Although quite a few people would have been able to recognize some common hieroglyphs, no more than five to ten per cent of the population could read and write proficiently. These skills, acquired through rigorous, sometimes laborious training at a scribal school, brought with them the possibility of a career in government. But on a more mundane level, literacy also conferred the ability to communicate with friends and family. Those Egyptians who *could* read and write seem to have been enthusiastic correspondents, concerning themselves with the usual range of weighty and trivial subjects. These are well illustrated in the letters of Thutmose, penned at the very end of the New Kingdom.

Thutmose was a scribe by profession, attached to the Theban necropolis during the second half of the reign of Ramesses XI. Thutmose's official title was 'scribe of the great and noble necropolis of millions of years of pharaoh (life, prosperity, health)', a post he held for at least sixteen years, and his duties included supervising the records of taxation of cereal farming. He lived in western Thebes but travelled to other parts of the country on business. One such trip took him to Middle Egypt, from where he sent numerous letters back home, to check on the state of his affairs and the health of his relatives, especially his mother Tanettabekhen and his brother Paykamun.

However, it was a much longer journey away from Thebes, in altogether more trying circumstances, that gave Thutmose the opportunity for his most extensive correspondence. In the tenth year of the 'Renaissance' (the official designation given to the last third of Ramesses XI's reign), Thutmose was conscripted for duty in the Egyptian army. The reason was a rebellion led by the disgraced Viceroy of Kush, Panehsy (no. 82). Leading the counter-attack on behalf of the government forces was the general Paiankh. Thutmose first travelled south to Edfu where he was met by Paiankh's men; he was then escorted to Abu (Elephantine), the traditional launching point for military expeditions against Nubia.

Once the campaign began, Thutmose found himself in an unaccustomed role, surrounded by people he did not know, in an alien land. His letters to his son Butehamun, at home in Thebes, spoke eloquently of his homesickness and increasing despair.

> *'Please tell Amun and the gods of the temple to bring me back alive from the enemy'*

he wrote to Butehamun; and, on another occasion,

> *'I tell Horus of Kubban, Horus of Aniba [both Nubian gods] and Atum, the lord of the earth, to give you life, prosperity, health; a long lifetime, and a good ripe old age; and to let Amun of the Thrones of the Two Lands, my good lord, bring me back alive from… the place where I am abandoned in this far-off land, and let me fill my embrace with you.'*

Thutmose wrote in similar vein to one of his friends, the guardian Kar:

> *'Tell Amun to bring me back sound from [this] hell-hole, the placewhere I am abandoned.'*

At other times, however, Thutmose's thoughts turned from his own situation to more down-to-earth matters concerning his household and business. He urged his son to look after members of the extended family. He also advised Butehamun not to neglect the cultivation of grain and the planting of vegetables. Of critical importance were the arrangements for the transport of the harvested grain, for if these were not properly made, the crop risked being lost and the family would face food shortages. Butehamun wrote to assure his father that donkeys had been readied for transporting grain; but he then evidently lost interest in the matter and went off on a tangent, detailing some of the minutiae of daily life back home. We can sense the father's exasperation in a subsequent letter to his son, giving the clearest of instructions:

'As soon as this water floods, you shall receive this transport boat which I have sent to you and give it to the fishermen and the Medjay (police) [to transport grain].'

Thutmose also knew from experience that management of the family's affairs required the maintenance of good discipline where contracted workmen were concerned. Keen that nothing should go awry during his absence, he wrote to Butehamun:

'Take care to reprimand any man who has quarrelled with another'.

If matters got out of control, the Medjay could always be called upon, and Thutmose was evidently on good terms with at least two officers, Kas and Hadnakht. The reference in one letter to a Sherden (foreign mercenary) called Hori illustrates the cosmopolitan nature of Theban society in the late New Kingdom.

Thutmose the disciplinarian also had a gentler side. In one of his letters home, he told Butehamun to look after the children and other family members, the conscript soldiers, the labourers in the fields and house guests. Thutmose's concern for his neighbours was obviously reciprocated, since some of his friends wrote back to him saying 'You are the one we wish to see'. Butehamun and some of Thutmose's friends were concerned enough about his condition to write to the general Paiankh in grovelling terms.

Thutmose could not push the uncertainties of his situation to the back of his mind for long, and in his letters home he soon returned to his own plight. The campaigning in Nubia had taken its toll on his health and he asked his son to help by making a libation to the god of Thebes:

> *'You shall take water to Amun of the thrones of the Two Lands and tell him to save [me]... Tell Amun to remove the illness which is in me.'*

The prayer was answered, for Thutmose later wrote that extra rations of bread, and especially beer, had made him well again. A popular member of the community whose family and business affairs occupied his thoughts while far from home, the scribe Thutmose presents a strangely familiar picture.

82 PANEHSY
STRONGMAN WHO CHALLENGED ROYAL POWER

Early in the second decade of Ramesses XI's reign, Thebes was racked by unrest and civil strife. Egypt's most important religious centre, the power-base of the Amun priesthood, was in upheaval. Pressures came from many sources. Disastrous harvests had caused a severe famine, which contemporary sources referred to – obliquely, yet graphically – as 'the year of the hyenas'. Gangs of marauding Libyans were attacking the city of Thebes with virtual impunity. Tombs and temples on the West Bank were subject to unprecedented levels of robbery, adding to the heightened sense of insecurity and crisis. As Theban society began to crumble, the king was in his Delta residence of Per-Ramesses: at a safe distance yet dangerously remote from events. With the High Priest of Amun, Amenhotep (son of Ramessesnakht, no. 79), seemingly powerless to act, a decisive leader was needed to restore order. That man was Panehsy, Viceroy of Kush.

As the king's representative in Nubia and Overseer of the Southern Countries, Panehsy had two major and immediate advantages: financial resources (derived from Nubia's famed gold reserves) and military forces (the Viceroy controlled a string of fortresses and garrisons that stretched from the First Cataract southwards into Upper Nubia). Panehsy's military role was reflected in his subsidiary titles – Overseer of the Army, Royal Scribe of the Army, and Foremost of the Troops of Pharaoh. Probably at the king's command, Panehsy and his army arrived in Thebes to put an end to the violence and looting. He was faced with the immediate problem of how to feed his soldiers. The city was in economic crisis, and the only major stocks of grain were held by the Amun priesthood. Panehsy acted decisively by assuming (or usurping) the important office of Overseer of Granaries, in order to gain access to these crucial supplies. Although this was a necessary step in the circumstances, it nevertheless put him in direct conflict with the High Priest, Amenhotep.

The two most powerful men in the country – one military, the other religious, both with economic and political muscle – now faced off against each other for ultimate authority. True to his military instincts, Panehsy besieged Amenhotep in his fortified temple compound at Medinet Habu (ancient Djeme). The High Priest appealed to the king for help and Ramesses, his authority weakened by recent events, perhaps felt he had no alternative but to yield to the interests of the Amun priesthood. Egypt stood on the brink of civil war.

Panehsy was not a man to take a challenge lying down. He marched north to engage the king's forces on their way from the royal residence. The Viceroy's army reached the settlement of Hardai in Middle Egypt, and ransacked it. It was a fleeting moment of triumph. The king's forces, under the command of an equally brilliant general, Paiankh, soon engaged Panehsy's troops. The superior strength of the royal army quickly proved itself on the battlefield. To avoid a crushing defeat, Panehsy was forced to retreat southwards, eventually ceding control of Upper Egypt and returning to his original power-base in Nubia. For the next few years, he faced continued military attack by Egyptian armies. Yet, in the land he knew best, the Viceroy could outwit his opponents. To Paiankh's frustration, Panehsy lived on in relative prosperity, eventually dying and being buried in Nubia.

In the course of a few turbulent years, his reputation had plummeted from national saviour to renegade. The twists and turns of his extraordinary career mirror the death-throes of imperial Egypt, as the Ramesside court, buffeted on all sides by unpredictable forces, faced its inevitable end.

83 HERIHOR
GREAT OVERSEER OF THE ARMY

The expulsion of Panehsy (no. 82) and his forces from Thebes by the General Paiankh marked a decisive new phase in the reign of Ramesses XI. Indeed, official documents proclaimed the beginning of a Renaissance, and for the next decade events were dated according to this era. But a rebirth of royal power was illusory. It was not Ramesses who had regained control of Thebes, but his general. Paiankh consolidated his power by adding the offices of vizier and High Priest of Amun to his control of the army. Judicial, administrative, religious and military authority were now vested in a single individual. However, the process still had some way to run before it reached its logical conclusion: the man responsible for the ultimate act of *lèse-majesté* would be Paiankh's successor, Herihor.

Herihor's early life and career remain shrouded in mystery. Some of his children were given Libyan names, suggesting a possible Libyan ancestry. Prisoners of war from Egypt's troublesome western neighbour had been settled in the Nile Valley since the early 19th Dynasty. They subsequently became assimilated and many of their descendants entered the Egyptian army, where their innate bravery found a suitable outlet. Herihor, too, is likely to have been an officer in the army before his meteoric rise to power as Paiankh's successor. There were certainly family ties between the two men, and Herihor may well have been hand-picked to take up Paiankh's baton. He showed straight away his intention to carry forward the same policies, not least in the way he aggregated to himself ever greater honours and jurisdictions. Where Paiankh had been merely general, Herihor now took the title generalissimo, Great Overseer of the Army. This he held in tandem with the vizierate and the High Priesthood of Amun. It was perhaps predictable, therefore, that when, in due course, Ramesses XI died, Herihor would take the ultimate step of proclaiming himself king.

His kingship is by no means universally attested. Its principal monument is the Temple of Khonsu inside the great enclosure of Amun-Ra at Karnak. As High Priest, Herihor had control over everything that happened inside Karnak; perhaps it was only here that his royal aspirations could be made a reality. If his kingship was limited in its geographical scope, he certainly made up for it by saturation coverage: the court of the Temple of Khonsu contains over a hundred representations of Herihor as king. He also took pains to stress his fecundity as a royal paterfamilias, showing himself with nineteen sons and five daughters. Egyptian monarchy demanded a royal couple at the pinnacle of society, and Herihor had at his side the lady Nedjmet. This union seems to have been a marriage of true love, the epithets given to Nedjmet by her husband suggesting real affection: 'great of favours, Lady of the Two Lands, possessor of charm, sweet of love, the King's Great Wife, his beloved.'

For a man of military background, Herihor seems, rather surprisingly, to have stressed the sacral aspects of kingship during his brief reign. The reliefs in the Temple of Khonsu show him wearing the priestly leopard skin, and he publicly acknowledged the religious office that had preceded his assumption of the kingship by taking 'High Priest of Amun' as his throne-name. The most prominent event of his reign was also intimately connected with the Amun cult: the construction of a new bark for Amun-Ra to be used in the annual Opet Festival. Herihor went to great lengths to acquire supplies of precious cedar wood from Lebanon for this project. The contemporary text known as the *Report of Wenamun*, which describes the journey of a royal envoy to Byblos 'to fetch timber for the great noble bark of Amun-Ra, King of the Gods', may be an account of the actual mission. As king, Herihor certainly ensured that scenes of him celebrating the Opet Festival were included in the decorative programme of the Temple of Khonsu.

The *Report of Wenamun* also noted the formal division of Egypt that had occurred after the demise of Ramesses XI, with Herihor ruling in the south from Thebes and Smendes ruling in the north from Tanis. Hence, while Herihor had been born under the centralized rule of the Ramessides, he would die in a divided country. His life and career spanned the transition between the last great period of pharaonic authority and the more uncertain times that followed.

PART 7

Twilight of the Gods
THIRD INTERMEDIATE PERIOD, LATE PERIOD AND PTOLEMAIC PERIOD

The ten centuries between the collapse of the New Kingdom and Egypt's absorption into the Roman empire constitute one-third of ancient Egyptian history, and witnessed a plethora of artistic and cultural developments, yet they remain one of the least-studied phases of pharaonic civilization. This is partly due to the fragmentary and often confusing nature of the evidence, and partly to the mistaken impression that Egypt after the New Kingdom was a culture in decline. Although the Third Intermediate Period, Late Period and Ptolemaic Period can, to some extent, be characterized as ancient Egypt's twilight years, they are none the less full of interest and of interesting individuals.

The end of Ramesses XI's reign was followed by the formal division of the country into northern and southern realms, with kings continuing to rule from the Delta while the High Priests of Amun exercised authority in Thebes and throughout much of Upper Egypt. There were ambitious men on both sides whose fortunes depended upon gaining and retaining royal favour. In the north, Wendjebaendjedet (no. 84) rose to prominence as one of the king's most trusted officials. In the south, the Libyan prince Osorkon (no. 85) succeeded – after an epic series of struggles – in claiming the kingship of Thebes for himself. Their stories illustrate the internal conflicts that beset Egypt's rival courts during the Third Intermediate Period.

National unity of a sort was re-established by the kings of the 25th and 26th Dynasties, even though the former were foreigners and the latter had come to power as foreign vassals. The Nubian pharaoh Piye (no. 86) seems to have regarded reunification as his sacred duty, since his devotion to the god Amun was as strong as any native Egyptian's. Having defeated the rival dynasts and asserted his sovereignty over the whole country, he promptly returned to his Nubian homeland, never to return. But his lasting achievement was to restore order and stability, allowing local dynasties of high officials to govern their own regions under the rule of law. The Theban aristocracy of this period is particularly prominent; men such as Harwa (no. 87), Montuemhat (no. 88) and Padiamenope (no. 89) commissioned for themselves funerary monuments on a truly regal scale. Indeed, Egyptian culture enjoyed something of a renaissance as the Late Period kings and their wealthy subjects sought inspiration from the great monuments of the past.

A new innovation was the political influence vested in the God's Wife of Amun, the most senior office in the Theban priesthood. By granting this title to his eldest daughter, a king could ensure royal control over the Amun cult, with its great wealth and extensive landholdings, and hence over Upper Egypt as a whole. The transfer of power in the south of the country from the Nubian 25th Dynasty to the Saite 26th Dynasty was achieved in this way, by having the incumbent God's Wife Shepenwepet II (the daughter of Piye) adopt as her successor princess Nitiqret (no. 90), daughter of the new Saite monarch Psamtik I. The magnificent river-borne procession that accompanied Nitiqret on her journey to Thebes, vividly described by the commander of the flotilla, Sematawytefnakht (I) (no. 91), must have been one of the great spectacles of the Late Period.

Unfortunately, a smooth succession did not take place at the end of the 26th Dynasty, because after Ahmose II (no. 92), the last Saite king, Psamtik III, lost his throne not to a rival royal family but to a Persian conqueror. During the years of occupation, liberation and re-occupation that followed, Egyptian officials often took a pragmatic stance, reaching accommodations with whichever regime was in power. The trials and tribulations of serving under successive Egyptian and Persian rulers are graphically documented in the autobiographical inscriptions of men like Wedjahorresnet (no. 93), Wennefer (no. 94) and Sematawytefnakht (II) (no. 96). Egypt enjoyed a final, brief period of independence and national renewal under the 30th Dynasty, before its last monarch, Nakhthorheb (no. 95), himself succumbed to a Persian invasion. Egypt would not truly regain national autonomy until the mid-twentieth century AD.

However, the second period of Persian domination was mercifully brief, and was brought to an end by an even mightier conqueror, in the person of Alexander the Great. For the next 300 years, Egypt was ruled by Greek-speaking Macedonians: first Alexander and his ephemeral heirs, then a new dynasty founded by one of Alexander's generals, Ptolemy (no. 98). Beyond the new maritime capital, Alexandria, literate Egyptians adopted a hybrid Graeco-Egyptian culture, influenced equally by their new rulers and their own, deep-rooted traditions. The effects of this cultural mixing can be seen in the art and in the wider world-view of the period, as exemplified in the tomb of the priest Padiusir (no. 97) and the historical writings of his near-contemporary Manetho (no. 99).

Under the Ptolemies, Egypt changed from being a North African nation with a primary interest in Nubia to a Mediterranean-oriented country whose fate was inextricably bound up with the other great powers in the region. In the centuries after Alexander, the baton of authority in the Mediterranean world had passed from Greece to Rome. Egypt with its legendary wealth was a tempting prize for Rome's ambitious rulers, and its fate was sealed long before its last resident ruler, Cleopatra VII (no. 100), made her ill-starred alliance with Mark Antony. But ancient Egypt did not altogether die with the tragic queen. Through its influence on Rome, and thence on Western civilization, the age-old culture of the pharaohs shaped the modern world. Two thousand years after Cleopatra, five thousand years after Narmer, interest in the pharaohs, their monuments and the lives of their subjects remains as powerful as ever. Ancient Egypt still holds us in its thrall.

84 WENDJEBAENDJEDET
ROYAL FAVOURITE

Alongside the famous contents of Tutankhamun's tomb, there is another golden treasure from ancient Egypt, almost as sumptuous but virtually unknown to non-specialists. This is the treasure of Tanis (ancient Djanet, modern San el-Hagar), dating from the 21st Dynasty. As might be expected, some of the most notable pieces, such as the gold funerary mask of Psusennes I, were commissioned for kings. However, a large proportion of the total hoard was made, not for a pharaoh, but for a non-royal individual, a man named Wendjebaendjedet. Inside his decorated burial chamber, set within the limestone walls of Psusennes I's own royal tomb, his funerary equipment included a granite sarcophagus (reused from the New Kingdom); a coffin of gilded wood containing a silver coffin; gold statuettes of gods and goddesses; a set of four divine figures in shrines; a green feldspar heart scarab on a gold chain; and a gold gadrooned cup shaped like a daisy, with inlays of coloured paste, inscribed with Wendjebaendjedet's name and titles. The sumptuousness of his grave goods demonstrates his status, yet there is no indication that he was related to the royal family. Who, then, was this uncommonly exalted commoner?

His background is obscure, although both his name and the fact that he was a priest of Osiris Lord of Djedet (Busiris, modern Abusir), suggest that this town in the central Delta was his birthplace. The name of his father is unknown, and only two members of his family, both women, are named on objects from his tomb: Tarudet and Hererit may have been his mother and grandmother, or alternatively his wife and mother-in-law. His priestly responsibilities extended beyond his home town to the dynastic capital, Tanis, where he was a priest and steward of the god Khonsu. The latter office would have brought him into contact with the royal family, and it seems that Wendjebaendjedet's qualities were recognized by the king.

Wendjebaendjedet was appointed to three important roles simultaneously, one religious, one military and one courtly. As Superintendent of the Prophets of All the Gods, he may have acted as the king's deputy in the daily cult activities at Tanis, standing in for Psusennes I at all but the most important ceremonies. As General and Army Leader of Pharaoh, he was second only to the Crown Prince in the military hierarchy. The titles member of the elite and Royal Seal-Bearer were mere indications of rank, held by numerous high officials in each reign; but to these Wendjebaendjedet added the unique distinction of Superintendent of the Sole Companions, suggesting that he was the king's chief courtier, the most favoured of all those with direct access to the monarch. This may be the clue to his extraordinary status, reflected in tomb equipment that was so far above the standard of normal non-royal burials. Among the gold statuettes, jewelry and vessels, there was also a ring inscribed with the name of Ramesses IX, evidently an heirloom from the royal treasury; and a magnificent footed cup in the shape of an open flower, its petals made alternately from gold and electrum, inscribed with the names of the king, Psusennes I, and his wife Mutnodjmet. There could be no better indication of Wendjebaendjedet's closeness to the royal couple.

At court he must have struck an imposing figure, adorned with earrings, a gold statuette of the goddess Isis suspended around his neck on a long gold chain. On the face of it, his combination of religious, military and civil offices would have given him great authority; but, on closer inspection, all his titles were connected with the king's private sphere, and all may have been tokens of royal esteem, not executive functions. Wendjebaendjedet stands as the most prominent ancient Egyptian example of that most pampered and envied of court figures, the royal favourite.

85 OSORKON
PRINCE CAUGHT UP IN A BITTER POWER STRUGGLE

The Third Intermediate Period was a turbulent time, with rival dynasties competing for power and regional governors constantly shifting their allegiances. A vivid insight into Egyptian politics during this period is provided by the autobiographical *Chronicle of Prince Osorkon*.

He was one of at least seven children, and was probably born and grew up in Thebes. Two of his sisters married local dignitaries, while Osorkon himself entered the priesthood of Amun, the most powerful institution in the whole of Upper Egypt. At an early age, he was appointed High Priest of Amun; but his rapid rise may reflect the political importance of his family rather than exceptional individual ability. He might have looked forward to a long and distinguished career at the head of the Amun priesthood, but a dramatic decision by his father Takelot was to change his life irrevocably.

Ever since the death of Ramesses XI, some 230 years before, Egypt had in effect been a divided state: power in the north was wielded by kings ruling from Memphis or the Delta, while authority in the south of the country resided in Thebes. Even if the city's governors paid lip service to the idea of a single pharaoh, in reality royal control ceased abruptly not far south of Memphis. Takelot, the most powerful man in Thebes, decided to dispense with the fiction of a united monarchy and formalize his position as *de facto* king of Upper Egypt. He therefore proclaimed himself pharaoh of a new, Theban, royal line, equal in every respect to the Libyan 22nd Dynasty ruling from Tanis.

The formal establishment of a rival dynasty unleashed the pent-up forces of internal strife, and Osorkon found himself in the middle of events. While he was in Middle Egypt, enemies tried to dislodge him from the High Priesthood of Amun. So he set sail for Thebes immediately, and had to overcome a number of minor rebellions en route. Once safely arrived in the city, he acted ruthlessly to quell all opposition and re-establish his authority. After making offerings to Amun in the temple, he had the leaders of the plot to unseat him executed; to send a powerful message to any other would-be rebels, their bodies were burned, denying them any chance of rebirth.

The tactic worked, and just two years after nearly losing his position, Osorkon was confident and powerful enough to carry out the duties of the High Priest during the three great annual Theban festivals. But the calm did not last. Osorkon's heavy-handed treatment of his opponents must have caused great resentment, and the plotters now found a new standard-bearer in the form of man called Pedubast who proclaimed himself king of Thebes, in opposition to Takelot. The result, inevitably, was civil war, which raged for nine, gruelling years. Once again, Osorkon was in the thick of the fighting.

Eventually, with neither side able to make a decisive breakthrough, an agreement was brokered by which Takelot remained king and Osorkon resumed the office of High Priest but relinquished his place in the succession. Hence, when Takelot died, the throne passed not to Osorkon but to a co-regency between Pedubast and another man named Iuput. Although by its very existence this regime perpetuated the territorial division of Egypt, it nevertheless showed its true, 'loyalist' colours by recognizing the sovereignty of the 22nd Dynasty ruling from Tanis. Osorkon was not a man to take lightly either this snub to his father's achievements, or his own exclusion from his rightful inheritance, the throne of Thebes. It was, therefore, inevitable that the unsatisfactory compromise that had ended the civil war would soon fall apart.

Hostilities broke out again just a couple of years after Takelot's death. Iuput was probably deposed or killed. But there was no easy victory for Osorkon. Instead, he was expelled once again from the High Priesthood of Amun, to be replaced by a Pedubast supporter. Worse still, he was forced to leave Thebes itself. His exile lasted nearly a decade. Osorkon and his siblings now joined forces to restore their fortunes. The initial moves were taken by Osorkon's younger brother, Bakenptah. With significant military support, he managed to secure for himself the governorship of Herakleopolis, dislodging those loyal to Pedubast. This new power-base provided the crucial springboard for an all-out assault on Thebes. Osorkon and his brother set sail for Upper Egypt at the head of their forces. In a surprisingly swift campaign, they defeated all their enemies and marked their victory by celebrating the festival of Amun. Takelot's heirs were back in full control of Thebes after three decades of conflict.

Now around fifty years old, Osorkon's appetite for power had not diminished in the years of fighting. He set the seal on his return by having himself proclaimed king (Osorkon III) at Thebes, installing his own son, another Takelot, as High Priest of Amun, and his daughter Shepenwepet as God's Wife of Amun. The kingship and the two highest religious offices of Thebes were now safely in the hands of Osorkon and his immediate family. Moreover, with the young Takelot succeeding his uncle as governor of Herakleopolis, Osorkon had secured undisputed authority over the whole of Upper Egypt.

The remainder of Osorkon's life seems to have passed in relative peace and stability. When he reached his mid-seventies, after twenty-five years on the throne, and a few years before his death, he appointed his elder son Takelot (III) as his formal co-regent, to ensure a smooth and undisputed transfer of power. Father and son made as their joint monument a new temple for the god Osiris, at Thebes' great temple of Karnak. In succession to Takelot, the High Priesthood of Amun was transferred to his son (Osorkon's grandson and namesake); while another member of the royal family, Peftjauawybast, took over at Herakleopolis. As the last ruling representative of the Theban 23rd Dynasty, his eventual fate would be decided not by internal political factions, but by intervention from a wholly unexpected direction.

86 PIYE
THE FIRST BLACK PHARAOH

Throughout the New Kingdom, Nubia's bountiful gold reserves filled Egypt's coffers and funded pharaonic building projects on a lavish scale. In Egyptian tombs of the period, Nubians are shown paying tribute – literally as well as metaphorically – to their Egyptian overlords; on temple walls, the message is even more explicit, as the king smites one or more token Nubians, symbolizing their utter subjugation to Egypt's might. After this state of affairs had existed for 500 years, the Egyptians could have been mistaken for thinking that Nubia was predestined to be their vassal. In fact, nothing could have been further from the truth.

During the Third Intermediate Period, while Egypt was politically fragmented and absorbed in its own divisions, Nubia was quietly rising from the ashes of Egyptian domination. In the fertile Dongola Reach, beyond the Third Cataract, a line of native, Nubian rulers emerged; unnoticed by Egypt, they re-established the once-great Kingdom of Kush. At its heart was the great temple of Amun-Ra at Gebel Barkal. Although this had been an Egyptian foundation, the cult of Amun had gained such a stronghold in the area that the Kushites continued to observe the daily rituals in the temple. Indeed they regarded themselves as particularly devout followers of Amun. This was what made them especially dangerous to an unsuspecting and enfeebled Egypt: in some ways, the Kushite dynasty saw itself as more Egyptian than the Egyptians.

In 747 BC, the throne of Kush passed to a man named Piye. Little is known about the first two decades of his reign, although his chosen throne-name – Usermaatra, after the great pharaoh Ramesses II – surely gave an indication of his sense of destiny. In 728 BC he burst onto the Egyptian stage, in response to the expansionary ambitions of Tefnakht, ruler of the Delta city of Sais. Tefnakht had already brought the entire western half of the Delta under his sway. He now laid siege to Herakleopolis (ancient Hnes) and succeeded in extending his control over much of Middle Egypt. Only Hermopolis stood between Tefnakht and the sacred sites of Upper Egypt, Abydos and Thebes itself. Reports of the situation reached Piye but he bided his time. The defection of the ruler of Hermopolis, Nimlot, to Tefnakht's side changed the whole situation. Piye immediately ordered his forces inside Egypt to re-conquer Hermopolis, and dispatched further contingents northwards to provide support. In the course of two battles waged near Herakleopolis, Tefnakht's southward expansion was halted.

When he had finished celebrating the New Year festival at Napata, at the beginning of his twenty-first year as king of Kush,

Piye decided to set forth for Egypt at the head of his army. His first stop was Thebes where, in the manner of a rightful pharaoh, he took part in the Opet Festival. After this brief pause, Piye continued northwards and besieged Hermopolis. With the city's food supplies exhausted and its population on the brink of starvation, Nimlot surrendered and sued for mercy. To show his disgust, Piye had his enemy's female relatives and retainers brought before him but, instead of looking at them, walked straight out and headed for his royal stables. He told Nimlot: 'I swear, as Ra loves me and as my nostrils are rejuvenated with life, it is more grievous in my heart that my horses have suffered hunger than any evil deed you have done in the prosecution of your desire.' Horses and horsemanship were key elements of Kushite court culture, and Piye had evidently inherited these national passions; but his indifference to the suffering of Nimlot's womenfolk also shows a ruthless streak. Piye was in no mood for compromise; nothing less than the complete surrender of Egypt would satisfy him.

True to form, his next move was to relieve the siege of Herakleopolis; its ruler, Peftjauawybast, greeted his Nubian liberators with joy. On the way north to the capital, another three towns surrendered to Piye's forces. Memphis itself, however, presented more of a challenge. The city shut its gates against the Kushite army and put up stiff resistance. Piye's tactics were as effective as they were inspired. He captured all the boats in the harbour of Memphis and used their masts and rigging to construct scaling ladders. With these, his soldiers managed to climb over the city walls. Fierce fighting ensued, with much loss of life, but the outcome was never in doubt: Piye appeared in the temple of Ptah, the city's grandest, to claim victory.

With the whole of Upper Egypt and the capital city in Nubian hands, the remaining Delta rebels knew they had no alternative but to surrender. In total, four kings, the prince of the West, four Great Chiefs of the Ma and a host of local chiefs and city mayors capitulated to Piye and his Nubian forces. His re-conquest of Egypt was complete and he headed for home. On his journey south, he paused only in Thebes, to present booty to the temple of Amun, and to have his relative, Amenirdis I, adopted by the incumbent God's

Wife of Amun as her successor. This would guarantee the Kushites' continued control of the Theban region. Piye then continued on to Napata, never again to set foot in Egypt.

He used the occasion of the next New Year festival to celebrate his famous victory by commissioning an enormous stela, copies of which were set up in the temples at Gebel Barkal, Karnak and Memphis. During his thrust north through Egypt, Piye must have seen at first hand many of the monuments built by the great pharaohs of the past, and they evidently left a lasting impression. He consciously modelled the style of his victory inscription on earlier texts, beginning an archaizing trend that was to characterize the court culture of the 25th Dynasty.

Surrounded by his five wives, six daughters and three sons, Piye must have been a satisfied man as he reached the end of his life. He had inherited a small state in Upper Nubia but would bequeath to his heir a kingdom that stretched over a thousand miles, from the Fourth Cataract to the Mediterranean Sea. He had reversed the pattern of history, conquering the erstwhile conquerors and imposing Nubian rule on the land of the pharaohs. Though he could not have realized it, his campaign of reunification would also, within a few years, bring to an end nearly three centuries of political division in Egypt, ushering in the final period of high culture known as the Late Period.

87 HARWA
STEWARD OF THE DIVINE ADORATRICE

In the Third Intermediate Period and the centuries following, Thebes was the largest and most important regional centre in Upper Egypt, the effective 'capital of the south'; its great temple of Amun-Ra at Karnak was the grandest, wealthiest and politically most influential religious establishment in the country. These two, closely intertwined factors gave the city a major voice in national affairs and its governors economic and political power to rival any Memphite official.

Few men exemplify this better than Harwa. He was born around 720 BC into a family of Theban priests. He followed this same career path, achieving one of the highest positions in the Amun priesthood, High Steward to the Divine Adoratrice. As one of the king's personal representatives at Thebes, the Divine Adoratrice held enormous symbolic power which, in reality, was exercised by her High Steward, as head of her household. Harwa served both Amenirdis I, installed by Piye, and her successor, Shepenwepet II, Piye's own daughter.

His authority and influence are highlighted by the fact that eight statues of him survive, a remarkable number for a person of non-royal birth. One of them shows Harwa with a large face, almond-shaped eyes and a thin-lipped mouth – the image of determination – and an enormously corpulent body, demonstrating his great wealth. The statues' inscriptions listed Harwa's many titles and offices and boasted of the esteem in which he was held by his royal mistress and the king. Equally striking are the new metaphors which Harwa used to describe himself: 'a refuge for the wretched, a float for the drowning, a ladder for him who is in the abyss.' The man of power was perhaps also a man of letters.

As politically the most influential person in Thebes, responsible for a territory stretching from Middle Egypt to the First Cataract, Harwa commissioned for himself a tomb of appropriate grandeur. Consciously modelled on the Osireion ('tomb' of Osiris) at Abydos, each part of the monument symbolized a different step on the path to eternal life. Yet, despite Harwa's long career, his tomb was never finished. However, one of his grave goods left no doubt as to his power and self-image. A servant figurine (*shabti*) with royal attributes suggests that he was effectively viceroy of Upper Egypt, governing on the king's behalf. Even so, this assumption of royal attributes by a commoner was unparalleled: perhaps even being Governor of Upper Egypt was not enough for a man of Harwa's vaunting ambition.

88 MONTUEMHAT
GOVERNOR OF THEBES IN UNCERTAIN TIMES

The Assyrian invasion of Egypt in 667 BC and the capture and sack of Thebes three years later echoed around the ancient world and fundamentally altered the politics of the Near East. Fearing the approaching onslaught, the last Kushite king of Egypt, Tanutamani, fled back to his dynasty's homeland in Upper Nubia, abandoning Thebes to its fate. Once the Assyrians had made their point, they withdrew back to their own Mesopotamian heartland, leaving Egypt in the hands of a satrap (governor), Nekau, and his son, Psamtik. Although technically an Assyrian vassal, Psamtik of Sais promptly declared himself king and ruled as an independent pharaoh. To begin with, his authority was confined to the north of the country, leaving a power vacuum in Upper Egypt. However, a Theban potentate named Montuemhat was able to ride the storm and survive every vicissitude. His is a remarkable story of resilience and survival in the face of political turmoil.

Montuemhat came from an important Theban family, which seems to have included among its members both Harwa (no. 87) and Padiamenope (no. 89). This local dynasty held all the main levers of power in Thebes. Montuemhat himself – named in honour of the ancient god of Thebes, Montu – combined several key offices: Prince of Thebes, Governor of Upper Egypt, and Fourth Prophet of Amun. This last gave him a role in the Karnak priesthood which remained one of the wealthiest and most influential bodies in the country.

He first achieved high office under the Kushite pharaoh Taharqo, and his subsequent career spanned half a century. He came through both the brief reign of Tanutamani and the Assyrian invasion unscathed. In the early years of the 26th Dynasty, he and the High Stewards of the God's Wife Shepenwepet II ruled Upper Egypt together as a virtually autonomous state, their jurisdiction reaching from Elephantine (ancient Abu) in the south to Hermopolis (ancient Khemnu) in the north. Through his wise administration, Montuemhat 'placed Upper Egypt on the right path when the whole land was upside down'.

His primary concern, in the wake of the Assyrian destruction of his home city, was to restore and rebuild the great temples of Thebes.

His accomplishments in this sphere were his proudest achievement, recorded in an autobiographical inscription at Karnak:

> *'I have renewed the temple of Mut-the-Great...*
>> *so that it is more beautiful than before.*
> *I adorned her bark with electrum, all its images*
>> *with genuine stones.*
> *I renewed the bark of Khonsu-the-Child... the bark of Amun,*
>> *Lord of the Thrones of the Two Lands...*
> *I rebuilt the divine boat of Osiris in Abydos,*
>> *when I found it gone to ruin.'*

The installation of princess Nitiqret (no. 90), daughter of Psamtik I, as God's Wife of Amun-elect marked the transfer of power in Thebes from the old regime to the Saite dynasty. As prince of Thebes, Montuemhat had to agree to provide Nitiqret with regular provisions: bread, milk, cake and herbs every day; and three oxen and five geese every month. Montuemhat's eldest son Nesptah and his wife Wedjarenes made similar commitments. Against expectations, Psamtik decided to retain Montuemhat's services, confirming him in his position. A man of such fortitude and experience was more useful on the king's side than agitating in the background.

With renewed security of tenure, Montuemhat turned his attention to posterity, in particular his magnificent tomb on the Asasif near Deir el-Bahri and the statues he intended to set up at Karnak. The tomb, featuring a sun-court, was decorated with exceptionally fine reliefs; its first court featured huge carved panels depicting symmetrically arranged pairs of papyrus plants. As for his statues, they revealed the artistic energy of Late Period Thebes, as well as the desire to hark back to earlier models, to reaffirm Egyptian cultural values in the face of foreign domination. Their quantity and quality have, as Montuemhat would have wished, made him one of the best-attested individuals from this turbulent period of Egyptian history.

89 PADIAMENOPE
OWNER OF THE LARGEST PRIVATE TOMB IN EGYPT

Like Montuemhat (no. 88), Padiamenope lived at Thebes through the turbulent years spanning the end of the 25th and the beginning of the 26th Dynasty. He, too, witnessed the flight of the last Nubian pharaoh, Tanutamani, and the subsequent sack of Thebes by the Assyrians, not only surviving these momentous events but prospering. He, too, was buried in a magnificent tomb, cut into the bedrock in the same part of the Theban necropolis. However, unlike his contemporary, Padiamenope remains something of an enigma. His tomb is the largest private funerary monument in the whole of Thebes, perhaps the whole of Egypt; yet the man himself never rose above the rank of Chief Lector-Priest. The corpus of inscriptions relating to Padiamenope is extensive, comprising *shabti*-figurines, an offering table, a temple text and at least seven statues; yet in none of these does he mention either the kings he served or – even more peculiarly – the name of his father. Padiamenope, it seems, was guarded about the source of his great wealth.

What we do know is that he was a Theban by birth and lived his entire life in that great religious city of Upper Egypt. His mother, Namenkhaset, played the sistrum and sang in the cult of Amun part time, in common with many wives of high officials. Padiamenope would therefore have grown up acquainted with some of the mysteries of Karnak temple. On reaching adulthood, he entered the priesthood, more specifically training as a lector-priest, one of the group of learned priest-scholars who guarded, interpreted and developed the liturgy for use in the great temples of the land. Padiamenope evidently excelled at this work, for he rose to be Chief Lector-Priest of Amun, Overseer of Scribes of the Divine Books and Keeper of His God's Secrets. While these positions gave him an important role within the temple cult, they did not equate to one of the great offices of state and he remained outside the upper echelons of the priesthood.

None the less, Padiamenope was able to commission for himself a truly stupendous tomb. Like those of his near-contemporaries, it was orientated towards a small way-station, built on the ruins of the causeway of Hatshepsut's mortuary temple. This small structure was used as a resting-place during the annual Beautiful Festival of the Valley, when the sacred image of Amun-Ra left its sanctuary at Karnak to pay a visit to Deir el-Bahri. Through the proximity of his tomb to the route taken by the divine image, Padiamenope hoped to share in the good fortune bestowed by Amun-Ra, through all eternity. The tomb itself was an impressive piece of architecture. Its sunken outer court measured 31.4 by 23.2 m (103 by 76 ft) and was reached by a flight of steps descending from ground level between two massive mudbrick walls supporting an arched gateway. The first court connected by means of a doorway with an inner court.

The numerous titles and epithets listed inside the tomb included several that hinted at special favour in royal circles: beloved sole companion (rather than the usual 'sole companion'), Overseer of All the King's Affairs, 'who is in the heart of his lord', 'king's beloved acquaintance', and 'revered in the king's presence'. Perhaps this helps to explain the apparent wealth of Padiamenope, even if he thought that it was better not to flaunt such patronage on public monuments like statues. The political upheavals during his lifetime seem to have taught him that discretion was the better part of valour.

In keeping with his professional interest in sacred writings, Padiamenope's tomb was decorated almost exclusively with religious texts; curiously, they most closely resemble those dating to the late Ramesside Period, some five hundred years earlier. It seems that the historical scholar wished to surround himself in the afterlife with the fruits of his research in the temple library. The 25th and early 26th Dynasties were a period of intense interest in earlier cultural forms, whether literary or artistic, and Padiamenope emerges as a leading figure in this archaizing movement.

90 NITIQRET (NITOCRIS)
GOD'S WIFE, KING'S SERVANT

The sacred office of God's Wife of Amun was not just of great religious significance, it was also politically important: when held by a close female relative, it gave the king the means of controlling the Theban priesthood and, by extension, the southern half of the country. For a monarch such as Psamtik I with a strictly provincial power-base in the northwestern Delta, this would have been a key objective. Moreover the legitimacy conferred by close association with the Amun cult would have been particularly attractive to a new dynasty, particularly one which had come to power as Assyrian vassals. Hence, in the ninth year of his reign, Psamtik I sent his eldest daughter to join the college of priestesses at Karnak with the aim of securing her eventual succession as God's Wife of Amun.

Nitiqret must have been very young when she was sent to Karnak in spring 656 BC, since she is known to have lived for another seventy years. On the appointed day, she was escorted to the quayside at the royal residence and went aboard her ship for the sixteen-day river journey to Thebes. Details of the voyage, which had all the ceremony of a royal progress, were recorded by the flotilla's proud commander, Sematawytefnakht (I) (no. 91).

On her arrival at Thebes, Nitiqret was taken immediately to the great temple of Amun-Ra at Karnak where she was formally welcomed by an oracle of the god. She was then introduced to the incumbent God's Wife of Amun, Piye's daughter Shepenwepet II. An agreement was reached between Psamtik I and the Theban hierarchy whereby Nitiqret would succeed to the office of God's Wife only after the death of both the current incumbent and her designated successor (Amenirdis II). The formalities over, Nitiqret's adoption as eventual heir was witnessed by 'all the prophets, priests and friends of the temple', and a formal record of the contract was made in writing.

Crucially, it signed over to Nitiqret all the property of the God's Wife of Amun 'in country and town'. Indeed, economic considerations were at the heart of the agreement. For his part, Psamtik I claimed that he had endowed Nitiqret 'better than those who were before her'. This was no idle boast, since her dowry included 1,800 arouras (486 ha, 1,118 acres) of land in Upper Egypt and its produce, together with daily and monthly supplies from the royal estate and the temples under the king's control in the Delta. In return for this sizeable endowment, Nitiqret was to receive daily and monthly supplies from some of Thebes' most powerful individuals, including Montuemhat (no. 88). Nitiqret's adoption as heiress to the God's Wife of Amun thus marked the formal recognition of Saite suzerainty in Thebes, the last stronghold of the previous Kushite dynasty: until the year before, all Theban documents had been dated according to the years of Tanutamani's reign, even though the last Kushite pharaoh had long since abandoned Egypt.

Although Nitiqret did not expect to become God's Wife for many decades, she came into her inheritance rather sooner than her adoption contract had stipulated. With the Kushites expelled from Egypt, it was no longer reasonable nor politically expedient for Psamtik I's appointee to wait such a long time to succeed. So, when Shepenwepet II died, some time in the latter years of Psamtik I's reign, the designated heiress Amenirdis II was passed over, retaining the deputy position of Divine Adoratrice, while Nitiqret became God's Wife. Once installed, she held office for the next quarter of a century, dying in 586 BC, in the fourth year of the reign of Apries. She was buried, with great ceremony, in a splendid tomb-chapel in the forecourt of Ramesses III's mortuary temple at Medinet Habu, at the heart of the Theban necropolis. The Delta princess had come to the end of her long journey.

91 SEMATAWYTEFNAKHT (I)
ROYAL FLOTILLA COMMANDER

On 2 March 656 BC a splendid flotilla set out from the royal residence, bound for the religious capital of Thebes, some 960 km (600 miles) to the south. The ships were fully crewed and laden with provisions.

This was no ordinary convoy: its purpose was to convey Nitiqret (no. 90), the king's daughter, to the great temple of Amun-Ra at Karnak. There, she would be received by the priesthood and acknowledged as the future God's Wife of Amun, the most important sacred office in Egypt after the High Priest himself.

In overall charge of the journey was the Flotilla Commander Sematawytefnakht, and the next sixteen days of sailing up the Nile were to be the pinnacle of his career, the most important two weeks of his life. His background, upbringing and rise to prominence are all obscure. He probably came from the town of Herakleopolis (ancient Hnes), a few days' sailing south of Memphis. By 656 BC he had become governor of the local region, the twentieth nome of Upper Egypt, known to the ancient Egyptians by the charmingly descriptive name of 'upper pomegranate-tree'. Sematawytefnakht was also Chief of the Harbour at the royal residence, responsible for all river-borne traffic in and out of the most prestigious port in the country. With a combination of courtly, military and logistical experience, Sematawytefnakht was the ideal choice to supervise Nitiqret's elaborate royal progress.

Planning for the journey had been going on for months in advance. Royal messengers had travelled upstream the length of the route, to persuade and cajole all the provincial governors through whose lands the flotilla would pass to supply provisions for the princess and her enormous retinue. Each nomarch would be responsible for providing the bread, beer, meat, poultry, fruit and vegetables to feed the convoy. In this way, the royal exchequer would be spared the entire burden of financing such a costly undertaking, and the regional potentates would be able to display their loyalty to the ruling dynasty.

By the time the day of departure dawned, all was ready. As marshals cleared the way, Nitiqret went in procession from the king's private apartments to the harbour side. Sematawytefnakht was probably at the quayside to supervise the embarkation. Sixteen days later, the flotilla under his command arrived safely at Thebes, to be met by throngs of people, shouting and clamouring for a glimpse of the princess. The second she stepped ashore, Sematawytefnakht's job was finished. He had enjoyed only a brief moment of fame, but it had been enough to secure his immortality.

92 AHMOSE II (AMASIS)
USURPER WHO MADE PEACE WITH THE GREEKS

The 26th Dynasty came to power as Assyrian vassals, when Assurbanipal installed Nekau I and his son Psamtik to rule Egypt after the invasion of 667 BC. However, little more than fifty years later, the Assyrian empire crumbled and its capital, Nineveh, was destroyed; Babylonia was the new power in the region. After another half-century, the plates shifted again, and Persia emerged as the dominant force in western Asia, with territorial ambitions stretching from the Aegean to the Indus. As Egypt contemplated the renewed threat from the east, its rulers were compelled to look for strategic support to the only other major force in the eastern Mediterranean, the Greek states.

It was into this complex and dangerous situation that Ahmose II was born, in the early years of the sixth century BC. Little is known of his background. Despite his classically Egyptian name, he was probably of Libyan ancestry, descended from prisoners of war who had settled in the Delta in Ramesside times. His distinctive physiognomy – a long face with eyes set high in his head – certainly suggests non-Egyptian ethnicity. Like many of his time, Ahmose saw the military as a route to the top. He joined the army and rose swiftly, achieving the rank of general towards the end of the reign of Apries (589–570 BC).

Apries was wary of Greek power and, in an attempt to keep it in check, dispatched the Egyptian army in 570 BC to attack the Greek city of Cyrene on the Libyan coast. Unfortunately, the king had not reckoned on his opponents' military skill. The Egyptian army suffered a disastrous defeat and the native troops rebelled, their resentment against Apries fanned by what they perceived as the privileges enjoyed by the foreign mercenaries fighting alongside them. As the leading Egyptian general, Ahmose was at the centre of the rebellion and seized his chance. Bolstered by the support of his troops, he ousted Apries and claimed the throne. Apries fled the country and sought refuge at the court of his arch-rival, Nebuchadnezzar II of Babylon. Three years later, Apries attempted a counter-coup against Ahmose II with Babylonian assistance. The two forces met in the Delta and Ahmose inflicted a crushing defeat. Apries was either killed in battle or captured and executed. The new pharaoh reigned unchallenged.

According to later Greek historians, Ahmose II's humble origins did not fit him for the highest office in the land, and he was incapable of behaving in a properly regal manner. However, this reputation probably reflected Ahmose's economic policies, which levied particularly high taxes on Greek traders living in Egypt, rather than his true character. The evidence from his forty-four-year reign (570–526 BC) suggests that he fulfilled the traditional duties of Egyptian kingship in an exemplary manner. He maintained a strong naval presence in the eastern Mediterranean and Red Sea (staffed with men like Wedjahorresnet, no. 93), to protect Egyptian trade routes. He was a master of domestic policy, reforming Egypt's judicial system and carrying out a substantial temple-building programme. He commissioned a shrine to the goddess Isis on the island of Philae and a more substantial temple in Memphis. This was the first major centre of the Isis cult in Egypt, paving the way for its great popularity and subsequent expansion across the Mediterranean and as far as Britain.

To boost the Egyptian economy, Ahmose II concentrated all Greek trading activity in the Delta city of Naukratis, where Greeks had first been encouraged to settle in the reign of Psamtik I. Ahmose's Greek policy was concerned with more than trade, however. Always astute in matters of foreign policy, he took pains to cultivate the friendship of the Aegean states, recognizing that a strong alliance offered the best defence against the Babylonians and Persians – and, indeed, against an invasion of Egypt by the Greeks themselves. Ahmose therefore exchanged diplomatic gifts with Greek rulers, reinforced his army with Greek mercenaries, and made the ultimate diplomatic gesture of friendship by paying for the reconstruction of the sanctuary of Apollo at Delphi – one of the most important sites of

Greek religion – after it had been destroyed by fire in 548 BC. One of Ahmose's wives may even have been the daughter of a Greek family living in Egypt.

Having come to the throne as a usurper, Ahmose II took steps to entrench his family's position. He had his daughter Nitiqret (II) appointed heir to the incumbent God's Wife of Amun, while his son Psamtik was designated heir apparent. Two further children, Pasenenkhonsu and Ahmose, seemed destined to perpetuate the dynasty. But it was not to be. Far to the east, Cyrus II ('the Great') had united the Medes and Persians in 550 BC and proceeded to conquer Babylon eleven years later, defeating its last king, Belsharusur (Belshazzar) – who did, indeed, fail to see the writing on the wall. Sweeping on westwards, Cyrus added the Greek states of Asia Minor to his expanding empire, and became the sole great power of the Levant. By 530 BC or thereabouts, the Persian army was in Egypt's back yard, waiting for any sign of weakness to attack.

The constant threat of Persian invasion overshadowed Ahmose II's last years as king. His personal determination, strength of character and astute diplomatic alliances succeeded in keeping the enemy at bay for a time. But at the moment of his death, the Persians invaded, led by their new king Cambyses. Ahmose's son, Psamtik III, was sadly unequal to the task of defending his inheritance, and Egypt swiftly capitulated. The age-old office of God's Wife of Amun was terminated. The rest of Ahmose's family either fled or were killed. The fate of Ahmose himself is also a mystery. He had presumably prepared a tomb within the precincts of the temple at Sais, but it has never been found. His reputation was to rest, not on a lavish burial or magnificent monument, but on his achievement in maintaining Egyptian independence against all the odds.

93 WEDJAHORRESNET
ADMIRAL WHO COLLABORATED WITH THE PERSIANS

When the Persian general Cambyses invaded Egypt in 525 BC, deposed the weak and ineffectual king Psamtik III and absorbed Egypt into an expanding Persian empire, the land of the pharaohs found itself politically subordinate to a radically different culture. The response of the Egyptian elite to this unprecedented challenge is graphically illustrated by the life of Wedjahorresnet. The ultimate pragmatist (some would say collaborator), he chose not to fight the Persian invaders but to win them over to his – and Egypt's – way of doing things, by a combination of loyalty and persuasion.

Wedjahorresnet came from the northwestern Delta city of Sais, which was the ancient cult centre of the warrior goddess Neith, and the home and power-base of the 26th (Saite) Dynasty. His father was a priest in the local temple, and Wedjahorresnet's own devotion to Neith was to be one of the driving forces of his life. He first achieved high office in the reign of Ahmose (no. 92) and, like his king, carved out a successful career in the military, reaching the exalted rank of Admiral of the Fleet. Little is known of Wedjahorresnet's naval activities, but under Ahmose's ephemeral successor, Psamtik III, they must have included battles against the Persians.

When the invasion came, the Egyptians reacted with horror. Wedjahorresnet himself described the Persian conquest in graphic terms as 'the monstrous cataclysm which happened in the entire land'. He boasted of having saved his city from the worst effects of the invasion, but it is equally clear that he did so not by resistance, but by collaboration with the Persians. Egypt's new ruler, Cambyses, lost no time in appointing Wedjahorresnet to high civilian office, making him a companion (interestingly, a traditional Egyptian rank denoting a member of the monarch's inner circle) and Controller of the Palace. Cambyses had evidently decided to retain the services of Egyptian officials who were willing to work with the new regime, while making sure that military power was firmly in loyal Persian hands. Wedjahorresnet could not have hoped to remain a high-ranking naval officer, but his leadership skills were clearly recognized and directed anew.

He set about using his influence to try and safeguard the traditions of his homeland. As personnel officer at the royal court, Wedjahorresnet took care to appoint new staff members from the ranks of the Egyptian nobility, thus ensuring cultural continuity at the centre of political power. When he gained further promotion, to the sensitive post of Chief Physician, he took it upon himself to go one stage further and convert the Persian conqueror into a model Egyptian pharaoh. He was especially concerned to protect his city and its temple from depredation and ruin, so he petitioned Cambyses to have foreigners expelled from the precinct of Neith at Sais so that it could be restored to its former state. For his part, Cambyses obviously recognized the political advantages of being seen to act as a model pharaoh, so he agreed to Wedjahorresnet's request and subsequently honoured the cult of Neith with a royal visit. Wedjahorresnet's lobbying, combined with pragmatism on both sides, saved the day for Sais.

Under Cambyses' successor, Darius I, Wedjahorresnet remained a key player at court. He was summoned by the Persian king to distant Susa, at the heart of the Persian empire, before being sent back to Egypt to restore its temples. Wedjahorresnet paid particular attention to the House of Life (temple scriptorium) at Sais, since this was the institution which, above all others, preserved and transmitted Egyptian religious and cultural traditions from one generation to another. Wedjahorresnet was ensuring not only the immediate survival of his local temple, but the long-term survival of his national identity.

It is entirely fitting that his lasting memorial, a statue inscribed with an account of his remarkable career, should have been set up in the temple of Neith. His hope was that his goddess would guarantee him eternal life. He had already repaid the compliment.

94 WENNEFER (ONNOFRI)
SNAKE DOCTOR AND POLITICAL SURVIVOR

Wennefer was a medical specialist, practised in the treatment of snake bites and scorpion stings. Exotic as his profession may have been, he could not have predicted that his life would involve extraordinary twists and turns of fate, mirroring Egypt's political travails in the second half of the 30th Dynasty.

Wennefer was born in the central Delta town of Behbeit el-Hagar (ancient Hebyt), in the twelfth Lower Egyptian nome (province). The provincial capital, Samannud (ancient Tjebnutjer), was less than 16 km (10 miles) away, and had only recently been propelled from regional to national importance after a local man, Nakhtnebef (Nectanebo I), had come to power as pharaoh and founder of the 30th Dynasty. Wennefer therefore grew up in the heartland of the new royal family, and this accident of geography and history influenced his later life profoundly.

Initially, however, he seemed destined to follow in his father's footsteps with employment in the local temple. Here he seems to have developed a more specialist interest in magic/medicine (the two were effectively indivisible in ancient Egypt). As Director of the *wab*-Priests of Sekhmet in Hetepet, he would have been involved in carrying out ritual sacrifices.

Sacred office and secular responsibility often went hand in hand in ancient Egypt. This was certainly the case for Wennefer who, in 362/361 BC, received his first royal commands, one religious, one administrative. His sacred task was to oversee the lavish funeral of the Apis bull and the search for its successor. On the secular side, his mission was no less important. When the satraps of the Asiatic coast revolted against their Persian overlords, the Egyptian king, Djedher (Teos), decided to take advantage of the situation and go to war himself against the Persian ruler Artaxerxes II; Wennefer was put in charge of keeping the expedition's official record. In a society where the written record carried enormous symbolic and religious weight, this was a highly significant appointment. It shows that Wennefer was already a trusted member of the dynasty's inner circle.

But events soon took a more sinister turn. Djedher marched with his army towards Asia to engage the Persian forces. No sooner had the king left Egypt than a letter was delivered to the ruler governing the country in Djedher's absence, implicating Wennefer in a plot. He was arrested, bound in copper chains, taken into the ruler's presence, and interrogated. By some stroke of luck or guile, Wennefer not only escaped punishment but also turned the situation to his advantage. The details are sketchy, but he emerged from the interrogation as a loyal confidant of the ruler (just as he had been of the king), given official protection and showered with gifts. He was even entrusted with a diplomatic mission of the greatest sensitivity, to sail to Asia at the head of a flotilla of transport ships and warships in order to find Djedher. Wennefer tracked the king down at Susa, before being sent back to Egypt.

On his arrival, Wennefer was welcomed and embraced by the Egyptian ruler's messenger; the two men spent the whole day together, with Wennefer recounting the details of his journey. Indeed, he became one of the closest and most loyal followers of the new king, Nakhthorheb (no. 95). On his monarch's behalf, Wennefer restored the mortuary cults of two kings from distant antiquity: Sneferu and Djedefra of the 4th Dynasty. For the 30th Dynasty and its supporters, the propaganda value in restoring these cults was obvious: it associated the new royal family with two of the most illustrious kings from the Pyramid Age.

Wennefer's reward for helping to legitimize Nakhthorheb's accession included a host of honorific titles, lucrative benefices in a number of Delta towns, and the privilege of a tomb near the Serapeum at Saqqara. His funerary monument was impressive indeed: with an avenue of sphinxes leading to a pylon gateway, a four-columned hypostyle hall and three small chapels, it was a veritable temple in miniature. Inside the burial chamber, his final resting-place was a diorite sarcophagus; his grave goods included eighty-two servant statuettes of faience.

In the central chapel of his temple-tomb, Wennefer had himself depicted resplendent in a large surcoat and a fringed Persian-style scarf, the characteristic costume of the 30th Dynasty elite. From relatively humble beginnings, he had acquired prominence, prestige and wealth through a combination of luck, astute manoeuvring, and hedging his bets at a time of great political uncertainty. His career had taken him from a town in the Delta to the heart of the Persian empire and back again: an extraordinary journey for a doctor of snake bites and scorpion stings.

95 NAKHTHORHEB (NECTANEBO II)
EGYPT'S LAST NATIVE RULER

The clash between the Greek world and the Persian empire, which formed the backdrop to the story of Wennefer (no. 94), also provided the context for the last native-born Egyptian to rule the Nile Valley until modern times. Nakhthorheb, better known as Nectanebo II, was the great-nephew of the founder of the 30th Dynasty, Nakhtnebef. He was still a young man, serving in the Egyptian army on campaign in Phoenicia, when Spartan mercenaries deposed his uncle, King Djedher, and installed Nakhthorheb in his place. The ousted monarch fled into the arms of Egypt's arch-enemy, Artaxerxes II of Persia, a desperate and fateful move that would ultimately spell the end of Egyptian independence.

The army returned to Egypt, but Nakhthorheb did not exactly receive a hero's welcome. He was besieged at Tanis by the prince of Mendes, a serious rival for the throne, and only saved by the military intervention of Agesilaos, the king of Sparta who had promoted Nakhthorheb's candidature in the first place. The young pharaoh must have realized the precariousness of his position, so he set about winning support from the most influential bodies in the land, the priesthoods of the great temples. The best way of doing this was to carry out the traditional kingly duty of embellishing and magnifying the homes of the gods (and, not incidentally, the wealth of their priests). Nakhthorheb's programme embraced additions to many of the existing cult centres, and the construction of an entirely new temple to Isis at Behbeit el-Hagar in the Delta. Statues of previous 30th Dynasty rulers were set up in sanctuaries throughout Egypt, and Nakhthorheb himself used sculpture to associate himself closely with Horus, the traditional god of kingship. Under the king's patronage, the arts and literature flourished, and Egyptian culture enjoyed something of a renaissance.

But indulging Egypt's sense of national identity could not mask the stark reality of the country's diminished power in the Near East, nor could it keep at bay the forces that sought to snuff out Egyptian sovereignty. The first challenge came in 351 BC, just a decade into Nakhthorheb's reign. The Persians, no doubt egged on by the exiled Djedher, attempted to invade Egypt. Nakhthorheb's forces prevailed, but this victory bred in the king an unwarranted and dangerous complacency. Thinking himself equal to any opposition, he neglected to make treaties with the Greeks and other regional powers. It was a fatal mistake. Seven years later, the Persians returned, this time led from the front by their great king Artaxerxes III. They massed at the fortified Delta city of Pelusium, facing Nakhthorheb's army of 100,000 men. Numbers alone, however, were not enough to save the Egyptians. The Persian forces captured Pelusium and pressed on to the capital, Memphis. Accepting the inevitable, Nakhthorheb fled the country.

His fate is unknown. He may have gone to Nubia, where pharaonic culture had implanted itself and would survive many more centuries. A more tantalizing possibility, reflected in medieval myth, is that he found his way to the court of Philip of Macedon, Persia's main adversary, there to attract the attentions of Philip's wife Olympias, and so father Alexander the Great. Such a story is impossible to verify, and perhaps unlikely, but it is a fact that Alexander and the Ptolemies honoured Nakhthorheb's memory and built shrines for his cult.

A more certain, though less edifying, fate awaited the unused stone sarcophagus of Egypt's last native pharaoh: it found its way to Alexandria and was used as a water-tank for public ablutions.

96 SEMATAWYTEFNAKHT (II)
EYEWITNESS OF ALEXANDER'S CONQUEST

With the long lens of history, the Persian invasion of 341 BC seems like a cataclysmic event, for it brought to an abrupt end the pattern of pharaonic government that had served ancient Egypt for a period of nearly 3,000 years. However, the events of the mid-fourth century BC may not have appeared as traumatic to those who lived through them. That, at least, is the impression given by one man who not only survived the Persian invasion and its aftermath, but evidently prospered under successive regimes.

Sematawytefnakht, like his namesake of three centuries earlier (no. 91), came from Herakleopolis in Middle Egypt. He was named after one of the local gods, Sematawy ('He who unites the Two Lands'), whose sanctuary lay inside the town of Herakleopolis. The chief local deity, however, was the ram-god Herishef. Sematawytefnakht's devotion to this latter god ran as a continuous thread throughout his life.

He began his career in the reign of Nakhthorheb (no. 95), and witnessed at first hand the Persian invasion. Although he later described this as a disaster, at the time he showed no hesitation in making his peace and ingratiating himself with the Persian ruler, Artaxerxes III. Indeed, Sematawytefnakht was appointed Chief Priest of Sekhmet: in effect, royal physician. In this capacity, Sematawytefnakht took his place at the heart of Artaxerxes III's court and accompanied his master back to Persia. From this vantage point, only a few years later, he witnessed the defeat of Artaxerxes' successor, Darius III, by the forces of Alexander the Great at the Battle of Issus in 333 BC. Once again, Sematawytefnakht found himself caught up in major events; once again, he escaped unscathed. He attributed his good fortune to the benevolent protection of his god Herishef:

'You protected me in the combat of the Greeks
When you repulsed those of Asia.
They slew a million at my sides
And no one raised an arm against me.'

Without doubt, good luck and political adroitness also played their part.

Sematawytefnakht's gleeful description of the Persian defeat seems curiously at odds with his personal advancement under Persian rule; but he was ever the loyal servant of those in power, and under Macedonian rule it would have been extremely unwise to express anything other than deep hostility to the memory of the Persians.

For much of the Egyptian population, who had suffered privations and brutality under Persian rule, Alexander the Great was welcomed as a liberator. Sematawytefnakht, too, saw the way the wind was blowing, and decided to return to Egypt. He reached his home town safe and sound, his head 'not robbed of a hair'. By the end of his career, he had accumulated a dazzling array of honours and offices. Besides royal physician, he was also Supervisor of the Riverbank; priest of the gods of the Oryx-nome; priest of Horus Lord of Hebnu; and priest of Sematawy, the god after whom he had been named. So, in his own words, he ended his life 'blessed by his lord, revered in his nome'.

Above all, Sematawytefnakht was a survivor. History may dub him a collaborator, but he was content to ascribe his good fortune to his god:

> *'As my beginning was good through you,*
> *So have you made my end complete.*
> *You gave me a long lifetime in gladness.'*

97 PADIUSIR (PETOSIRIS)
DEVOTED SERVANT OF HIS LOCAL GOD

While some Egyptians, like Sematawytefnakht (no. 96), may have actively collaborated with the Persian conquerors, others, particularly in the provinces, evidently hunkered down, continued with normal life as far as possible, and quietly maintained native traditions in steely defiance of the foreign invaders. One such was Padiusir (Petosiris in Greek) of Hermopolis, known to his friends as Ankhefenkhons.

Padiusir came from a powerful local family connected with the city's temple of Thoth. Padiusir's grandfather, Djedthothiuefankh ('Thoth says he will live'), and father, Nes-Shu, had served in turn as High Priest of Thoth under the pharaohs of the 30th Dynasty. In Padiusir's own generation, the office passed first to his elder brother Djedthothiuefankh and then to Padiusir himself. Padiusir and his brother lived through the Persian invasion of 341 BC. Indeed, it was during this very period that Padiusir succeeded as 'the High Priest who sees the god in his shrine, who carries his lord and follows his lord, who enters into the holy of holies, who performs his functions together with the great prophets.' His conduct and accomplishments during a politically difficult time are a testament to his personal piety and his determination to maintain Egypt's age-old traditions. His own description of events cannot be bettered:

> 'I spent seven years as controller for this god, administering his endowment without fault being found, while the ruler of foreign lands was protector of Egypt, and nothing was in its former place, since fighting had started inside Egypt, the South being in turmoil, the North in revolt..., all temples without their servants; the priests fled, not knowing what was happening.
>
> When I became controller for Thoth Lord of Hermopolis, I put the temple of Thoth back in its former condition, I caused every rite to be as before, every priest to serve in his proper time... I made splendid what was found ruined anywhere. I restored what had decayed long ago, and was no longer in its place.'

In a stark illustration of the collapse of traditional Egyptian kingship, Padiusir even carried out a temple foundation ceremony usually reserved for the pharaoh:

> 'I stretched the cord, released the line, to found the temple of Ra in the park. I built it of fine white limestone, and finished with all kinds of work; its doors are of pine, inlaid with Asiatic copper.

I made an enclosure around the park, lest it be trampled by the rabble.'

Under Persian rule, there was an ever-present risk of social unrest. Nevertheless, Padiusir maintained all the traditional rites as best he could, taking pains to 'consult the scholars' to ensure that everything was done by the book.

To compound the political and social upheaval of the Persian occupation, Padiusir's personal life was struck by tragedy when his son Thothrekh ('Thoth knows') died young. Private sadness combined with piety to produce in Padiusir an unusually thoughtful outlook on life, recorded in inscriptions on the walls of his magnificent family tomb at Tuna el-Gebel. He emphasized, above all, that life should be lived according to 'the way of god': law-abiding and pious, but also successful and happy. In return for a lifetime of loyal service to his town and his god, Padiusir asked for a few simple rewards: 'Length of lifetime in gladness of heart; a good burial after old age; my corpse interred in this tomb beside my father and elder brother.' This simple statement encapsulated the Egyptians' most deeply held wishes: a strong family and a blessed afterlife. That Padiusir achieved both demonstrates the resilience of the ancient Egyptian governing class and of pharaonic culture against the vicissitudes of history.

98 PTOLEMY I
MACEDONIAN GENERAL WHO FOUNDED A DYNASTY

When Alexander the Great conquered Egypt in 332 BC, he was welcomed as a saviour. He might not have been an Egyptian, but he had delivered the country from the harsh rule of the hated Persians, and that was cause enough to recognize him as a legitimate pharaoh. For the next three centuries, until its absorption into the Roman world, Egypt was ruled by a Greek-speaking elite, but one that, as far as we can tell, was largely accepted as legitimate by the native population.

This was due in large measure to the efforts and character of the man who set Egypt on its new course, and after whom the period of Greek rule is named: Ptolemy.

Ptolemy son of Lagus was born in 367 or 366 BC, in the kingdom of Macedon. His mother Arsinoe may have been related to the royal family and as a boy Ptolemy was enrolled in the corps of pages at the court of King Philip. He therefore came into contact with Philip's son and heir, Alexander, and the two became close childhood friends. Ptolemy's name (Ptolemaios) derived from the epic form of the Greek word for war, *polemos*, and the boy was true to his designation. He excelled in martial activities, and fought alongside Alexander when, as king, the latter conquered most of the known world, from the shores of the Aegean to the jungles of India. As a distinguished general, Ptolemy was chosen to be one of Alexander's seven bodyguards, the inner circle of the king's most trusted companions.

Alexander's sudden death in Babylon in June 323 BC threw his empire, and his advisers, into turmoil. For the next eighteen years, Ptolemy was embroiled in the complex world of Macedonian politics, as Alexander's heirs struggled over the division of his enormous territory. Ptolemy's initial move was to prove far-sighted, or perhaps it was mere luck. Five months after Alexander's death, he arrived in Egypt to rule as satrap, having been appointed to this position – no doubt after much urging – by Alexander's half-brother and successor, Philip Arrhidaeus. Ptolemy was about forty-four years old, but he was certainly in no mood to hang up his sword and live out his days in luxury.

Ptolemy's greatest rival was Perdiccas, the man who had inherited Alexander's signet-ring and thus effectively controlled the Council of State set up to rule the empire. Perdiccas had exploited his position by seizing Alexander's Babylonian territories, and proceeded to annex the Greek colony of Cyrene, on the coast of Libya, towards the end of 322 BC. This was a direct challenge to Ptolemy, since Cyrene could provide a forward base for an attack on Egypt itself. Indeed, this attack came a year later, but Ptolemy was ready. Perdiccas was stopped in his tracks and assassinated. Ptolemy was confirmed as ruler of Egypt and Cyrene. He hijacked Alexander's body as it made its way from Babylon back to Macedon, and brought it to Egypt as a totem to legitimize his own rule.

But Ptolemy the general was still restless for further military glories. Over the next sixteen years, he involved himself in campaign after campaign, winning territory and losing it again in a seemingly endless succession of battles. Lebanon, Palestine, Cyprus, even the Cyclades: all were fought over, all lost. By 306 BC, Ptolemy seems to have decided to consolidate his rule and satisfy himself with Egypt and Cyrene: easily defended, wealthy, and undeniably prestigious. However, setting himself up as a new pharaoh was not entirely straightforward. Under Philip Arrhidaeus and his successor Alexander IV (Alexander the Great's posthumous son by Roxane), Ptolemy had technically been only satrap of Egypt. None of Alexander the Great's heirs had gone so far as to claim royal titles. Even when Alexander IV was murdered, in 311 BC, Ptolemy continued to have documents dated by his reign, for another six years. This official fiction gave Ptolemy some breathing space, as he worked out how he wished to rule Egypt, now that the Macedonian royal line was extinct. He gave a clear sign of his intentions in a proclamation of 311, carved in hieroglyphics, in which he restored the land and possessions of two of Egypt's most important cult temples. The rebirth of pharaonic rule was in the offing.

In November 305 BC, Ptolemy took the plunge. First he adopted the traditional Macedonian title of *basileus* ('king'), then a full pharaonic titulary. Once installed as king, he back-dated his reign (in good Egyptian fashion) to the death of Alexander the Great and set about creating a dynamic, hybrid Egypto-Greek civilization on the banks of the Nile. He established a new cult, of Serapis (Osiris-Apis), as the focus for worship by the Egyptian Greeks, many of whom had settled in Egypt under his encouragement. He developed Alexandria as a great cultural, political and religious centre, eclipsing the ancient capital of Memphis and confirming the Mediterranean orientation of Ptolemaic rule. Emulating such illustrious pharaohs as Amenhotep III (no. 52) and Ramesses II (no. 70), he even had himself deified, though at a safe distance from Egypt: the people of Rhodes consecrated a sacred precinct to him, the Ptolemaeum, and gave him the epithet Soter, 'saviour'. Finally, he restored the age-old institution of co-regency to ensure a smooth succession for his preferred heir. Ptolemy II Philadelphus (his younger son by his third wife, Berenice) was crowned in 284 BC. Eighteen months later, at the age of eighty-four, Ptolemy I died, the only one of Alexander's heirs to pass away from natural causes.

To historians of the Greek world, Ptolemy's greatest achievement was his magisterial account of Alexander the Great's battles, still one of the major sources for these momentous events. To Egyptologists, he was the founder of a new dynasty, and the instigator of a new age that witnessed the final flowering of Egyptian civilization – albeit with a Greek flavour.

99 MANETHO
THE FATHER OF EGYPTIAN HISTORY

Manetho is a paradox: his chronological system for ancient Egypt's rulers is still widely used and his name is famous to this day among Egyptologists, yet none of his writings survives intact and virtually nothing is known about his life. He seems to have been born at the end of the fourth century BC, at Sebennytos (modern Sammanud) in the central Delta. His career flourished in the reigns of the first two Ptolemies. Like so many of his time, he entered the priesthood, perhaps serving in the temple of Ra at Heliopolis, one of the most important cults in Egypt. His name in its Egyptian form, Meryen-netjeraa, meant 'Beloved of the Great God', suggesting that piety ran in the family. In his priestly capacity, he may have been involved with the foundation of the cult of Serapis by Ptolemy I, since a statue base inscribed with Manetho's name was found in the temple of Serapis at Carthage. Beyond these scanty details, however, Manetho the man remains a mystery.

His enduring fame rests not on the incidents of his life, but on his writings. The temples were Egypt's centres of learning, their archives the nation's repositories of knowledge. Manetho evidently had access to one or more temple libraries and used them as the source material for a number of treatises: on Egyptian religion, cult practice, medicine, and natural history. He seems to have written primarily for the (substantial) non-Egyptian population, especially the new Macedonian ruling class; perhaps he saw it as his duty to inform them of the culture and customs of their new realm. His lasting achievement was in the same vein: a monumental, three-volume history of Egypt, the *Aegyptiaca*. It is tempting to associate its composition with the foundation of the great library at Alexandria by Ptolemy II. Certainly, Manetho's work was encyclopedic in scope. In it, he organized the innumerable kings of Egypt since the foundation of the state into more easily manageable groupings, based upon presumed family links. Manetho's thirty dynasties, the 1st starting with Menes (Narmer, no. 1) and the 30th ending with Nectanebo II (Nakhthorheb, no. 95), have remained the basic chronological scheme for ancient Egypt ever since.

Like most authors of the time, Manetho was keen to entertain as well as to educate his readership. So, to the basic outline of dynasties, he added the length and principal events of each reign and observations on each king's character. Here, though, he departed from the temple records and included anecdotes drawn from folklore, and perhaps also from the works of his fellow historian, Herodotus. Manetho's more whimsical and outlandish statements about pharaonic peccadilloes have discredited his reputation in the eyes of later scholars. However, none of his works has survived intact – the *Aegyptiaca* is known only from fragments quoted in the works of later authors – so it is impossible to make an accurate and objective assessment of his scholarship. Whatever his level of accuracy, few authors could hope to have their central thesis used throughout the world two millennia after their death. That is the scale of Manetho's achievement.

100 CLEOPATRA VII
TRAGIC QUEEN WHO BECAME A LEGEND

Cleopatra: the very name conjures up images of unimaginable luxury and opulence, of love and betrayal, of beauty and tragedy – of the exoticism and mystery that are the enduring hallmarks of ancient Egypt. The story of Cleopatra and her entanglement with the Roman empire has been told and re-told, from Shakespeare to Hollywood, reflecting the prejudices and predilections of each generation. Yet at its heart is the life of a real woman, an uncommonly gifted ruler, who tried in vain to defend her land, Egypt, against the unstoppable might of Rome. Her tragedy was the tragedy of an entire civilization.

Cleopatra was born in 69 BC, the third child of Ptolemy XII. The identity of her mother is not certain but, given the Macedonian dynasty's preference for consanguineous marriages, she was probably one of Ptolemy's own sisters. Egypt was a rich country, but under Ptolemy XII it lacked political stability. When Cleopatra was just ten years old, she had to witness the indignity of her father travelling to Rome to beg for its support. It was the beginning of a doomed relationship between the ancient world's most venerable civilization and its newest upstart. Not only did Ptolemy have to pay a huge sum of money for the promise of Roman backing – the equivalent of Egypt's entire annual revenue – but his absence also prompted the outbreak of factional fighting back home. His two eldest daughters, Cleopatra VI and Berenice, were alternately proclaimed monarch in opposition to their father. Berenice went one stage further, marrying a foreign prince and raising an army to support her claim. It was only defeated with Roman assistance, and Berenice was executed for her treachery. At the age of fifteen, Cleopatra VII thus became heir-apparent. She had experienced an early lesson in the internecine rivalry that would plague her for the rest of her life.

Three years later, Ptolemy XII died, leaving the throne jointly to Cleopatra and her eldest half-brother, Ptolemy XIII. She was seventeen, he a child of ten; in effect, therefore, she was sole monarch. In the first year of her reign, 51 BC, she made it clear that she intended to honour Egypt's religious traditions by attending the funeral of the Apis bull at Memphis. She also adopted the vulture-headdress of Egyptian queens, and further endeared herself to the Egyptian people by her ability to speak their language. But cultural solidarity alone was not enough to guarantee stability. A bad harvest in 50 BC put Cleopatra's government under pressure, and her brother's supporters tried to have her removed from power. Warned in time, she escaped to Syria and raised an army to win back her birthright. Her forces marched on Egypt and engaged her brother's troops at Pelusium. The encounter ended in a stalemate, but drew the intervention of a Roman army under Julius Caesar – not out of any particular interest in Cleopatra's fate, but to settle a grudge with his rival Pompey who had sought sanctuary with Ptolemy XIII. Having entered Alexandria, Caesar acted as judge and jury in the dynastic dispute, summoning the warring siblings and coming down in favour of Cleopatra. Ptolemy XIII's supporters were not going to give up without a fight, and they besieged the royal party on the off-shore island of Pharos. A complicated struggle ensued which ended with the defeat of the Egyptian rebels and Ptolemy's death by drowning. Resisting the temptation to annex Egypt, Caesar instead had Cleopatra marry her surviving half-brother, Ptolemy XIV, and he proclaimed them joint rulers, maintaining the custom of co-regency. His interest was not entirely altruistic, however: he and Cleopatra had become lovers.

Despite the myths, Cleopatra was no beauty; her coin portraits show her with a hooked nose and jutting chin. But she was intelligent and sharp-witted, and she had at her disposal the greatest prize of all: Egypt. For an ambitious man like Caesar, that was an irresistible combination. At his invitation, she visited Rome in 46 BC, with her brother-husband, her retinue, and her young child by Caesar, whom she had named Ptolemy Caesarion. The royal party stayed for more than a year. Cleopatra's departure was prompted by Caesar's assassination on the Ides of March, 44 BC. She left the city immediately and was back in Alexandria by July. Two months later, Ptolemy XIV was also dead. Although Cleopatra's guilt cannot be proved, the finger of suspicion points clearly at her, since she had most to gain. She adopted her young son as her co-regent (Ptolemy XV), not least to secure his future. For Caesar's will had named his great-nephew Octavian as heir.

Caesar's death prompted a chain of events that ensnared Cleopatra in the power-politics of the Roman world. She was courted by his friends and murderers alike, eventually throwing in her lot with Mark Antony who had inherited control of Rome's eastern provinces. History repeated itself as Cleopatra became the lover of a second powerful Roman leader. She offered Mark Antony funds for his Parthian campaign in return for his political support – which even extended to the murder of her sole surviving sister and dynastic rival, Arsinoe. In 40 BC, now in her late twenties, Cleopatra bore Mark Antony twin children, a boy named Alexander Helios and a girl, Cleopatra Selene. In Egypt, a period of relative peace and prosperity followed, during which a third child (Ptolemy Philadelphus) was born. Meanwhile, Mark Antony's military adventures turned from disaster – against the Parthians – to victory against the Armenians. The latter was celebrated with a spectacular ceremony, the Donations of Alexandria, in which Mark Antony proclaimed Cleopatra 'Queen of Kings and of her Sons who are Kings', made symbolic grants of land to their three children, and publicly recognized Ptolemy XV as Caesar's true heir. His clear intention was to see all Roman lands ruled by his lover and her children, with himself as the puppet-master.

The inevitable confrontation with Octavian was not long in coming. Rome's new strong-man declared war on Cleopatra in 32 BC, and the two sides came to blows the following year. The decisive battle, at Actium off the west coast of Greece, was a disaster for the Egyptian forces. Cleopatra and Mark Antony fled back to Alexandria. Her plot to escape with Ptolemy XV to India was foiled, and she resigned herself to her inevitable fate. With her former allies defecting to Octavian, she offered to abdicate in favour of her children if it would save her life and Egypt's destiny, but to no avail. Octavian reached the outskirts of Alexandria and accepted the surrender of the Egyptian fleet; on 1 August 30 BC he entered the royal capital.

Thinking Cleopatra had been killed, Mark Antony stabbed himself. She tried to commit suicide on learning of her lover's death, but was overpowered and taken prisoner. Octavian allowed her to attend

Mark Antony's funeral, and then to take her own life. The two were buried side by side in the royal mausoleum. Octavian promptly had Ptolemy XV murdered and he formally annexed Egypt to Rome: the fate that Cleopatra had tried so hard to avoid.

Three thousand years of Egyptian independence were at an end. The land of the pharaohs would now be plundered as the grain-basket of the Roman empire. Cleopatra herself, however, achieved the sort of immortality of which her pharaonic predecessors could only have dreamed. In the age of celluloid, she has become the person-ification of ancient Egypt. Her story has beguiled audiences across the world and will undoubtedly continue to do so for generations to come, a symbol of our enduring fascination with the lives of the ancient Egyptians.

CHRONOLOGY AND KING LIST

The dates of ancient Egypt are generally assumed to be among the most secure in the ancient world – accurate to within two centuries *c*. 3000 BC; accurate to within two decades *c*. 1300 BC; and precise from 664 BC. But this still means that there are no precise dates for most of the period covered by this book. Different books give different dates for the same event, with the result that, for example, Narmer might have become king in 3100, 3050 or 2950 BC and the Battle of Kadesh might have taken place in 1297, 1286 or 1275 BC. Nevertheless, although there is not complete agreement among experts, there are options which are widely favoured. The dates used in this book are listed below, alongside the names of the kings of ancient Egypt.

Egyptologists normally employ a method of dividing the kings of ancient Egypt into 31 dynasties, following the practice of the Egyptian priest, Manetho, who wrote a history of his nation shortly after 300 BC. In general these dynasties correspond to particular ruling families, although in the more obscure eras of history some dynasties appear to be little more than convenient groupings of kings, some of whom were contemporary rulers in different parts of Egypt. In fact, Manetho is quite clear about this last point – that often there was more than one line of kings in Egypt.

Modern Egyptologists have grouped the dynasties into broader periods known as 'Kingdoms', when, normally, there was only one king throughout Egypt. The Old Kingdom (*c*. 2575–2125 BC) is the age of the Great Pyramid and the Great Sphinx. The Middle Kingdom (*c*. 2000–1630 BC) was an age of renewed national unity, and of a great flowering of art and literature. The New Kingdom (*c*. 1539–1069 BC) is often described as the imperial, or golden, age of ancient Egypt – the time of Amenhotep III, Akhenaten and Ramesses II, when Egypt was the richest and most powerful nation in the world. The Late Period (664–332 BC) became the final assertion of ancient Egyptian independence in the wider world, after which the country was conquered by Alexander the Great and later was absorbed by the Roman empire.

Early Dynastic Period

'DYNASTY 0'

c. 3100 BC
Existence uncertain
Ka (?)
Scorpion (?)

1ST DYNASTY

c. 2950–*c*. 2775
Narmer
Aha
Djer
Djet
Den
Anedjib
Semerkhet
Qaa

2ND DYNASTY

c. 2750–*c*. 2650
Hetepsekhemwy
Nebra

Ninetjer
Weneg (?)
Sened (?)
Peribsen
Khasekhem(wy)

3RD DYNASTY

c. 2650–*c*. 2575
Netjerikhet (Djoser)
Sekhemkhet
Khaba
Sanakht
Huni

Old Kingdom

4TH DYNASTY

c. 2575–*c*. 2450
Sneferu
Khufu (Cheops)
Djedefra
Khafra (Chephren)
Menkaura (Mycerinus)

Shepseskaf

5TH DYNASTY

c. 2450–*c*. 2325
Userkaf
Sahura
Neferirkara Kakai
Shepseskara Izi
Neferefra
Niuserra Ini
Menkauhor
Djedkara Isesi
Unas

6TH DYNASTY

c. 2325–*c*. 2175
Teti
Userkara (?)
Pepi I
Merenra Nemtyemsaf
Pepi II

7TH/8TH DYNASTY
c. 2175–*c.* 2125
Numerous ephemeral
kings

First Intermediate Period

9TH/10TH DYNASTY
c. 2125–*c.* 1975
Several kings, including:
Khety I
Khety II
Merikara

11TH DYNASTY
c. 2080– *c.* 1940
Intef I
Intef II
Intef III

Middle Kingdom

Mentuhotep II
c. 2010–*c.* 1960
Mentuhotep III
c. 1960–*c.* 1948
Mentuhotep IV
c. 1948–*c.* 1938

12TH DYNASTY
c. 1938–*c.* 1755
Amenemhat I
c. 1938–*c.* 1908
Senusret I
c. 1918–*c.* 1875
Amenemhat II
c. 1876–*c.* 1842
Senusret II
c. 1842–*c.* 1837
Senusret III
c. 1836–*c.* 1818
Amenemhat III
c. 1818–*c.* 1770
Amenemhat IV
c. 1770–*c.* 1760
Sobekneferu
c. 1760–*c.* 1755

13TH DYNASTY
c. 1755–*c.* 1630
Seventy kings, including
(order uncertain):
Sobekhotep I
Amenemhat V
Ameny Qemau

Sobekhotep II
Hor
Amenemhat VII
Ugaf
Khendjer
Sobekhotep III
Neferhotep I
Sahathor
Sobekhotep IV
Sobekhotep V
Ay (I)

Second Intermediate Period

Mentuemsaf
Dedumose
Neferhotep II

14TH DYNASTY
Numerous ephemeral
kings

15TH DYNASTY
c. 1630–*c.* 1520
Six kings, including:
Salitis
Sheshi
Khyan
Apepi *c.* 1570–*c.* 1530
Khamudi
c. 1530–*c.* 1520

16TH DYNASTY
Numerous ephemeral
kings

17TH DYNASTY
c. 1630–*c.* 1539
Numerous kings,
probably ending:
Intef V
Intef VI
Intef VII
Sobekemsaf II
Senakhtenra (Taa?)
Seqenenra Taa (II)
Kamose *c.* 1541–*c.* 1539

New Kingdom

18TH DYNASTY
c. 1539–*c.* 1292
Ahmose *c.* 1539–*c.* 1514
Amenhotep I
c. 1514–*c.* 1493
Thutmose I
c. 1493–*c.* 1481

Thutmose II
c. 1481–*c.* 1479
Thutmose III
c. 1479–*c.* 1425
and Hatshepsut
c. 1473–*c.* 1458
Amenhotep II
c. 1426–*c.* 1400
Thutmose IV
c. 1400–*c.* 1390
Amenhotep III
c. 1390–*c.* 1353
Amenhotep IV
(Akhenaten)
c. 1353–*c.* 1336
Smenkhkara
c. 1336–*c.* 1332
Tutankhamun
c. 1332–*c.* 1322
Ay (II) *c.* 1322–*c.* 1319
Horemheb
c. 1319–*c.* 1292

19TH DYNASTY
c. 1292–*c.* 1190
Ramesses I
c. 1292–*c.* 1290
Seti I *c.* 1290–*c.* 1279
Ramesses II
c. 1279–*c.* 1213
Merenptah
c. 1213–*c.* 1204
Seti II *c.* 1204–*c.* 1198
Amenmesse
c. 1202–*c.* 1200
Siptah *c.* 1198–*c.* 1193
Tawosret *c.* 1198–*c.* 1190

20TH DYNASTY
c. 1190–*c.* 1069
Sethnakht
c. 1190–*c.* 1187
Ramesses III
c. 1187–*c.* 1156
Ramesses IV
c. 1156–*c.* 1150
Ramesses V
c. 1150–*c.* 1145
Ramesses VI
c. 1145–*c.* 1137
Ramesses VII
c. 1137–*c.* 1129
Ramesses VIII
c. 1129–*c.* 1126

Ramesses IX
c. 1126–*c.* 1108
Ramesses X
c. 1108–*c.* 1099
Ramesses XI
c. 1099–*c.* 1069

Third Intermediate Period

21ST DYNASTY
c. 1069–*c.* 945
Smendes *c.* 1069–*c.* 1045
Amenemnisu
c. 1045–*c.* 1040
Psusennes I
c. 1040–*c.* 985
Amenemope
c. 985–*c.* 975
Osochor (Osorkon
'the elder')
c. 975–*c.* 970
Siamun *c.* 970–*c.* 950
Psusennes II
c. 950–*c.* 945

22ND DYNASTY
c. 945–*c.* 715
Shoshenq I
c. 945–*c.* 925
Osorkon I *c.* 925–*c.* 890
and Shoshenq II
c. 890
Takelot I *c.* 890–*c.* 875
Osorkon II *c.* 875–*c.* 835
Shoshenq III
c. 835–*c.* 795
Shoshenq IV
c. 795–*c.* 785
Pimay *c.* 785–*c.* 775
Shoshenq V
c. 775–*c.* 735
Osorkon IV *c.* 735–*c.* 715

23RD DYNASTY
c. 830–*c.* 715
Takelot II *c.* 840–*c.* 815
Pedubast I *c.* 825–*c.* 800
and Iuput I *c.* 800
Shoshenq VI
c. 800–*c.* 780
Osorkon III
c. 780–*c.* 750
Takelot III *c.* 750–*c.* 735
Rudamun *c.* 755–*c.* 735

Peftjauawybast
c. 735–*c.* 725
Shoshenq VII
c. 725–*c.* 715

24TH DYNASTY
c. 730–*c.* 715
Tefnakht *c.* 730–*c.* 720
Bakenrenef
c. 720–*c.* 715

25TH DYNASTY
c. 800–657
Alara *c.* 800–*c.* 770
Kashta *c.* 770–*c.* 747
Piye *c.* 747–*c.* 715
Shabaqo *c.* 715–*c.* 702
Shabitqo *c.* 702–690
Taharqo 690–664
Tanutamani 664–657

Late Period

26TH DYNASTY
664–525
Nekau I 672–664
Psamtik I 664–610
Nekau II 610–595
Psamtik II 595–589
Apries 589–570
Amasis 570–526
Psamtik III 526–525

27TH DYNASTY
(PERSIAN) 525–404
Cambyses 525–522
Darius I 521–486
Xerxes 486–466
Artaxerxes I 465–424
Darius II 424–404

28TH DYNASTY
404–399
Amyrtaeos 404–399

29TH DYNASTY
399–380
Nepherites I 399–393
Psammuthis 393
Hakor 393–380
Nepherites II 380

30TH DYNASTY
380–343
Nectanebo I 380–362
Teos 365–360
Nectanebo II 360–343

31ST DYNASTY (PERSIAN)
43–332
Artaxerxes III 343–338
Arses 338–336
Darius III 335–332

Macedonian Period
332–309
Alexander III (the Great)
332–323
Philip Arrhidaeus
323–317
Alexander IV 317–309

Ptolemaic Period
309–30
Ptolemy I 305–282
Ptolemy II 285–246
Ptolemy III 246–221
Ptolemy IV 221–205
Ptolemy V 205–180
Ptolemy VI 180–145
Ptolemy VIII and
Cleopatra II 170–116
Ptolemy IX 116–107
and Cleopatra III
116–101
Ptolemy X 107–88
Ptolemy IX (restored)
88–80
Ptolemy XI
and Berenice III 80
Ptolemy XII 80–58
Cleopatra VI 58–57
and Berenice IV 58–55
Ptolemy XII (restored)
55–51
Cleopatra VII and
Ptolemy XIII 51–47
Cleopatra VII and
Ptolemy XIV 47–44
Cleopatra VII and
Ptolemy XV 44–30

Roman Period
30 BC–AD 395

SOURCES OF QUOTATIONS

8 | Metjen
Allen, J.P., in Metropolitan Museum of Art, *Egyptian Art in the Age of the Pyramids* (New York, 1999), 213

10 | Khufu
Dodson, A., *Monarchs of the Nile* (London, 1995), 29–32

14 | Pepiankh
Lichtheim, M., *Ancient Egyptian Autobiographies Chiefly of the Middle Kingdom* (Freiburg & Göttingen, 1988), 18–20

15 | Unas
Lichtheim, M., *Ancient Egyptian Literature, Vol. I. The Old and Middle Kingdoms* (Berkeley, 1975), 36–38

16 | Metjetji
Ziegler, C., in Metropolitan Museum of Art, *Egyptian Art in the Age of the Pyramids* (New York, 1999), 413

18 | Weni
Lichtheim, M., *Ancient Egyptian Literature, Vol. I. The Old and Middle Kingdoms* (Berkeley, 1975), 18–23

19 | Harkhuf
Lichtheim, M., *Ancient Egyptian Literature, Vol. I. The Old and Middle Kingdoms* (Berkeley, 1975), 23–27

20 | Pepi II
Lichtheim, M., *Ancient Egyptian Literature, Vol. I. The Old and Middle Kingdoms* (Berkeley, 1975), 23–27
Parkinson, R.B., *Voices from Ancient Egypt. An Anthology of Middle Kingdom Writings* (London & Norman, 1991), 56

21 | Pepinakht-Heqaib
Lichtheim, M., *Ancient Egyptian Autobiographies Chiefly of the Middle Kingdom* (Freiburg & Göttingen, 1988), 15–16

22 | Tjauti
Darnell, J., *Theban Desert Road Survey in the Egyptian Western Desert, Vol. 1. Gebel Tjauti Rock Inscriptions 1–45 and Wadi el-Hôl Rock Inscriptions 1–45* (Chicago, 2002), 31

23 | Ankhtifi
Lichtheim, M., *Ancient Egyptian Literature, Vol. I. The Old and Middle Kingdoms* (Berkeley, 1975), 85–86

24 | Hemira
Vassilika, E., *Egyptian Art* (Cambridge, 1995), 22

25 | Intef II
Lichtheim, M., *Ancient Egyptian Literature, Vol. I. The Old and Middle Kingdoms* (Berkeley, 1975), 94–95

26 | Tjetji
Lichtheim, M., *Ancient Egyptian Literature, Vol. I. The Old and Middle Kingdoms* (Berkeley, 1975), 91–93

30 | Hekanakht
Parkinson, R.B., *Voices from Ancient Egypt. An Anthology of Middle Kingdom Writings* (London & Norman, 1991), 103–07

31 | Sarenput
Wilkinson, T., after Gardiner, A.H., 'Inscriptions from the tomb of Si-renpowet I, prince of Elephantine', *Zeitschrift für Ägyptische Sprache und Altertumskunde* 45 (1908), 123–40

33 | Khnumhotep II
Breasted, J.H., *Ancient Records of Egypt* (Chicago, 1906), vol. i, §§619–39

34 | Ikhernofret
Wilkinson, T., after Lichtheim, M., *Ancient Egyptian Literature, Vol. I. The Old and Middle Kingdoms* (Berkeley, 1975), 123–25

35 | Senusret III
Lichtheim, M., *Ancient Egyptian Literature, Vol. I. The Old and Middle Kingdoms* (Berkeley, 1975), 198
Clayton, P.A., *Chronicle of the Pharaohs* (London & New York, 1994), 84–87

36 | Horwerra
Parkinson, R., *Voices from Ancient Egypt* (London & Norman, 1991), 97–99

41 | Ahmose son of Abana
Breasted, J.H., *Ancient Records of Egypt* (Chicago, 1906), vol. ii, §§1–16, 38–39, 78–82

42 | Ahmose Pennekhbet
Breasted, J.H., *Ancient Records of Egypt*
(Chicago, 1906), vol. ii, §§17–25, 344

43 | Hatshepsut
Robins, G., *Women in Ancient Egypt*
(London, 1993), 45–52
Breasted, J.H., *Ancient Records of Egypt*
(Chicago, 1906), vol. ii, §§304–21

44 | Senenmut
Dorman, P.F., *The Monuments of
Senenmut. Problems in Historical
Methodology* (London & New York,
1988)

45 | Thutmose III
Clayton, P.A., *Chronicle of the Pharaohs*
(London & New York, 1994), 109
Lichtheim, M., *Ancient Egyptian
Literature, Vol. II. The New Kingdom*
(Berkeley, 1976), 33

46 | Menkheperraseneb
Breasted, J.H., *Ancient Records of Egypt*
(Chicago, 1906), Vol. 11, §§772–76

47 | Rekhmira
Breasted, J.H., *Ancient Records of Egypt*
(Chicago, 1906), Vol. II, §§663–762

49 | Qenamun
Davies, N. de G., *The Tomb of Ken-Amun
at Thebes* (New York, 1930)

51 | Sennefer
Caminos, R.A., 'Papyrus Berlin 10463',
Journal of Egyptian Archaeology 49
(1963), 29–37

55 | Amenhotep son of Hapu
Fletcher, J., *Egypt's Sun King:
Amenhotep III* (London, 2000), 98–99

56 | Akhenaten
Murnane, W., *Texts from the Amarna
Period in Egypt* (Atlanta, 1995), 73–106
Clayton, P.A., *Chronicle of the Pharaohs*
(London & New York, 1994), 120–26

58 | Meryra
Davies, N. de G., *The Rock Tombs of
el Amarna, Part 1. The Tomb of Meryra*
(London, 1903)

60 | Mahu
Murnane, W., *Texts from the Amarna
Period in Egypt* (Atlanta, 1995), 147–51

61 | Huy
Davies, N. de G. & Gardiner, A.H., *The
Tomb of Huy, Viceroy of Nubia in the
Reign of Tut'ankhamun* (London, 1926)

66 | Horemheb
Murnane, W., *Texts from the Amarna
Period in Egypt* (Atlanta, 1995), 227–40

70 | Ramesses II
Shelley, P.B., 'Ozymandias'
Kitchen, K.A., *Pharaoh Triumphant:
The Life and Times of Ramesses II,
King of Egypt* (Warminster, 1982)

72 | Khaemwaset
Kitchen, K.A., *Pharaoh Triumphant:
The Life and Times of Ramesses II, King
of Egypt* (Warminster, 1982), 103–9

74 | Didia
Wilkinson, T., after Lowle, D.A.,
'A remarkable family of draughtsmen-
painters from early nineteenth-dynasty
Thebes', *Oriens Antiquus* 15 (1976),
91–106

78 | Ramesses III
de Buck, A., 'The Judicial Papyrus of
Turin', *Journal of Egyptian Archaeology*
23 (1937), 152–64

80 | Naunakht
Černý, J., 'The will of Naunakhte and the
related documents', *Journal of Egyptian
Archaeology* 31 (1945), 29–53

81 | Thutmose
Wente, E.F., *Late Ramesside Letters*
(Chicago, 1967)

86 | Piye
Clayton, P.A., *Chronicle of the Pharaohs*
(London & New York, 1994), 190–92

88 | Montuemhat
Lichtheim, M., *Ancient Egyptian
Literature, Vol. III. The Late Period*
(Berkeley, 1980), 29–33

96 | Sematawytefnakht (II)
Lichtheim, M., *Ancient Egyptian
Literature, Vol. III. The Late Period*
(Berkeley, 1980), 42–43

97 | Padiusir (Petosiris)
Lichtheim, M., *Ancient Egyptian
Literature, Vol. III. The Late Period*
(Berkeley, 1980), 44–54

FURTHER READING

General:
Rice, M., *Who Was Who in Ancient Egypt* (London & New York, 2002)

Kings and members of royal families:
Clayton, P.A., *Chronicle of the Pharaohs* (London & New York, 1994)
Dodson, A. & Hilton, D., *The Complete Royal Families of Ancient Egypt* (London & New York, 2004)
Tyldesley, J., *Chronicle of the Queens of Egypt* (London & New York, 2006)

1 | Narmer
Wilkinson, T.A.H., *Early Dynastic Egypt* (London & New York, 1999), 67–70
Wilkinson, T.A.H., 'What a king is this: Narmer and the concept of the ruler', *Journal of Egyptian Archaeology* 86 (2000), 23–32

2 | Merneith
Wilkinson, T.A.H., *Early Dynastic Egypt* (London & New York, 1999), 74–75

3 | Den
Wilkinson, T.A.H., *Early Dynastic Egypt* (London & New York, 1999), 75–78

4 | Khasekhemwy
Wilkinson, T.A.H., *Early Dynastic Egypt* (London & New York, 1999), 91–94, 246

5 | Djoser
Kahl, J., 'Old Kingdom: Third Dynasty' in Redford, D. (ed.), *The Oxford Encyclopedia of Ancient Egypt* (New York, 2001), vol. 2, 591–93
Kahl, J., Kloth, N. & Zimmermann, U., *Die Inschriften der 3. Dynastie: eine Bestandsaufnahme* (Wiesbaden, 1995)
Metropolian Museum of Art, *Egyptian Art in the Age of the Pyramids* (New York, 1999), esp. 169–87
Verner, M., 'Old Kingdom: An Overview' in Redford, D. (ed.), *The Oxford Encyclopedia of Ancient Egypt* (New York, 2001), vol. 2, 585–91
Weill, R., *Les Origines de l'Egypte Pharaonique, 1ère Partie. La 11e et la 111e Dynasties* (Paris, 1908)
Wilkinson, T.A.H., *Early Dynastic Egypt* (London & New York, 1999), 95–98, 247–52

6 | Hesira
Hoffmann-Axthelm, W. (tr. Koehler, H.M.), *History of Dentistry* (Chicago, Berlin, Rio de Janeiro & Tokyo, 1981), 20–21
Kahl, J., Kloth, N. & Zimmermann, U., *Die Inschriften der 3. Dynastie: eine Bestandsaufnahme* (Wiesbaden, 1995)
Metropolitan Museum of Art, *Egyptian Art in the Age of the Pyramids* (New York, 1999), 188

7 | Imhotep
Kahl, J., Kloth, N. & Zimmermann, U., *Die Inschriften der 3. Dynastie: eine Bestandsaufnahme* (Wiesbaden, 1995)
Ray, J., *Reflections of Osiris. Lives from Ancient Egypt* (London, 2001), 5–22
Wildung, D., *Egyptian Saints: Deification in Pharaonic Egypt* (New York, 1977), 31–81

8 | Metjen
Metropolitan Museum of Art, *Egyptian Art in the Age of the Pyramids* (New York, 1999), 208–13
Wilkinson, T.A.H., *Early Dynastic Egypt* (London & New York, 1999), 147

9 | Hetepheres
Metropolitan Museum of Art, *Egyptian Art in the Age of the Pyramids* (New York, 1999), 216–19

10 | Khufu
Dodson, A., *Monarchs of the Nile*, 2nd edition (Cairo, 2000), 29–32
Kuper, R. & Förster, F., 'Khufu's "mefat"-expeditions into the Libyan Desert', *Egyptian Archaeology* 23 (2003), 25–28
Lehner, M., *The Complete Pyramids* (London & New York, 1997), 108–19

11 | Hemiunu
Metropolitan Museum of Art, *Egyptian Art in the Age of the Pyramids* (New York, 1999), 229–31

12 | Perniankhu
Metropolitan Museum of Art, *Egyptian Art in the Age of the Pyramids* (New York, 1999), 150, 163–64, 299

13 | Ptahshepses
Breasted, J.H., *Ancient Records of Egypt* (Chicago, 1906), vol. 1, §§254–62
Verner, M., *The Mastaba of Ptahshepses* (Prague, 1977)

14 | Pepiankh
Blackman, A.M., *The Rock Tombs of Meir, IV* (London, 1924)
Lichtheim, M., *Ancient Egyptian Autobiographies Chiefly of the Middle Kingdom* (Freiburg & Göttingen, 1988), 18–20

15 | Unas
Altenmüller, H., 'Old Kingdom: Fifth Dynasty' in Redford, D. (ed.), *The Oxford Encyclopedia of Ancient Egypt* (New York, 2001), vol. 2, 597–601
Hassan, S., 'The causeway of *Wnis* at Sakkara', *Zeitschrift für Ägyptische Sprache und Altertumskunde* 80 (1955), 136–39, pls XII–XIII
Lehner, M., *The Complete Pyramids* (London & New York, 1997), 154–55

16 | Metjetji
Metropolitan Museum of Art, *Egyptian Art in the Age of the Pyramids* (New York, 1999), 408–17

17 | Mereruka
Duell, P., *The Mastaba of Mereruka* (Chicago, 1938)
Porter, B. & Moss, R.L.B., *Topographical Bibliography of Ancient Egyptian Hieroglyphic Texts, Reliefs, and Paintings*, 2nd edition (rev. Malek, J.), vol. III (Oxford, 1978–81), Part 2, 525–37

18 | Weni
Eyre, C.J., 'Weni's career and Old Kingdom historiography' in Eyre, C.J., Leahy, A. & Leahy, L.M. (eds), *The Unbroken Reed: Studies in the Culture and Heritage of Ancient Egypt in Honour of A.F. Shore* (London, 1994), 107–24
Lichtheim, M., *Ancient Egyptian Literature, Vol. I. The Old and Middle Kingdoms* (Berkeley, 1975), 18–23
Richards, J., 'Text and context in late Old Kingdom Egypt: the archaeology and historiography of Weni the Elder', *Journal of the American Research Center in Egypt* 39 (2002), 75–102
Richards, J., 'The Abydos cemeteries in

the late Old Kingdom' in Hawass, Z. (ed.), *Egyptology at the Dawn of the Twenty-first Century: Proceedings of the Eighth International Congress of Egyptologists, Cairo* (Cairo, 2003), 400–7

19 | Harkhuf
Lichtheim, M., *Ancient Egyptian Literature, Vol. I. The Old and Middle Kingdoms* (Berkeley, 1975), 23–27
Wilkinson, T., 'Egyptian explorers' in Hanbury-Tenison, R. (ed.), *The Seventy Great Journeys in History* (London & New York, 2006), 29–32

20 | Pepi II
Dodson, A., *Monarchs of the Nile*, 2nd edition (Cairo, 2000), 40–42
Lehner, M., *The Complete Pyramids* (London & New York, 1997), 161–63

21 | Pepinakht-Heqaib
Habachi, L., *Elephantine IV. The Sanctuary of Heqaib* (Mainz, 1985)
Lichtheim, M., *Ancient Egyptian Autobiographies Chiefly of the Middle Kingdom* (Freiburg & Göttingen, 1988), 15–16

22 | Tjauti
Darnell, D. & Darnell, J., 'Exploring the "Narrow Doors" of the Theban Desert', *Egyptian Archaeology* 10 (1997), 24–26
Darnell, J., *Theban Desert Road Survey in the Egyptian Western Desert, vol. 1. Gebel Tjauti Rock Inscriptions 1–45 and Wadi el-Hôl Rock Inscriptions 1–45* (Chicago, 2002)

23 | Ankhtifi
Lichtheim, M., *Ancient Egyptian Literature, Vol. I. The Old and Middle Kingdoms* (Berkeley, 1975), 85–86
Vandier, J., *Mo'alla: La tombe d'Ankhtifi et la tombe de Sebekhotep* (Cairo, 1950)

24 | Hemira
Vassilika, E., *Egyptian Art* (Cambridge, 1995), 22–23

25 | Intef II
Darnell, J., *Theban Desert Road Survey in the Egyptian Western Desert, vol. 1. Gebel Tjauti Rock Inscriptions 1–45 and Wadi el-Hôl Rock Inscriptions 1–45* (Chicago, 2002), 41
Dodson, A., *Monarchs of the Nile*, 2nd edition (Cairo, 2000), 46–49

Parkinson, R., *Voices from Ancient Egypt*
(London & Norman, 1991), 112–13

26 | Tjetji
Blackman, A.M., 'The stele of Thethi,
Brit. Mus. No. 614', *Journal of Egyptian
Archaeology* 17 (1931), 55–61
Lichtheim, M., *Ancient Egyptian
Literature, Vol. I. The Old and Middle
Kingdoms* (Berkeley, 1975), 90–93
Robins, G., *The Art of Ancient Egypt*
(London, 1997), fig. 85

27 | Mentuhotep II
Arnold, D., *The Temple of Montuhotep
at Deir el-Bahari* (New York, 1979)
Bourriau, J., *Pharaohs and Mortals*
(Cambridge, 1988), 10–20
Dodson, A., *Monarchs of the Nile*,
2nd edition (Cairo, 2000), 49–54

28 | Meketra
Kemp, B.J., *Ancient Egypt. Anatomy of
a Civilization* (London & New York,
1989), 151–53, fig. 81
Winlock, H.E., *Models of Daily Life
in Ancient Egypt* (New York, 1955)

29 | Amenemhat I
Dodson, A., *Monarchs of the Nile*, 2nd
edition (Cairo, 2000), 55–58
Lichtheim, M., *Ancient Egyptian
Literature, Vol. I. The Old and Middle
Kingdoms* (Berkeley, 1975), 114

30 | Hekanakht
Allen, J.P., *The Heqanakht Papyri*
(New York, 2002)
Parkinson, R., *Voices from Ancient Egypt*
(London & Norman, 1991), 101–7
Ray, J., *Reflections of Osiris. Lives from
Ancient Egypt* (London, 2001), 23–39

31 | Sarenput
Gardiner, A.H., 'Inscriptions from the
tomb of Si-renpowet 1, prince of
Elephantine', *Zeitschrift für Ägyptische
Sprache und Altertumskunde* 45 (1908),
123–40

32 | Hapdjefa
Breasted, J.H., *Ancient Records of Egypt*
(Chicago, 1906), vol. i, §§535–93
Griffith, F.L., *The Inscriptions of Siût and
Dêr Rîfeh* (London, 1889)

33 | Khnumhotep
Breasted, J.H., *Ancient Records of Egypt*
(Chicago, 1906), vol. i, §§619–39

Newberry, P.E., *Beni Hasan, I*
(London, 1893)

34 | Ikhernofret
Breasted, J.H., *Ancient Records of Egypt*
(Chicago, 1906), vol. i, §§661–69
Lichtheim, M., *Ancient Egyptian
Literature, Vol. I. The Old and Middle
Kingdoms* (Berkeley, 1975), 123–25.
Schäfer, H., *Die Mysterien des Osiris unter
König Sesostris III* (Leipzig, 1904)

35 | Senusret III
Arnold, D., *The Pyramid Complex of
Senwosret III at Dahshur: Architectural
Studies* (New York, 2002)
Bourriau, J., *Pharaohs and Mortals*
(Cambridge, 1988)
Dodson, A., *Monarchs of the Nile*, 2nd
edition (Cairo, 2000), 58–64
Delia, R.D., 'Senwosret III' in Redford, D.
(ed.), *The Oxford Encyclopedia of
Ancient Egypt* (New York, 2001), vol. 3,
268–69

36 | Horwerra
Parkinson, R., *Voices from Ancient Egypt*
(London & Norman, 1991), 97–99

37 | Sobekhotep III
Ryholt, K., *The Political Situation in Egypt
During the Second Intermediate Period
c. 1800–1550 B.C.* (Copenhagen, 1997),
222–24, 343–45
Spalinger, A., 'Sobekhotep III', in Helck,
W. & Westendorf, W. (eds), *Lexikon der
Ägyptologie* (Wiesbaden, 1984), vol. 5,
1039–41

38 | Apepi
Ryholt, K., *The Political Situation in Egypt
During the Second Intermediate Period
c. 1800–1550 B.C.* (Copenhagen, 1997)
Säve-Söderbergh, T., 'The Hyksos rule in
Egypt', *Journal of Egyptian Archaeology*
37 (1951), 53–71

39 | Taa II
Polz, D.C., 'Seventeenth Dynasty'
in Redford, D. (ed.), *The Oxford
Encyclopedia of Ancient Egypt* (New
York, 2001), vol. 3, 273–74
Ryholt, K., *The Political Situation in Egypt
During the Second Intermediate Period
c. 1800–1550 B.C.* (Copenhagen, 1997)
Winlock, H.E., 'The tombs of the kings of
the Seventeenth Dynasty at Thebes',

Journal of Egyptian Archaeology 10
(1924), 217–77

40 | Ahmose Nefertari

Robins, G., *Women in Ancient Egypt*
(London, 1993), 43–45

41 | Ahmose son of Abana

Breasted, J.H., *Ancient Records of Egypt*
(Chicago, 1906), vol. ii, §§1–16, 38–39,
78–82

Helck, W., 'Ahmose, Sohn der Abina', in
Helck, W. & Otto, E. (eds) *Lexikon der
Ägyptologie* (Wiesbaden, 1975), vol. 1,
110–11

42 | Ahmose Pennekhbet

Breasted, J.H., *Ancient Records of Egypt*
(Chicago, 1906), vol. ii, §§17–25, 344

Helck, W. 'Ahmose Pennechbet', in
Helck, W. & Otto, E. (eds) *Lexikon der
Ägyptologie* (Wiesbaden, 1975), vol. 1,
110

43 | Hatshepsut

Breasted, J.H., *Ancient Records of Egypt*
(Chicago, 1906), vol. ii, §§304–21

Lipinska, J., 'Hatshepsut' in Redford,
D. (ed.), *The Oxford Encyclopedia of
Ancient Egypt* (New York, 2001), vol. 2,
85–87

Ray, J., *Reflections of Osiris. Lives from
Ancient Egypt* (London, 2001), 40–59

Robins, G., *Women in Ancient Egypt*
(London, 1993), 45–52

Roehrig, C.H., Dreyfus, R. and Keller,
C.A. (eds), *Hatshepsut: From Queen to
Pharaoh* (New York, 2005)

Tyldesley, J., *Hatchepsut: The Female
Pharaoh* (London, 1996)

44 | Senenmut

Dorman, P.F., *The Monuments of
Senenmut. Problems in Historical
Methodology* (London &
New York, 1988)

Dorman, P., 'Senenmut' in Redford,
D. (ed.), *The Oxford Encyclopedia of
Ancient Egypt* (New York, 2001), vol. 3,
265–66

Ray, J., *Reflections of Osiris. Lives from
Ancient Egypt* (London, 2001), 57–58

Tyldesley, J., *Hatchepsut: The Female
Pharaoh* (London, 1996), 177–209

45 | Thutmose III

Breasted, J.H., *Ancient Records of Egypt*
(Chicago, 1906), vol. ii, §§391–540

Cline, E.H. & O'Connor, D. (eds),
Thutmose III: A New Biography (Ann
Arbor, 2006)

Lipinska, J., 'Thutmose III' in Redford,
D. (ed.), *The Oxford Encyclopedia of
Ancient Egypt* (New York, 2001), vol. 3,
401–3

46 | Menkheperraseneb

Breasted, J.H., *Ancient Records of Egypt*
(Chicago, 1906), vol. ii, §§772–76

Davies, N. de G. & Davies, N. de G.,
*The Tomb of Menkheperraseneb,
Amenmose, and Another* (London, 1933)

Porter, B. & Moss, R.L.B., *Topographical
Bibliography of Ancient Egyptian
Hieroglyphic Texts, Reliefs, and
Paintings* (Oxford, 1927), vol. 1, 117–19

47 | Rekhmira

Breasted, J.H., *Ancient Records of Egypt*
(Chicago, 1906), vol. ii, §§663–762

Dorman, P. 'Rekhmire' in Redford, D.
(ed.), *The Oxford Encyclopedia of
Ancient Egypt* (New York, 2001), vol. 3,
131–32

48 | Dedi

Porter, B. & Moss, R.L.B., *Topographical
Bibliography of Ancient Egyptian
Hieroglyphic Texts, Reliefs, and
Paintings* (Oxford, 1927), vol. 1, 153–54

49 | Qenamun

Davies, N. de G., *The Tomb of Ken-Amun
at Thebes* (New York, 1930)

50 | Nakht

Davies, N. de G., *The Tomb of Nakht
at Thebes* (New York, 1917)

Shedid, A.G. & Seidel, M., *The Tomb
of Nakht* (Mainz, 1996)

51 | Sennefer

Caminos, R.A., 'Papyrus Berlin 10463',
Journal of Egyptian Archaeology 49
(1963), 29–37

Carter, H., 'Report upon the tomb of
Sen-nefer found at Biban el-Molouk
near that of Thotmes 111 No. 34',
*Annales du Service des Antiquités de
l'Egypte* 2 (1901), 196–200

Fletcher, J., *Egypt's Sun King:
Amenhotep III* (London, 2000), 13–14

Porter, B. & Moss, R.L.B., *Topographical
Bibliography of Ancient Egyptian
Hieroglyphic Texts, Reliefs, and
Paintings* (Oxford, 1927), vol. 1, 125–27

Simpson, W.K. 'Sennefer', in Helck, W. & Otto (eds), *Lexikon der Ägyptologie* (Wiesbaden, 1984), vol. 5, 855–56

Virey, P., 'La tombe des vignes à Thèbes', *Recueil des travaux relatifs à la philologie et à l'archéologie égyptiennes et assyriennes* 20 (1898), 211–23; 21 (1899), 127–33, 137–49; 22 (1900), 83–97

52 | Amenhotep III

Fletcher, J., *Egypt's Sun King: Amenhotep III* (London, 2000)

Kozloff, A. & Bryan, B., *Egypt's Dazzling Sun: Amenhotep III and his World* (Cleveland, 1992)

O'Connor, D. & Cline, E.H. (eds), *Amenhotep III: Perspectives on His Reign* (Ann Arbor, 1998)

53 | Tiye

Aldred, C., *Akhenaten, King of Egypt* (London, 1988), 146–52, 219–22

Eaton-Krauss, M., 'Tiye' in Redford, D. (ed.), *The Oxford Encyclopedia of Ancient Egypt* (New York, 2001), vol. 3, 411

Fletcher, J., *Egypt's Sun King: Amenhotep III* (London, 2000)

Robins, G., *Women in Ancient Egypt* (London, 1993), 21–55

54 | Userhat

Beinlich-Seeber, C. & Shedid, A., *Das Grab des Userhat (TT56)* (Mainz, 1987)

55 | Amenhotep son of Hapu

Fletcher, J., *Egypt's Sun King: Amenhotep III* (London, 2000), 98–99

Vandersleyen, C.A.P., 'Amenhotep, son of Hapu' in Redford, D. (ed.), *The Oxford Encyclopedia of Ancient Egypt* (New York, 2001), vol. 1, 70

Wildung, D., *Egyptian Saints: Deification in Pharaonic Egypt* (New York, 1977)

56 | Akhenaten

Aldred, C., *Akhenaten: King of Egypt* (London & New York, 1988)

Freed, R., Markowitz, Y.J. & D'Auria, S.H. (eds), *Pharaohs of the Sun* (London, 1999), esp. 81–95

Montserrat, D., *Akhenaten: History, Fantasy and Ancient Egypt* (London & New York, 2000)

Murnane, W., *Texts from the Amarna Period in Egypt* (Atlanta, 1995), 73–106

Reeves, N., *The Complete Tutankhamun*

(London & New York, 1990), 18

Reeves, N., *Akhenaten: Egypt's False Prophet* (London & New York, 2001)

57 | Nefertiti

Freed, R., Markowitz, Y.J. & D'Auria, S.H. (eds), *Pharaohs of the Sun* (London, 1999), esp. 81–95

Murnane, W., *Texts from the Amarna Period in Egypt* (Atlanta, 1995), 74

Robins, G., *Women in Ancient Egypt* (London, 1993), 53–55

Tyldesley, J., *Nefertiti* (London, 1998)

58 | Meryra

Davies, N. de G., *The Rock Tombs of El Amarna, Part I. The Tomb of Meryra* (London, 1903)

Murnane, W., *Texts from the Amarna Period in Egypt* (Atlanta, 1995), 151–62

59 | Bak

Freed, R., Markowitz, Y.J. & D'Auria, S.H. (eds), *Pharaohs of the Sun* (London, 1999), 116, 128, 131, 244

Murnane, W., *Texts from the Amarna Period in Egypt* (Atlanta, 1995), 128–30

60 | Mahu

Davies, N. de G., *The Rock Tombs of El Amarna, Part IV* (London, 1906)

Freed, R., Markowitz, Y.J. & D'Auria, S.H. (eds), *Pharaohs of the Sun* (London, 1999), 147

Murnane, W., *Texts from the Amarna Period in Egypt* (Atlanta, 1995), 147–51

61 | Huy

Davies, N. de G. & Gardiner, A.H., *The Tomb of Huy, Viceroy of Nubia in the Reign of Tut'ankhamun* (London, 1926)

Reeves, N., *The Complete Tutankhamun* (London & New York, 1990), 32

62 | Tutankhamun

Freed, R., Markowitz, Y.J. & D'Auria, S.H. (eds), *Pharaohs of the Sun* (London, 1999), esp. 81–95

Reeves, N., *The Complete Tutankhamun* (London & New York, 1990)

63 | Ankhesenamun

Freed, R., Markowitz, Y.J. & D'Auria, S.H. (eds), *Pharaohs of the Sun* (London, 1999), 36, 94 n. 61, 161, 178, 180, 200

Reeves, N., *The Complete Tutankhamun* (London & New York, 1990)

64 | Maya

Martin, G.T., *The Hidden Tombs of Memphis* (London & New York, 1991), 147–88

Murnane, W., *Texts from the Amarna Period in Egypt* (Atlanta, 1995), 215

Reeves, N., *The Complete Tutankhamun* (London & New York, 1990), 31

van Dijk, J., 'The Overseer of the Treasury Maya: A Biographical Sketch' in *The New Kingdom Necropolis of Memphis: Historical and Iconographical Studies*, unpublished dissertation, Rijksuniversiteit Groningen, 1993, 65–83

65 | Ay

Aldred, C., *Tut-ankh-amun and His Friends* (Santa Barbara, 1987)

Murnane, W., *Texts from the Amarna Period in Egypt* (Atlanta, 1995), 107–20, 219–20

Reeves, N., 'The royal family' in Freed, R., Markowitz, Y.J. & D'Auria, S.H. (eds), *Pharaohs of the Sun* (London, 1999), 81–95

Reeves, N., *The Complete Tutankhamun* (London & New York, 1990)

Schaden, O., *The God's Father Ay* (Ann Arbor, 1982)

Vinson, S., 'Ay' in Redford, D. (ed.), *The Oxford Encyclopedia of Ancient Egypt* (New York, 2001), vol. 1, 160

66 | Horemheb

Freed, R., Markowitz, Y.J. & D'Auria, S.H. (eds), *Pharaohs of the Sun* (London, 1999), 177, 180

Hornung, E., *Das Grab des Haremhab im Tal der Könige* (Bern, 1971)

Martin, G.T., *The Memphite Tomb of Horemheb, Commander-in-Chief of Tutankhamun* (London, 1989)

Murnane, W., *Texts from the Amarna Period in Egypt* (Atlanta, 1995), 227–40

Ray, J., *Reflections of Osiris. Lives from Ancient Egypt* (London, 2001), 60–77

67 | Sennedjem

Hayes, W.C., *The Scepter of Egypt, Part II* (New York, 1959), 414

Porter, B. & Moss, R.L.B., *Topographical Bibliography of Ancient Egyptian Hieroglyphic Texts, Reliefs, and Paintings* (Oxford, 1927), vol. 1, 1–5

68 | Urhiya and 69 | Yupa

Kitchen, K.A., 'The family of Urhiya and Yupa, High Stewards of the Ramesseum: Part II, The Family Relationships' in Ruffle, J., Gaballa, G.A. & Kitchen K.A. (eds), *Orbis Aegyptiorum Speculum. Glimpses of Ancient Egypt. Studies in Honour of H.W. Fairman* (Warminster, 1979), 71–74

Kitchen, K.A., *Pharaoh Triumphant: The Life and Times of Ramesses II, King of Egypt* (Warminster, 1982), 30, 70, 112, 139, 140, 171

Ruffle, J., 'The family of Urhiya and Yupa, High Stewards of the Ramesseum: Part I, The Monuments' in Ruffle, J., Gaballa, G.A. & Kitchen K.A. (eds), *Orbis Aegyptiorum Speculum. Glimpses of Ancient Egypt. Studies in Honour of H.W. Fairman* (Warminster, 1979), 55–70

70 | Ramesses II

Kitchen, K.A., *Pharaoh Triumphant: The Life and Times of Ramesses II, King of Egypt* (Warminster, 1982)

71 | Raia

Martin, G.T., *The Hidden Tombs of Memphis* (London & New York, 1991), 124–30

Martin, G.T., *The Tomb-Chapels of Paser and Ra'ia at Saqqâra* (London, 1985)

72 | Khaemwaset

Kitchen, K.A., *Pharaoh Triumphant: The Life and Times of Ramesses II, King of Egypt* (Warminster, 1982), 103–9

Ray, J., *Reflections of Osiris. Lives from Ancient Egypt* (London, 2001), 78–96

73 | Mes

Gaballa, G.A., *The Memphite Tomb-chapel of Mose* (Warminster, 1977)

Gardiner, A.H., *The Inscription of Mes* (Leipzig, 1905)

Kitchen, K.A., *Pharaoh Triumphant: The Life and Times of Ramesses II, King of Egypt* (Warminster, 1982), 128–29

74 | Didia

Lowle, D.A., 'A remarkable family of draughtsmen-painters from early nineteenth-dynasty Thebes', *Oriens Antiquus* 15 (1976), 91–106, pls I–II

75 | Merenptah
Kitchen, K.A., 'New Kingdom: Nineteenth Dynasty' in Redford, D. (ed.), *The Oxford Encyclopedia of Ancient Egypt* (New York, 2001), vol. 2, 534–38
Lichtheim, M., *Ancient Egyptian Literature, Vol. II. The New Kingdom* (Berkeley, 1976), 73–77
Sourouzian, H., *Les monuments du roi Merenptah* (Wiesbaden, 1989)

76 | Paneb
Černý, J., 'Papyrus Salt 124 (Brit. Mus. 10055)', *Journal of Egyptian Archaeology* 15 (1929), 243–58
Vernus, P. (tr. Lorton, D.), *Affairs and Scandals in Ancient Egypt* (Ithaca & London, 2003)

77 | Bay
Dodson, A., *Monarchs of the Nile*, 2nd edition (Cairo, 2000), 141
Grandet, P., 'L'execution du chancelier Bay: O.IFAO 1864', *Bulletin de l'Institut Français d'Archéologie Orientale 2000* (2000), 338–45

78 | Ramesses III
de Buck, A., 'The Judicial Papyrus of Turin', *Journal of Egyptian Archaeology* 23 (1937), 152–64
Grandet, P., 'Ramesses III' in Redford, D. (ed.), *The Oxford Encyclopedia of Ancient Egypt* (New York, 2001) vol. 3, 118–20
Leahy, A., 'Sea Peoples' in Redford, D. (ed.), *The Oxford Encyclopedia of Ancient Egypt* (New York, 2001), vol. 3, 257–60
Redford, S., *The Harem Conspiracy: The Murder of Ramesses III* (Chicago, 2002)
Vernus, P. (tr. Lorton, D.), *Affairs and Scandals in Ancient Egypt* (Ithaca & London, 2003)

79 | Ramessesnakht
Bierbrier, M., *The Late New Kingdom in Egypt c. 1300–664 BC. A Genealogical & Chronological Investigation* (Warminster, 1975), 10–12

80 | Naunakht
Černý, J., 'The will of Naunakhte and the related documents', *Journal of Egyptian Archaeology* 31 (1945), 29–53

81 | Thutmose
Wente, E.F., *Late Ramesside Letters* (Chicago, 1967)

82 | Panehsy
Dodson, A., *Monarchs of the Nile*, 2nd edition (Cairo, 2000), 152–53
Janssen-Winkeln, K., 'Das Ende des Neuen Reiches', *Zeitschrift für Ägyptische Sprache und Altertumskunde* 119 (1992), 22–37
van Dijk, J., 'The Amarna Period and the later New Kingdom' in Shaw, I. (ed.), *The Oxford History of Ancient Egypt* (Oxford, 2000), 272–313, esp. 308–9

83 | Herihor
Epigraphic Survey, Chicago, *The Temple of Khonsu, vol. 1, Plates 1–110. Scenes of King Herihor in the Court with Translation of the Texts* (Chicago, 1979)
Taylor, J.H., 'Nodjmet, Payankh and Herihor: the end of the New Kingdom reconsidered' in Eyre, C.J. (ed.), *Proceedings of the Seventh International Congress of Egyptologists* (Leuven, 1998), 1143–55

84 | Wendjebaendjedet
Coutts, H. (ed.), *Gold of the Pharaohs. Catalogue of the Exhibition of Treasures from Tanis* (Edinburgh, 1988)
Kitchen, K.A., *The Third Intermediate Period in Egypt (1100–650 B.C.)*, 3rd edition (Warminster, 1995), 265
Montet, P., *La nécropole royale de Tanis, II. Les constructions et le tombeau de Psousennes* (Paris, 1951)

85 | Osorkon
Aston, D.A., 'Takeloth II – A king of the "Theban Twenty-third Dynasty"?', *Journal of Egyptian Archaeology* 75 (1989), 139–53
Caminos, R.A., *The Chronicle of Prince Osorkon* (Rome, 1958)
Dodson, A., *Monarchs of the Nile*, 2nd edition (Cairo, 2000), 169–73

86 | Piye
Kitchen, K.A., *The Third Intermediate Period in Egypt (1100–650 B.C.)*, 3rd edition (Warminster,1995), 362–63, 378
Morkot, R., *The Black Pharaohs* (London, 2000)

87 | Harwa
Lichtheim, M., *Ancient Egyptian Literature, Vol. III. The Late Period* (Berkeley, 1980), 24–28
Tiraditti, F., 'Three years of research in the tomb of Harwa', *Egyptian Archaeology* 13 (1998), 3–6

88 | Montuemhat
Leclant, J., *Montouemhat, Quatrième Prophète d'Amon, Prince de la Ville* (Cairo, 1962)
Lichtheim, M., *Ancient Egyptian Literature, Vol. III. The Late Period* (Berkeley, 1980), 29–33
Russman, E.R., 'Relief decoration in the tomb of Montuemhat', *Journal of the American Research Center in Egypt* 31 (1994), 1–19

89 | Padiamenope
Anthes, R., 'Der Berliner Hocher des Petamenophis', *Zeitschrift für Ägyptische Sprache und Altertumskunde* 73 (1937), 25–35, pls V–VI
Aston, D.A., 'The Theban west bank from the Twenty-fifth Dynasty to the Ptolemaic Period' in Strudwick, N. & Taylor, J.H. (eds), *The Theban Necropolis: Past, Present and Future* (London, 2003), 138–66
Bianchi, R.S., 'Petamenophis' in Helck, W. & Otto (eds), *Lexikon der Ägyptologie* (Wiesbaden, 1984), vol. 4, 991–92
Eigner, D., *Die monumentale Grabbauten der Spätzeit in der thebanischen Nekropole* (Vienna, 1984)
Porter, B. & Moss, R.L.B., *Topographical Bibliography of Ancient Egyptian Hieroglyphic Texts, Reliefs, and Paintings* (Oxford, 1927), vol. 1, 66–67
von Bissing, F., 'Das Grab des Petamenophis in Theben', *Zeitschrift für Ägyptische Sprache und Altertumskunde* 74 (1938), 2–26

90 | Nitiqret and 91 | Sematawytefnakht (I)
Caminos, R.A., 'The Nitocris Adoption Stela', *Journal of Egyptian Archaeology* 50 (1964), 71–101, pls 7–10
Kitchen, K.A., *The Third Intermediate Period in Egypt (1100–650 B.C.)*, 3rd edition (Warminster, 1995)

92 | Ahmose II (Amasis)
Josephson, J.A., 'Amasis' in Redford, D. (ed.), *The Oxford Encyclopedia of Ancient Egypt* (New York, 2001), vol. 1, 66–67

93 | Wedjahorresnet
Bares, L., *Abusir IV: The Shaft Tomb of Udjahorresnet at Abusir* (Prague, 1999)
Lloyd, A.B., 'The inscription of Udjahorresnet: a collaborator's testament', *Journal of Egyptian Archaeology* 68 (1982), 166–80

94 | Wennefer
Ray, J., *Reflections of Osiris. Lives from Ancient Egypt* (London, 2001), 117
von Känel, F., 'Les mésaventures du conjurateur de Serket Onnophris et de son tombeau', *Bulletin de la Société Française d'Egyptologie* 87–88 (1980), 31–45

95 | Nakhthorheb
Dodson, A., *Monarchs of the Nile*, 2nd edition (Cairo, 2000), 200–201
Josephson, J.A., 'Nektanebo', in Redford, D. (ed.), *The Oxford Encyclopedia of Ancient Egypt* (New York, 2001), vol. 2, 517–18
Ray, J.D., 'Late Period: Thirtieth Dynasty' in Redford, D. (ed.), *The Oxford Encyclopedia of Ancient Egypt* (New York, 2001), vol. 2, 275–76
Ray, J., *Reflections of Osiris. Lives from Ancient Egypt* (London, 2001), 113–29
Spencer, N., 'The great naos of Nekhthorheb from Bubastis', *Egyptian Archaeology* 26 (2005), 21–24

96 | Sematawytefnakht (II)
Clère, J.J., 'Une statuette du fils aîné du roi Nectanebô', *Revue d'Egyptologie* 6 (1951), 135–56, esp. 152–54
Gardiner, A.H., *Egypt of the Pharaohs* (Oxford, 1961), 379–80
Lichtheim, M., *Ancient Egyptian Literature, Vol. III. The Late Period* (Berkeley, 1980), 41–44
Tresson, P., 'La stèle de Naples', *Bulletin de l'Institut Français d'Archéologie Orientale* 30 (1930), 369–91

97 | Padiusir (Petosiris)
Lefebvre, G., *Le Tombeau de Petosiris* (Paris, 1924)
Lichtheim, M., *Ancient Egyptian Literature, Vol. III. The Late Period* (Berkeley, 1980), 44–54

98 | Ptolemy I
Bevan, E., *The House of Ptolemy. A History of Egypt under the Ptolemaic Dynasty* (Chicago, 1968)
Ellis, W.M., *Ptolemy of Egypt* (London & New York, 1994)
Hölbl, G., *A History of the Ptolemaic Empire* (London, 2001)
Hölbl, G. (tr. Schwaiger, E.), 'Ptolemaic Period', in Redford, D. (ed.), *The Oxford Encyclopedia of Ancient Egypt* (New York, 2001), vol. 3, 76–85

99 | Manetho
Redford, D., 'Manetho' in Redford, D. (ed.), *The Oxford Encyclopedia of Ancient Egypt* (New York, 2001), vol. 2, 336–37
Waddell, W.G., *Manetho* (Loeb Classical Library, 1940)

100 | Cleopatra VII
Flamarion, E., *Cleopatra. From History to Legend* (London, 1997)
Hölbl, G., *A History of the Ptolemaic Empire* (London, 2001)
Hughes-Hallett, L., *Cleopatra: Histories, Dreams and Distortions* (London, 1990)
Samson, J., *Nefertiti and Cleopatra: Queen-Monarchs of Ancient Egypt* (London, 1985)
Walker, S. & Higgs, P. (eds), *Cleopatra of Egypt. From History to Myth* (London, 2001)

INDEX

INDEX

254; *see also* Serapeum
Apries 236–7
Armant 60, 182
army: 18th Dynasty development 97;
   Amarna Period 155; in Egyptian
   campaigns 44–5, 115–16, 131, 184, 185,
   213, 244; foreigners 180–81; role of, in
   dynastic change 169, 174, 181, 210
Asiatics 5, 14, 38, 84, 98–100
Asklepius 18; **3**
assassinations 75, 174, 202, 205
Assyria(ns) 116, 229, 231, 236
Asyut 81
Aten 141, 144–5, 146, 148, 149–52, 156,
   160, 163
Augustus *see* Octavian
Avaris 99, 104–5
Ay 147, 161, 162, 164, 166, 167–70, 175

Babylon(ians) 132, 236–7
Bak 141, 152–4; **16**
Bay 173, 200–202
Bedouin 107
Behbeit el-Hagar 241, 244
Beit Khallaf 14
Beni Hasan 83, 84–5
boats 45, 71, 87, 104, 113, 158, 234–5
bureaucrats xiii, 2, 13, 15, 20, 97, 137
Busiris xii, 61, 62, 220
Butehamun 173, 210, 211
Buto 5, 16, 197
Byblos 11, 38, 98

Caesar, Julius 254
Cambyses 238, 239–40
Carter, Howard 160
Christie, Agatha 78
Cleopatra VII xi, 219, 253–6
Coffin Texts 70
Coptos 58, 59, 60, 120
Crete 120
Cusae 34, 99

Dahshur 22, 25, 28, 89, 91
Darius I 240
Dedi 123–4
Deir el-Bahri 68, 69–70, 71, 110, 111, 113,
   114, 140, 230, 232
Deir el-Ballas 69, 101
Deir el-Medina 19, 140, 173, 178, 198;
   see also Place of Truth
Den 6, 7–9
Dendera 19, 61, 69
dentist 13, 15–16

deserts 8, 58–9, 123–4
Didia 171, 194–5
Djedefra 28
Djedher 241–2
Djer 7, 87
Djet 6
Djoser (Netjerikhet) 3, 12–15, 16, 17, 18, 38
doctors 92, 241
domestication of animals 42
dwarf 23, 31–2; *see also* pygmy

Early Dynastic Period xii, 1–21
Edfu 19, 60
Elephantine 5, 24, 45, 46, 53, 60, 78–80,
   229
Elkab xii, 11, 69, 104, 107, 132

famine 22, 38, 61, 64, 196, 212
Fayum 21, 40, 76, 99, 131
Festivals: Beautiful Festival of the
   Valley 127, 232; New Year's 119;
   Opet 132, 161, 176, 185, 215, 226;
   Osiris 85–8; *see also* sed-festival
First Intermediate Period 50, 54, 55,
   58–67, 81, 123
foreigners *see* Apepi; Asiatics; Assyria(ns);
   Babylon(ians); Bay; Didia; Libya(ns);
   Nubia; Osorkon; Persia(ns); Piye;
   Urhiya; Yupa
furniture 25–6; **5**

Gebel Barkal 225, 227
Gebelein 11, 69, 99
Giza 22, 32, 172, 190; *see also* Khufu, Great
   Pyramid of
God's Wife of Amun 103, 109, 218, 224,
   226, 229, 233–4, 235, 238
Greeks 236–8, 244

Hapdjefa 56, 81–3
harem 44, 108, 131, 187, 205
Harkhuf 24, 46–9, 50, 51
Harwa 218, 227–8, 229
Hathor 36, 62, 93, 133, 134, 181, 188
Hatshepsut 97, 108–12, 113, 115, 117, 129; **11**
Hekanakht 56, 76–8
Heliopolis 14, 19, 53, 132, 150, 193
Hemaka 9
Hemira 56, 61–2
Hemiunu 23, 29–31
Heqaib *see* Pepinakht-Heqaib
Herakleopolis xii, 55, 58, 174, 223, 224,
   225, 226, 235, 245
Herihor 173, 214–16

INDEX